DAYS THAT WERE

GERALD WARNER BRACE

DAYS
THAT
WERE

With illustrations by the author

NEW YORK · W · W · NORTON & COMPANY · INC ·

Copyright © 1976 by Gerald Warner Brace.

All rights reserved. Published simultaneously in Canada by George J. Mc-
Leod Limited, Toronto. Printed in the United States of America.

First Edition

Library of Congress Cataloging in Publication Data
Brace, Gerald Warner, 1901–
  Days that were

  Autobiography.
  1. Brace, Gerald Warner, 1901–   —Biography—youth. I. Title.
PS3503.R14Z513   813'.5'2 [B]   76–16110
ISBN 0–393–07509–5

1 2 3 4 5 6 7 8 9 0

T

CONTENTS

One	OLD LITCHFIELD	11
Two	GRANDFATHER'S WORLD	26
Three	LIFE AT CHES-KNOLL	39
Four	DEER ISLE	61
Five	KENNEBAGO	78
Six	CAMPING	85
Seven	THE DONALDSONS	103
Eight	THE GUNNERY	127
Nine	THE STANLEY HOUSE	145
Ten	LOOMIS	154
Eleven	AMHERST AND CARRIE JOHNSON	170
Twelve	VERMONT	182
Thirteen	ONDAWA FARM	193
Fourteen	FROST, WHICHER, MEIKLEJOHN, AND OTHERS	200
Fifteen	FUSSING	217
Sixteen	LINCOLN	224
Seventeen	ABROAD	231

DEDICATION

If I should dedicate this book to all the old-timers I admired and loved, the list would seem absurdly long. I have been very fortunate in the friends and relations of my early days. In my mind they constitute a true nobility. They represented in their lives and beings the lofty idealism of a time now gone: they were confident and faithful and serene and wise, and infinitely kind to my youthful self. Some of them were scholars of the old school, like my Uncle Jim Croswell ("the nicest man who ever lived"), or my Uncle Harry Donaldson (the foremost authority on the rat), or my "Uncle" Lincoln Hendrickson (the classicist of Yale), or Dean Briggs of Harvard. Some were hardworking country folk, especially the good women who took me in as though I belonged to them—like Carrie Gale Johnson of Amherst and Mary Hancock of Vermont. There were the Buffum family of Ondawa Farm and the Fairleys of Jamaica Plain and Cape Rosier and Ellen Coolidge of Boston. There were many others.

DAYS THAT WERE

ONE

OLD LITCHFIELD

M Y GREAT-GRANDFATHER, John Pierce Brace, lived in Litchfield, Connecticut, a century and a half ago and I feel as though I knew him well. He was a writer of poetry and fiction, a walker and trout fisherman, a geologist and botanist who corresponded with Silliman of Yale and Gray of Harvard (who married his niece Jane Loring) and a teacher whom his most celebrated pupil, Harriet Beecher, called the best teacher of writing she ever knew. Later in his life he moved to Hartford and became the editor of *The Hartford Courant*, where he wrote strong anti-slavery editorials and was depressed eventually to a state of misery by the tragedy of the Civil War. He had graduated from Williams College in the class of 1814, and taught school for a year in Northampton, Massachusetts. After that he went back to Litchfield and took charge of the school for girls that his Aunt Sarah Pierce had established there. But he records in his journal that soon after his return to Litchfield he set out to walk north to Sheffield, some forty miles, where he called on a girl named Huldah whom he was interested in—and during the evening visit he was so weary from his walk and she was so weary from being out at a dance the night before that they sat in glum silence, and that for them was the end of it. He went on with his trip into New York State the next day and devoted himself to picking up geological and botanical specimens, but I think he never saw Huldah again. In the course of time he married Lucy Porter, from Portland, Maine, who had first come to Litchfield to visit her sister, who was the second wife of Lyman Beecher, and Harriet Beecher's stepmother.

Litchfield in those times was a town of extraordinary distinction and beauty. It seems to have been inhabited by the very cream of our colonial society who had built their big clapboarded houses on the wide and spacious streets along with the Phelps Tavern of 1787 and the Meeting House of 1828 with its classic portico and Wren spire. It is beautifully evoked in Harriet Beecher Stowe's novel *Old Town Folks*, which is far and away the most authentic novel ever written about old New England: she names the town Cloudland and gives it those qualities we still dream of as belonging to the lovely austerities of our puritan past, the plain living and high thinking, the pure country pleasures, the surrounding beauty, the sense of elevation both moral and actual. The old Calvinistic tough-mindedness had mellowed, and a very humanistic half-romantic attitude was creeping in, and the village and people of Litchfield were aglow with a new faith in the goodness and delight in pleasant and virtuous living.

The school founded by Miss Sarah Pierce in 1792 was called the Litchfield Female Academy, and everyone, including Harriet Beecher, agreed that it was the most enlightened and advanced girls' school of its time, and a pioneer in offering young women a chance at higher education. A few boys came to it too, as Mrs. Stowe records in her novel, but it was mainly for girls, who came from all parts of the settled country—from the South and Midwest as well as New York and New England. They boarded, of course under strict supervision, with selected families in the village. They studied mathematics, chemistry, natural philosophy, history (particularly modern European and the American Revolution), logic, composition, geography and map study, English grammar, and music and painting. They took their work very seriously. And again and again in their journals they have left a record of their happiness at being there, and their devotion to the place and the school and its teachers. One Caroline Chester in 1816, for example, wrote, "Long after I have left school will memory delight to recur to the happy *year* which I spent with Miss Pierce and ever shall I remember with affection her numerous kindnesses to me, her advice, her repeated instructions —And not to her alone do I feel indebted for my lessons have generally been recited to Mr. Brace for whom I feel that RESPECT & GRATITUDE which is due to an instructor who takes so much pains, and feels so much interested in the improvement of those under his care." Another girl named Anna Shepard wrote to her family in New York in 1818: "[Litchfield] only wants the Tioga and Susquehanna rivers to make it the most delightful place I have ever seen. The society far exceeds the local situation with all its beauty, and there are schools where every science may be studied, charitable institutions for the dissemination of knowledge are established. . . ." She also records that "Our school is very interesting, all united like sisters," and adds, "One question (in class) Mr. Brace could not answer was, what is the physical cause of blushing?" May one suspect the girls of having a little fun with their young teacher? She notes finally that "Our subject for composition this week is, what is the disposition, is it innate or acquired? This exceeds my faculties for reasoning. It is more than I can answer. . . ."

"There are but few subjects more interesting to community than the education of women," J.P.B. said in his commencement address at the close of the school on October 25, 1819. "Who ever dared, until lately, breathe the idea, that woman should have any influence beyond the precincts of her kitchen, or any knowledge beyond an acquaintance with the recipe-book? In man's hour of folly, he might worship her beauty; in his hours of sickness require her assistance but, who then ever thought of her, as the companion of his hours of study, the adviser in his hours of difficulty, & the strengthener

in his hours of trial?" And while such declarations may not
satisfy today's more militant advocates of women's "libera-
tion," they stand up as a clear and valid beginning of the
movement that is now gathering such enormous power in our
world.

This history of Miss Pierce's Female Academy, and J. P.
Brace's part in it, is recorded in two large volumes called
Chronicles of a Pioneer School, compiled and edited by Emily
Noyes Vanderpoel, and published respectively in 1903 and
1927—and the word "Pioneer" refers not to primitive colo-
nists in an unsettled country but to these determined advocates
of female education who were its earliest promoters. And
while the name "college" was not used, the operation seems to
me to have been conducted on a collegiate level, with the same
academic purpose in view, long before Mary Lyon established
the first official women's college at Mount Holyoke in 1837.
It was in 1832, when J.P.B. moved to Hartford to take charge
of the Hartford Female Seminary and then became editor of
The Hartford Courant, that the Litchfield school lost its mo-
mentum and finally ceased to operate—and thereby gave up
the chance to go on as the major forerunner of American women's colleges. By 1832 it had won recognition as the
best school of its kind in the country. It was his deliberate
purpose, J.P.B. wrote, "to change the whole character of *female education.*"

The other major institution in Litchfield in these early
1800's was the Law School, which was also of top rank, and
attracted some eminent names both as students and faculty. It
was established by Judge Tapping Reave, and enrolled what
has been called "the very flower and nobility of American
genius." And the social consequences were very exciting for
the girls as well as the boys, with country picnics and dances
and theatricals and a few love affairs and marriages—all
doubtless conducted with decorum and restraint. My Auntie
Emma used to say that when Lucy Porter came from Port-

land, Maine, to visit her sister, the second Mrs. Lyman Beecher, she rode the last part of her journey in a stage with a young law student sitting on each side of her, and as they came into Litchfield she smiled sweetly and said to them, "Gentlemen, I think it is time you let me have my muff back." Each had supposed he was holding her hand inside her muff. Like her sister, she was considered a very elegant young lady indeed—always cool and poised and perfectly trained in social behavior. In her Litchfield visit she met my great-grandfather and they fell in love and were married and in due course she became my great-grandmother.

She was not one of his students, but up to that time he confesses that he was quite susceptible to girls. He accused himself of "flirtations." His character, he said, was "made up of susceptibility, excitability, romance, & imagination." He gave up the satirical habits he had borrowed from Alexander Pope, and succumbed to the romanticism of Byron, Moore, Scott, and Southey—especially, as he says, Byron. This was when he was in his mid-twenties, and he had a busy time keeping his cool among the delightful girls he was surrounded by, who all seem to have vied with each other in copying and keeping the poems that he wrote. He was particularly fond for a while of the girl from Sheffield, in Massachusetts, Huldah Maria Ensign, and almost, as he said, "popped the question" when he walked up to visit her but was made faint-hearted by his weariness and his youth. "I accuse her of caprice in my journal," he wrote, "but it is more probable the caprice was my own." He also said, "She had a large hazel eye with a mild sensible expression, beautiful auburn hair of the real purple tinge. Her face when animated was beautiful." He was still very young then—only eighteen or nineteen, and had first met his Huldah when she came to school in Litchfield, and during his first year of teaching in Northampton he wrote what he called a parody of a Thomas Moore poem, "The Vale of Avoca," and dedicated it to her.

There is not in New England, a damsel so fair
As that girl with the dark eyes and bright auburn hair;
The last lingering pulsation of life shall depart,
Ere that maiden's image shall fade from my heart.

As he looks back over his life from an age of fifty-five or so, he takes pride in his work in changing, as he put it, "the whole character of *female education*." "I was one of the first," he wrote, "if not the very first to introduce a more scientific course in female education. I had, for this purpose, to prepare lectures on Philosophy, Rhetoric, Logic, the philosophical principles of Grammar, etc." But then as he assesses his career and disposition he adds the following note about what happened in his mid-twenties: "In the meantime a change had come over my own character. The foolish indulgence of morbid melancholy had become a habit & was almost periodical. I knew its folly; I knew that its causes were imaginary. I knew full well that I could resist its influence, and yet, I went into it with my eyes open, & indulged in all its excesses. It might have terminated in confirmed insanity. It did alienate many very valuable friends, broke off an interesting engagement with a talented and beautiful girl. I was cured of it, in the winter of 1819 by the efforts of *Lucy Porter* and *Catherine Beecher*." Lucy, of course, became his wife, and Catherine was the extraordinarily brilliant elder sister of Harriet and Henry Ward. The "talented and beautiful girl" was probably Huldah Ensign. And there is no doubt that he led a life of effective self-control and achievement as scholar and teacher and writer and editor, but he did have an introspective habit of melancholy that always hovered about him.

Mrs. Stowe has painted a life-sized portrait of him in *Old Town Folks*—with affection and admiration and a very discerning intelligence. She presents him in his role as head of the school: "He, our master, talking of everything under the sun, past, present, and to come,—of the cathedrals and pictures of Europe, describing those he had not seen apparently with as

minute a knowledge as those he had,—of plants and animals,
—of the ancients and the moderns,—of theology, metaphys-
ics, grammar, rhetoric, or whatever came uppermost,—always
full and suggestive, startling us with paradoxes, provoking
us to arguments, setting us out to run eager tilts of discus-
sion with him, yet in all holding us in a state of unmeasured
admiration. Was he conscious, our great man and master, of
that weakness of his nature which made an audience, and an
admiring one, always a necessity to him? Of a soul naturally
self-distrustful and melancholy, he needed to be constantly reinforced and built up in his own esteem by the support of others. What seemed the most trenchant self-assertion in him was,
after all, only the desperate struggle of a drowning man to
keep his head above water; and though he seemed at times to
despise us all, our good opinion, our worship and reverence,
were the raft that kept him from sinking." She describes the
intense adventure of their schooling under "Mr. Rossiter,"
their reading of Virgil in Latin and Aeschylus's *Prometheus
Bound* in Greek, "the Calvinism of the old Greek tragedian,"
she goes on to say, "mingling with the Calvinism of the pulpit
and of modern New England life." "Bless me," she writes,
"how we did study everything in that school! . . . Mr. Rossiter had the most withering scorn for ordinary sentimental
nonsense and schoolgirl platitudes . . . we wrote on such subjects as 'The Difference between the Natural and Moral
Sublime,' 'The Comparative Merits of the Athenian and Lace-
daemonian Systems of Education.' Sometimes, also, we wrote
criticism, and if, perchance, the master picked up some
verbose Fourth of July oration or some sophomorical newspaper's declamation, he delivered it over to our tender mer-
cies with as little remorse as a huntsman feels in throwing a
dead fox to the dogs. Hard was the fate of any such composition thrown out to us. With what infinite zeal we attacked it!
how we riddled and shook it! how we scoffed and sneered,
and jeered at it! how we exposed its limping metaphors, and
hung up in triumph its deficient grammar! Such a sharp set of

critics we became that our compositions read to each other, went through something of an ordeal."

Mr. Rossiter in the novel was surely no more complicated and brilliant and formidable than the John Pierce Brace of the real Litchfield. It seems remarkable that Mrs. Stowe could so lovingly admire him and acknowledge her debt to him yet see him so discerningly. She recognized the doubts in his mind that prevented him from going into the ministry and turned him into scholarship and teaching and writing. She saw the strength of his intelligence and character, and noted his humor and humanity as well as his self-consciousness and his tendency to melancholy, and the kind of vanity that needed the esteem of others. He becomes actually the real hero of her novel in the admirable strength of his mind and heart—whereas the conventional hero, who presumably writes the story, is a rather neutral echo of her husband, Calvin Stowe, who seems to have been a man without much personality, though he is always patient and reliable.

There are three published novels by J.P.B. *The Fawn of the Pale Faces* was published by Appleton in 1853, and in the next year he finished *Roaring Brook, A Tale of the Past*, published eventually in Mrs. Van der Poel's volume of miscellany, *More Chronicles of a Pioneer School*, in 1927. These two are similar in material and motive, and belong to the Fenimore Cooper school of frontier adventure, involving Indian raids and capture and pursuit. They are realistic and probably authentic in their picture of the early times—even then at a distance of two centuries; but they are full of the moral and heroic stereotypes of the period. They are quite "readable," I hasten to add. We follow the desperate pursuit through the wilds of forest and stream to the eventual rescue of the captive maidens and the vengeful killing of the hostile Indians. They are in fact so similar in plot and theme that it is hard to remember which is which: in one the hero is wild and undisciplined in his youth but is brought to a sense of his puritan duty by the loss of his foot in the climactic battle and is cared for by the loyal and patient heroine, Martha; in the other the "hero" appears as two brothers, one the wild one, the other grave and responsible—and of course the wild one is killed in the battle and the virtuous one is rewarded by the hand and heart of his beloved Jane, though she did a little pine for the warm and spontaneous affection of the lost brother. "She was not exacting," we are told, "but her heart was lonely. . . . The character of our young Puritan may not interest the ladies, but we must portray his faults as well as his excellencies. We hold him as a warning to those of both sexes who suppose that sensitive hearts are wrong in demanding constant declarations of attachment."

These two Cooper-like stories do lack the epic strength and sweep of the master—as well as the extraordinary vitality and energy of the gifted pupil, Harriet Beecher Stowe. They are part of a genre art of the period, a bit like Currier and Ives prints giving stylized views of the life and times of long ago, but I think with an authentic understanding—not so much of Indian and forest action as of the hearts and minds of the Connecticut Puritans he knew so well. The stern repressions, the suspicion of exuberance of spirit, the awful fear of sin, the faith in the all-powerful and unpredictable and often cruel decrees of God—these with the competence and courage and mutual loyalties of family and community are what we can value most highly in the writing. They stand as minor documentary evidence about the ways of our ancestors.

But in 1847 he produced a book so odd and strange that I find it almost impossible to give an intelligible account of it. The title is *Tales of the Devils*, the author is given as J. P. Brace, A.M.,* Late Principal of the Hartford Female Seminary, the publisher S. Andreas and Son, Hartford.

The work may be described as a macabre satire—though not a humorous one, and not in any sense a dance. The object of the attack seems to be the Byronic attitudes and values that

---

* I do not know where or when he earned the A.M. degree, or in what field of study.

the author may have once held, and now renounces with intense moral loathing. This "Byronism" was of course one of the cults of Regency romanticism earlier in the century that exalted the heroic aristocrat as a splendid cultural champion who lived far above the petty limitations of ordinary men. It is to be remembered that Harriet Beecher Stowe had gone through a similar cycle of devotion to and disillusion with Byron when she published her sensational attack on him in *Lady Byron Vindicated* in 1869—more than twenty years after *Tales of the Devils*. And of course Thackeray had been lambasting Regency romanticism ever since his parodies of it appeared in *Punch* in the late 1830's. The Victorians tended to react very harshly against the worldly dreams of their early youth.

What *Tales of the Devils* actually does is to give us a post-mortem sequel to the life of a notorious hero-villain named Ernest Maltravers, a creation of the prolific and popular novelist, Edward Bulwer-Lytton, who represents in his early fiction all the exalted worldliness of the Regency era. He had written several novels—*Pelham* is an early one, and *Eugene Aram* and *Paul Clifford*—in which the hero can behave like a supervillain and get away with it by dint of nerve and iron-clad sophistication. But why J.P.B. should have selected Ernest Maltravers as his target seems to me a mystery. The attack is savage and positive. We are told that Maltravers has passed his life amid scenes "of cruelty and blood, of debauchery and lust," and now at his death must face up to the consequences—which involves a trial in a court of demons where he is condemned to be a corrupter of the good and innocent folk of earth and because he fails in this mission and even defies the power of the devil himself he is again tried, found guilty of "haughtiness, contumacy and pride," and is sentenced "to be driven from this assembly, in the form of a female skunk, to be the parent of skunks, and to lead the life, suffer the disgrace, and die the death of that despised animal; and as fast as death ends one body, your soul shall animate another, through successive generations, until Robert Woods shall pay the debt all mortals owe."* In the end, as we are told, "the pangs of renewed corporal existence fall on the haughty Ernest Maltravers, and when perception again returned, he found himself in the body of that loathsome animal in the forest paths of the estate of his despised son!"

Bulwer-Lytton's portrait of his hero is carried out in two novels: *Ernest Maltravers*, and its sequel, *Alice or The Mysteries*, and it is difficult for a twentieth century skeptic to realize quite how dangerous such a character seemed to the Victorian moralists. Ernest is depicted as a proud, gifted, conscientious gentleman, a poet, an athlete, a scholar—an idealized Byron, in fact, who loved an innocent girl and seduced her with honorable intentions to marry her, but was thwarted and lost her, and only after extraordinary complications and tragedies and melodramas was he able to reunite himself with her and confound his enemies and settle down in peace and great prosperity.

Like all of Bulwer's work these Maltravers novels are filled with the sort of splendid rhetoric that Thackeray derided in his burlesque *Novels by Eminent Hands*—the writing that the romantic Edgar Allen Poe found "richly and glowingly intellectual . . . unsurpassed by any writer living or dead." But Thackeray's view was the more orthodox Victorian one, and was echoed by Hawthorne (J.P.B.'s puritan contemporary) who considered Bulwer "the very pimple of the age's humbug," and by Tennyson who attacked him as the worst kind of Regency dandy in *Punch* in 1846:

> What profits how to understand
> The merits of a spotless shirt
> A dapper boot—a little hand—
> If half the little soul is dirt.

* Robert Woods was his illegitimate son who had succeeded, in spite of his birth, as one of "the leaders of his party, and the first men of the land."

But even so, *Tales of the Devils* does seem to me to carry its attack on Bulwer and his school to an unhealthy extreme, and I am distressed that my respected great-grandparent allowed his normally humane and mellow view of behavior to be so perverted. He is unjust both to the original Ernest Maltravers, whose actions seem to us now quite fantastically honorable, and to that harmless and kindly creature, the skunk, who seeks only to be left in peace. But as I said, the book is a strange one, and it may intend some edge of satiric humor which I have failed to do justice to.

Yet there is also an odd footnote to this affair that may throw a bit of light on it. J.P.B. had quite an extensive library, and among other things he collected many contemporary documents and articles and journals which he had had bound in book form—and one such volume contains an account of a man named Philander Brace who was tried by the vigilantes in San Francisco in 1847 and was condemned and hanged as an outlaw and murderer. He went to his death in a fury of eloquent invective against his accusers and executioners, and up to the very end he damned and berated everyone in hearing distance. Since all Braces in the country, so far as I know, stem from the same Stephen Brace of Hartford in the seventeenth century, I can only suppose that Philander must have been a cousin of some sort. He was described as a celebrated outlaw, who had originally been corrupted and led astray by the reading of Regency romances—the old Newgate Crime novels of Bulwer-Lytton and Harrison Ainsworth. He went west from New York State, where his family had gone to live, and decided to emulate his heroes of fiction by launching on a glamorous career as a gunman and highwayman and horse thief, justifying himself by his romantic conception of himself as a man of superior gifts and privileges, like Byron's Don Juan or the Giaour, for example, or Bulwer's Alton Locke or Ainsworth's gallant outlaw Dick Turpin, the hero of *Rookwood*, who became the legend and model of all aspiring supermen.

By the 1840's the reaction against Gothic celebration of

crime had set in strongly—in Dickens, for example, with his
Oliver Twist, and notably in Thackeray with his Fielding-
like satire *Barry Lyndon* which chronicles the unhappy fate of
a self-appointed heroic rascal. I think with his *Tales of the
Devils* my conscientious great-grandparent was doing his bit
to dispose of the glamorous ghost of the villain-hero of the
romances as well as of his very distant cousin Philander, the
account of whose death he had kept among his papers. But it
still doesn't seem fair that he took out his moral indignation
by an attack on Ernest Maltravers, who as I said hardly deserved such condemnation—and indeed was quite a noble
character. But there is no arguing with true moral indignation,
especially the Puritan and mid-Victorian kind. In 1854 he
wrote an editorial in *The Hartford Courant* on the deception
to be found in romantic novels. "The perusal of the Ainsworth School of novels has been peculiarly deleterious," he
wrote. "More bad habits have been formed and wrong notions
acquired by the perusal of these exciting exhibitions of the
success of vice, than the world is aware of."

At his death in 1872 he was widely recognized as a great
and good man. The long eulogy in *The Hartford Courant*
speaks of his "vast and multifarious acquirements" in law and
medicine and theology—in history and minerology and bot-
any, and even in out-of-the way subjects, such as heraldry,
astrology, cyphers, and the composing of music. "His ingenuity, invention, patience, and vast memory, with his passion
for imparting knowledge made him an unequaled teacher,"
and it goes on to cite Harriet Beecher Stowe's remembrance
of him as "one of the most stimulating and inspiring instructors I ever knew." Another account of him states that "No
other teacher in the United States has ever had so many influential and intelligent pupils." His niece Jane Loring (Mrs. Asa
Gray) writes about "his activity and energy, his originality
and immense variety of information and versatility, and his
merry laugh and fun . . . his absurd way of looking at what
are generally only bemoaned,—the toothache, or getting his

pocket picked!" She speaks also of his long visits to Cambridge and his "helping Dr. Gray over plants." All in all, he represents the New England ideal of a "Renaissance Man," a scholar and teacher and poet and novelist and critic who took all human achievement as his province. There is a beautiful daguerreotype portrait of him in the prime of his age and strength, in formal broadcloth and white linen collar and stock, seated, his right hand holding the head of a cane, his light hair thick and a little wind-blown, his face expressing a serene and strong repose—and the effect of it is immediate and vital, as though he would in a moment speak and smile. As I said, I feel very close to him. I think he was admirable and lovable. It may be that the century that has passed since his death has changed us more than I can realize, and we might find it difficult to communicate—especially on matters of religious belief and morals, though even there I think we would bridge our generation gap more easily than a good many present-day fathers and sons can. With all his faith and sternness of principle he seems to have been a warmly humanistic being, with an eager response to the pleasure and beauty of the world and an infinite curiosity about its ways. In fact, he shares some of the talents of his wife's fabulous cousin, Rufus Porter, the "American Leonardo," the mural painter, musician, astounding and ingenious inventor of everything from the Colt six-shooter to a transcontinental airship, the first editor of *The Scientific American* Magazine, which still flourishes, and the original inspiration for Mark Twain's Connecticut Yankee. J.P.B. was the more scholarly and philosophical, and was not a practical inventive genius like Rufus Porter, but his curiosity and knowledge in the affairs of his world were immense and inclusive. In many ways nineteenth century New England was the best of times and places, and an able man could aim to be in full control of his destiny. Everything seemed possible, the old wrongs and sorrows could be overcome by men of good will and intelligence—at least, that was the all but universal faith in the confident time before the

Civil War. It is my impression that J.P.B. was discouraged and disillusioned by that tragic catastrophe, and it is of course well known that such an originally hopeful and buoyant observer as Mark Twain grew increasingly bitter and finally wholly pessimistic, as he was when he wrote *The Mysterious Stranger*, for example. But now as we look back at the world of Litchfield and Hartford before the war—and even after—we see lives rich in faith and hope and love and a great deal of beauty.

TWO

GRANDFATHER'S WORLD

A LL TIMES ARE TIMES of hope Life without hope would be insupportable, but the range between great hopes and small hopes is very large. In my grandfather's time, which spanned the Victorian century, the best people, the social and intellectual leaders, were filled with a glowing certainty that what some of them called the Kingdom of God was slowly and surely taking shape. Optimism prevailed not only with the devout and conventional Christians, but with most of the poets and scientists and philosophers. My grandfather, the son of J.P. Brace, was a scholar and a historian and what today would be called a sociologist who wrote such books as *The Unknown God* and *Races of the Old World* and *Gesta Christi*, which dealt with the origins and impact of Christianity. He had read Darwin's *The Origin of Species* thirteen times; he was a friend and correspondent of John Stuart Mill, and of Sir Charles Lyell, the pioneer modern geologist, and of Asa Gray who had married his cousin Jane Loring, and of James Bryce, the author of *The American Commonwealth*—in fact he seemed to know most of the eminent scholars of his day in western Europe and America. He spent much of his life trying to improve the lot of the children of the New York poor, and wrote a book called *The*

Dangerous Classes of New York which is now in its second century and still valid. But always he worked with great expectations of progress, of a slow but sure triumph over the social evils of poverty and moral degradation.

The fight for the good life still goes on, but the hope of success is rather less than it used to be, and the shocks of failure are rather greater. The idea grows that nothing short of a profound reorganization of our political and economic system will save us, but in the last century, as well as in much of this one, the loose and liberal ways of American life seemed to hold infinite promise. My grandfather counted on the vastness of Western land to absorb and sustain the poor of the Eastern cities, and for a couple of generations his scheme worked well—but of course the West is no more the land of opportunity. He also counted on the charity of the benevolent and honorable rich to subsidize his projects, but so far as I know he never seriously challenged an economy that encouraged such colossal inequalities of the infinitely rich and the infinitely poor. He took our economic and social arrangements as basic to our ways of life, as the given hypothesis which we must all accept and build on, but he believed that by individual effort and good will we could collaborate to make things work well—which is the general belief that the average American citizen still holds. But few citizens have ever devoted such time and effort and conviction to achieving the better life of his vision. In his day and long afterwards he was loved and admired by the great and the small people of his world. His name was Charles Loring Brace.

He had grown up in Hartford, and was a close friend of Horace Bushnell and the Colts and the Olmsted brothers, John and Frederick Law. After he graduated from Yale he taught school in Winchendon Massachusetts, for a year or so and then went to New York to study theology and supported himself by teaching Latin and writing articles for the newspapers. In 1851, at the age of twenty-five, he traveled abroad with the two Olmsteds, and after visiting Ireland, where he met his future wife, he went on to Germany and gathered material for his book, *Home Life in Germany*, and thence finally to Hungary. There he found the sort of political oppression that he naturally hated, and because he was outspoken in his defense of Kossuth and the native Hungarian patriots he was arrested by the governing authorities and accused of being a foreign agent and a subversive. It was a serious and dangerous charge: he was allowed no communication and no defense, and was threatened with death. In his book *Hungary in 1851* he describes his repeated trials by a hostile tribunal. One of his imprisoned mates, it so happened, was a Catholic priest, soon to be released, and together in the course of saying their prayers under the watchful eyes of their jailers they managed to exchange the necessary messages in Latin, and eventually the word got to the American consul, a Mr. McCurdy, who made strong and successful representations. The story became a *cause célèbre* and the book was in time widely read. Kossuth wrote that "the book . . . had done more for him than any other thing."

This story was told to us as children, and it was as remote from our lives as the stuff of King Arthur and Robin Hood that we knew almost by heart. But our imaginations easily encompassed dungeons and threatened death and secret messages and we realized that our grandfather was one with the heroes of legend.

He lived, of course, the life of a gentleman. He was a Yale graduate, a member of the Century Club, and after the death of his father he settled in the ample Hudson River gothic house he had built in the seventies on a hill he called Chesknoll at Dobbs Ferry—a three-acre estate which is still there. The house was designed by his friend Calvert Vaux. In his day there was a panoramic view of the river and the Palisades on the western shore, and there was a grove of giant chestnut trees; there were all the amenities of country life, with a fine big garden, a stable and coachhouse, a chicken yard, and open fields and woods ranging up to higher hills to the east. There were a cook, a couple of housemaids, a German governess called Fräulein, a gardener and coachman named Patrick—it seems strange to me still to think of the place as ever having been new because when I first lived there only twenty-five years or so after it was built, it had the look and feel of an old establishment with long-settled traditions. That is, of course, in part a small boy's view of permanence, but I think the illusion of it was strong in those times and that big house and its grounds still seem fixed and changeless in my memory.

I don't really know where the money for his good life came from, but he must have inherited a modest estate from his father—which he used to build Ches-knoll. He had a salary, of course, as executive secretary of the Children's Aid Society, which was his major work, and he published eight or nine books and wrote editorials for *The New York Times*. I don't believe my grandmother, who was a Neill from Belfast, Ireland, brought him very much in the way of property. But he seemed to enjoy all the amenities of comfortable family living, not only on his Dobbs Ferry estate but in many trips abroad and one to California, and long summer sojourns to Lake Placid in the Adirondacks. All in all, he led a productive and satisfying life. He sent his two sons to Yale, and gave his two daughters the best available social education. The family lived together with love and respect and happiness.

It seems to have been a world that a man could take hold of. Even in view of the vast underground of poverty and misery he lived with confidence that he and his friends and cohorts were doing the right thing and were slowly and surely solving the age-old problems of social evil. In his day it seemed that he knew everyone worth knowing, and could rally all those who consented to his cause. His world was a finite one, but its opportunities seemed infinite—the sea, for example, or the wild lands and unknown regions of the earth, or the challenge of expanding business, all such areas could be made use of by the right sort of people, who could achieve decent order and prosperity without predatory violence. It was a question of sufficient effort and good will, which he abundantly possessed—he and all his loyal friends and relations together who assumed a cultural responsibility for their times. And actually the idea of organizing and implementing social conscience, of doing something practical to make life better for the poor, was very largely a nineteenth century development —partly because the poor were in worse plight than they had ever been and partly because of what Shaw flippantly—too flippantly—called the rise of middle class morality, which may be considered a hold-over from Puritanism mixed with democracy. The old Catholic notion that the poor were always with us and were doomed to suffer had given way to a troubled sense of a social injustice that might be partially, at least, alleviated. Good men were needed for the work, and good intentions, and a strong appeal to both private and public virtue. The great writer and prophet of the age was Charles Dickens.

My grandfather's extraordinary ability to "take hold" of his life and times sets him apart from the rest of us. With his combined vision and energy he aided and influenced the lives of more than half a million boys and girls of New York City. He established schools and convalescent homes and the famous News Boys Lodging House. Above all he gathered up thousands of the homeless children of the city and sent them off to the farm states. To many cautious observers it seemed a too risky venture, but the records show that it succeeded. The children were pathetically eager to learn the ways of farm life, and they rejoiced in being clean and clothed and fed. They were tough and illiterate, but they actually seemed to fit in happily with their new opportunities and new families. My Uncle Rob, who was my father's younger brother, made it the main project of his life to keep track of the children (mostly boys) who had been taken "west" to the farms and ranches, and he saw to it that all was going well for them. He lived always in the consciousness of their love and trust. Many who had begun their lives as abandoned waifs in the streets of New York grew up to be leading citizens of the new and expanding West. The operation turned out to be one of the major events in our nation's social history.

My grandfather had the kind of talent that we give the name of genius to. His father, John, was distinguished as a teacher and writer and editor, and was influential in his time, but he has been mostly lost in the past; his son, my own father, who took over his work as director (or secretary, as they modestly called themselves) of The Children's Aid Society, was a good and capable executive but was not driven by the need to do miracles.

He, my father, C.L.B. II, was as gentle and kind a man as ever lived, and for thirty-five years he carried on his father's work in the expanding and increasingly complicated economy of the twentieth century. But he had been trained at Yale Sheff as a civil engineer, and at the time of his father's death in 1892 he was working as a builder of railroad bridges in Minnesota—he lived in Minneapolis, with his wife (my mother) and two daughters. He was persuaded to give up his job in engineering and come East to take over his father's house and estate and as much of his career as he could manage.

So the Ches-knoll life continued, with less distinguished society (my grandfather's acquaintance was quite fabulous) but with the same family warmth, with visits from Aunts Emma and Leta Croswell, and Uncle Rob and Neill cousins and my mother's sister May Sherwood and her family from San Francisco and Hendricksons from New Haven and Donaldsons from Philadelphia. My brother Charlie (C.L.B. III) and sister Betty were born there. I wasn't, though. For reasons never clear to me, my family had rented a house in Islip, Long Island, and my mother arranged my birth there, late in September of 1901—doubtless later than she intended (my older sisters remember the long period of waiting). But I never saw Islip, and have never seen it, and am always a little embarrassed when I have to name it as my birthplace. None of us, I think, have ever returned there. It must have been a pleasant place in those days, with cool sea breezes, but its name has an absurd connotation. Anyway, Ches-knoll was the home of my early childhood, and for the first ten years of my life I lived there with great and steady happiness.

It was a life of protected innocence and a very limited experience with the realities. In my family were no improprieties of any sort—no bad language, no enmities, not much rebellion. My oldest sister Dorothy did at times seem bossy and much too literal in her notion of what was allowable in a little brother. Old-fashioned moral stringencies were taken for granted by all of us, though. I don't remember ever hearing a profane word uttered in our house—except once when an unhappy little girl visitor could do nothing but snivel and cry and I was at last driven to utter a blasphemous "Oh, hell—do shut up!"—at least it was so reported by my sisters. It was clearly an act of desperation, and no one scolded me. Perhaps on another occasion I was caught in some sort of innocent profanity because I was required by my mother to rinse out my mouth in soapy water, but I can only remember that the ordeal was not half as bad as it was intended to be—except for the indignity of it. Another time she actually spanked me because I had torn the pants of a brand new Sunday suit—but again it was the indignity that hurt, and I cried from the shame of it. None of us—no one we knew—rebelled against the code of what we believed to be the moral imperatives, and when later we read the iconoclasts like Samuel Butler and Bernard Shaw we were delighted by their outrageous wit but paid no serious attention to their basic motives. Actual moral and cultural revolution, outside the pages of a book or the stage, was not a viable reality.

My mother was splendidly beautiful in the fashion of Victorian heroines, and she accepted literally the codes of moral and social behavior. She was upright, almost austere, but full of anxieties and powerful affections—she took her responsibilities as wife and mother of five very hard, and was constantly concerned about household problems. She had no practical abilities—she couldn't cook an egg, as we used to say,

she did no actual housework, no sweeping or dusting or bed-
making, she certainly couldn't hammer a tack or screw a
screw, but she saw to it that such work was done. She could
order supplies with perfect assurance—I remember her morning telephone calls to Acker, Merrill, and Condit, and the
long listing of supplies—and she could arrange the meals with
the cook and write the menus neatly on a pad. She saw to it
that we lived well—and I'm sure food in those days had a
quality of freshness and flavor it has lost. She told us very little about her father's household, and it is my impression that
she was unhappy, at least when she was a young woman. As
a girl she had a stepmother she was very fond of, who died
too early in life, and her widower father sent her off to live
with the Braces and then sternly disapproved when she and
my father fell in love and married. He accused my father of
being a fortune hunter and disowned his daughter and behaved like the father of the heroine in Henry James's *Washington Square* (and since they were both well-known New
York doctors I have often wondered if there could have been
some actual connection: James was one who could pick up
and make use of current gossip). But unlike the fiction, her
true story had a happy outcome. She was loved and cherished
by her new family and her husband. She was a beautiful and
faithful wife and mother and lived a life of devotion and duty.
And as my father often told us, she was an heiress with an
income from her grandfather's estate—and he always pointed
out the advantage of marrying money. I should add that by
the time the estate was portioned out among her five children
as well as her sister's three it had considerably dwindled away
and was drained by bad managers and lawyers, but in its original condition it was substantial. Her stern father had had no
control over it; in fact no one except the impersonal legal ad-
ministrators seemed to have had any responsibility for it.

At any rate, when she came to be the chatelaine of Ches-
knoll in 1892, she was a happy and hopeful and well-to-do
young wife and mother of two girls, full of faith and devo-

tion to all Braces and to her sister May. As I have said, I keep seeing her as the perfect Victorian heroine, the picture of austere beauty, with the manners and tastes that were wholly natural and right for all occasions. Yet actually she was quite self-conscious, and rose to social challenges only by summoning up her will and courage. She was the kind of timid woman who could do her duty in the face of terrible fear—she had the makings in her of a saint and martyr, and would have been faithful to her death if life had ever demanded it.

Yet except for the ordinary domestic tribulations, and for the original melodrama of her marriage, she lived a good and peaceful life. Her great talent was to be a perfectly genuine gentlewoman, who wholly loved her husband and children, and saw to it that they were properly cared for and managed. She was not particularly musical or artistic, though she was trained in all ladylike arts; she had no philosophical or intellectual teaching above the level of a finishing school—her thinking on all serious matters was conventional for her time and class. She could easily be shocked by new ideas, and of course by improprieties, and she was rigorous in the enforcement of the social and moral codes of her world. Like other ladies of her day, she insisted on an extreme and almost inhuman modesty of female behavior—though I must add, to be fair to her, that she went in for vigorous outdoor activity such as camping and sailing, and she spoke almost boastfully of how she and her sister May played baseball with the boys on the streets of lower New York in her girlhood, an activity I could never really imagine as she described it, though I knew that May had always been good at sports and was in her day a famous golfer. Nor could I picture an old New York where Eighteenth Street was a peaceful uptown residential district with trees and gardens.

But my mother seldom talked about her own family. My father used to say that the heroic Vermonter Seth Warner was one of her forebears, though I never knew what the true connection was. I have at least claimed him as an ancestor,

and view with pride his monumental statue in Old Benning-
ton. She also said that her grandfather John Franklin Gray
walked from his home in Sherburn, Massachusetts, to New
York where he entered medical school and became a doctor—
but her news of her family was quite skimpy. One of them,
possibly an uncle or great uncle, I have found since, named
Schiller Gray, after the German romantic poet, was apparently an adventurer with great nerve and few principles who
went in for very shady get-rich-quick schemes and among
other activities pretended to be a doctor and practiced ille-
gally—though my mother never mentioned him: some of the
facts came to light in the legal efforts to untangle the confusion of her grandfather's trust fund. Aside from her sister
May the only member of her own family that she felt close
to was her stepmother, who died when my mother was a girl
of twelve, Sarah McKaye Warner, a woman of extraordinary
charm and brilliance, a pianist of professional ability whose
friends and admirers collaborated on a book of commemora-
tive tributes to her character and genius. It was after that
event that my mother sought refuge, as it were, in the Brace
family and was taken in and made one of them. Sarah, or
Saidie as her friends called her, was a sister of Steele and
Percy McKaye, who were well known authors of drama and
poetry in their day. Theirs was a world, as I have said, of in-
terconnections and relationships, with a great deal of deserved
and undeserved mutual admiration.

My name, I should add, came from a younger brother of
my mother, Gerald Warner, who died as a child long before
my birth. I have no knowledge of him except for an
old-fashioned brown portrait that makes him seem remote
and somehow inhumanly Victorian, all curly and plump. My
Auntie May Sherwood also named her son Warner, so they
both took pride in the name in spite of their vain and difficult
father. But so far as I know, there are no male Warners to
carry on the surname—not in that branch, I mean.

The Sherwoods lived in Berkeley in California, and every

two years or so they came east to visit us at Ches-knoll—a
wonderful festivity of gifts and hilarity and music. They arrived with violin and cello and a lute and I remember them
playing far into the night after I was sent up to bed—or so it
seemed. They lived what sounded like a life of high adventure in the unknown West, and were full of stories and pictures of climbs in the Sierras. They were good at tennis and
golf. Uncle Harry Sherwood owned a big store in San Francisco, a sort of Western S.S. Pierce, I gathered, and came with
presents for all. And he was actually a cousin of my father's,
his mother being a sister of my grandmother Neill—and was
at Yale with my father as well, and very much a part of that
interrelated small world I've been describing. He had a white
trimmed beard and was very generous, but I remember nothing else about him. I think he was a charter member of the
Sierra Club. While my mother was alive and active we kept in
touch with our California cousins, but the connections grew
more and more tenuous and are actually all but lost. Yet I
think of that depth of love and good will among us in the past
that seemed as durable and sure as anything in life, and I realize again how helpless we are in the hands of time.

My mother believed in God and heaven, and made us go
to the Episcopal Church, and my father stayed home—he said
he was a Unitarian and didn't have to go to church. He always made a joke of it, and whether he was ever really a Unitarian or not I never knew. His father had once studied to be a
Congregational minister, but was unable to tie himself down
to any sect, and may have encouraged his son in the more liberal tenets of the Unitarians. And it comes to me that my
Irish grandmother was herself a Unitarian, though how that
happened I don't know—it sounds improbable, but she was
certainly an Ulster Protestant. At any rate, the Episcopal rituals did seem very irksome and dreary to me as a small boy,
and I disliked the well-fed clergyman who presided with professional unction and specially annoyed me by the trick of beginning to read the responses before the congregation finished

reading their part—a trifling item, indeed, but it remains vivid for me after all these years. It seems to be part of the professonal habit of unctuous Episcopal clergymen because I have heard others doing it, as though they couldn't wait to get the ritual over and done with. I realize now that there is a sort of reassurance in the professional speed and rhythm of the service which moves along like a recitative, over and over forever, Sunday after Sunday, but in my boyhood I resented it as if it had been designed to annoy and baffle me.

My grandfather inherited a rational and scholarly habit of thought from his father J.P.B., and as I have said was a friend and correspondent of such men as Darwin and Sir Charles Lyell and Asa Gray, but he—like them—remained a faithful Christian to the end. My father, however, paid little attention to questions of faith at all, and would have shrugged himself off as an agnostic if anyone had pressed him for answers: he took life as it came, did his duty, believed in honesty and fair dealing, and indulged himself in a romantic love of music and painting and the beauties of forest and sea coast. He delved also into the picturesque aspects of history and antiquity. He would have called himself a Christian and a Protestant, but without much positive conviction. Like his fellow husbands of his era, he left the problem of serious religious observances to his wife, and himself lived in a state of hopeful uncertainty. He seldom went to church but never discouraged those who did. His greatest pleasure was to visit the forests of the Adirondacks and northern Maine where he could paddle a canoe and fly-fish for trout, and he lived his life in a dream of the transcendent beauty of natural wildness.

In earliest times there must have been Sunday evening family prayers, perhaps established by my grandfather, because I have a tableau in my mind of all of us humbly on our knees on the floor of the library—but the glimpse of it is very remote and small. I doubt if my father gave it much encouragement, and as we grew older and more worldly we probably rebelled, but in those times it was a normal practice in good and dutiful Christian families. And though I have, like count-less others in our times, rejected the old rituals of faith, I am profoundly aware of how much we have lost—and how lost we ourselves are in a life that allows us fewer and fewer illusions and hopes. Even then our religion had begun to lose its old purpose. And of course it established a moral foundation we could count on and agree to—and abandon at our clear and evident peril. Illusion or delusion, it made living a game worth whatever effort we could give to it, a game to be played according to the long-established rules of cultural Christian tradition.

My mother's pieties were both modest and anxious. She seldom insisted on them or forced them on anyone; she made no display of them, and she had no intellectual command over them, but she lived in sad bewilderment at the spread and strength of modern skepticism. Her pure and rigorous code seemed no longer valid in the changing world. We hardly ever spoke of such matters, of course, but I know she was troubled by some of the minor moral irregularities in the novels I began to write many years later, and she would be overwhelmed by the moral and religious anarchy of the present world. So, of course, would most of the conservative folk of her generation, but few among even the high-minded ones were as anxious as she was in her support of purity and faith. She tried, as I have said, to make good Episcopalians of us in our early youth, with little or no help from my father, and late in life she gave up on the formal church and communed more directly with her god. Her faith, she felt, was worth living and dying for.

THREE

LIFE AT CHES-KNOLL

T HAT BIG HOUSE at Ches-knoll made us all very happy—
at least it seemed always so to me, the youngest. I was
probably never really aware of adolescent ordeals in
my sisters and brother, though I am sure nothing sinister ever
happened in their early lives. Since I was from five to twelve
years younger than they, I looked on them as worldly young
adults—especially, of course, my brother Charlie who was an
ambitious athlete who tried to teach me how to throw curves
with a baseball. I was surprised one spring morning to see him
slipping out the door before breakfast in a track suit of white
shorts and T shirt and jogging off down the road, and I confidently and somewhat hilariously set off in pursuit, thinking I
could certainly keep up with that easy pace. The whole operation seemed somehow silly to me, but on the first hill I panted
and gasped and quit and went home. Training, I realized, was
a serious matter. It was my first encounter with what I recognized as a genuine athlete working out in a genuine athletic
uniform—in those days shorts and a T shirt on a youth would
ordinarily have seemed indecent for public wear.

Charlie went to a private school called Mackenzie and on
one occasion I sadly betrayed him. My neighbor playmate
Bob Forsythe and I were out around our barn one morning
(I don't know why we weren't at school) and saw a figure of
a boy disappear behind a chicken yard fence. Assuming it was

a sinister stranger, we ran to report to my mother, who at once telephoned to the local school for delinquent boys and explained that we had a runaway, probably in our barn. In time a posse appeared and began searching the premises, and I have a vivid memory of a grim looking man climbing on some grain storage bins and firmly seizing a human leg— which turned out to be Charlie's. We were all acutely embarrassed, Charlie most of all, and I still feel my guilt at having betrayed him to authoritarian adults. He was ordinarily a brave and confident person, but some sort of misery had driven him to play hooky and take refuge in our barn, and there he was, caught and exposed as a delinquent. The posse went away in some disgust; Charlie, doubtless after a talking-to, returned to school; and I was left with unanswered questions about the mysterious secret life of my big brother. I must add here that during all of his too-short life, he not only tolerated me but treated me as a partner in many a splendid enterprise, especially when I was big enough to go on coast-wise cruises with him, and canoeing and camping and climbing. He was seven years older than I, and very adventurous and eager for experience and romantic, and he loved physical prowess and competition and was a bad loser. It was a bitter experience for him to have been caught playing hooky so publicly and ignominiously.

My best friends and companions in the Dobbs Ferry years were the three Forsythes, Willie and Jack and Bob, who lived on the second floor of the steam laundry building belonging to Miss Masters School, the grounds of which bordered ours, just down the hill. They were Irish and Catholic, and my mother was doubtful about the propriety of our being friends: I remember one day when a group of *their* friends were climbing in a big beech tree on our land she appeared in a fury and demanded to know who they were and what right they had to be climbing in our beech tree, and they slunk away and left me in a state of embarrassed astonishment. But such was the innocence of class distinctions in that time that no re-

CHES-KNOLL
G.W.B.

percussions ever seemed to occur—at least not very seriously. The poor micky boys, as we all called them, kept mostly to the lower levels of the village and only rarely ventured up into the hills. And if sides had to be chosen, the three Forsythes always banded with me against the enemies from below, and kept our hill secure. They were, in fact, faithful and constant friends, and we roamed about our hills together and coasted down the steep roads in winter and hitched rides on the sleighs. I recollect an angry driver brandishing his horse whip at us for daring to hitch our sleds to his sleigh on an uphill climb. In good snow we could coast from our house down across Broadway and down Tom's Hill, very steep, to the railroad station just above the level of the river—a feat long since rendered impossible by reason of motor traffic and new buildings and pavements. We believed we were champion coasters, and we kept at it happily into the cold twilight of the afternoons. No one knew about skiing in those days—except for some wildly impractical notions of strapping on barrel staves, we had only the faintest glimmer of what the possibilities were. When I finally took to skis at the age of twenty-five I regretted the lost opportunities of my early years, but I must say also that there was a good deal of fine adventure in our coasting: sometimes we would get together on a ripper, which is what we called a bobsled, and go whizzing down the plowed roads with reckless speed, but more often we would roam the region with our Flexible Flyers, which could of course be steered, unlike the old-fashioned sleds we called pig-stickers. (I have a vivid little memory of my bearded Uncle Rob coasting on a pig-sticker down the steep hills to the station to take the train to New York.)

The Forsythes gave me my earliest lessons in the realities of plain living. They were both generous and rough, gentle and profane, kind and harsh, and they nearly always took my part against my adversaries—of which I had very few. They were warm-hearted and loyal—they shared in the fantastic chivalric code we all got from reading Howard Pyle's King

Arthur books, which we used to act out in dramatic episodes, with even my sister Betty, five years older than I, playing Queen Guinevere. But of course the code included a lot of brutality and the wholesale slaughter of our enemies—who consisted of a few neighboring boys we decided we didn't like. I remember once how we waylaid a fat boy named Cummings whom we designated as an enemy and we cruelly beat him up in a gang attack, carried out with self-righteous satisfaction: it didn't occur to me until later that we were acting more like savages than the gentle knights of our romantic visions. I must have been eight years old, and along with Cummings and other presumably nice little boys and girls was attending what was probably the second grade at Miss Masters' school—where the lowest grades were coeducational under the benevolent direction of Miss Jones—and during recess we ran out into an open glade to play, and it was there my tough young friends were lying in preplanned ambush, and jumped on poor, fat Cummings like savages and after a brief interval of kicking and pounding ran off again into the woods. So far as I know, nothing ever came of the affair—no adult inquiry, no retribution, no discovery of my part in the conspiracy, though I am sure my schoolmates must have been stunned at the brief outbreak of apparent underworld violence. And Cummings remained subdued and scared for some time, nor did he try to get back at me, though he must have known that the attackers were my friends. They were, of course, the micky boys respectable folk lived in fear of.

Another hapless boy on whom a good deal of violence was committed was Bobby Frazer, whose father was a doctor who lived nearby. We were the same age—and he too was a Miss Masters pupil—as was his year-older sister, Mary. We played regularly together, and at intervals fought quite bitterly—and beating up Bobby Frazer became an almost ritualistic event. I have led a peaceful life—I am not much of a fighter under most circumstances—but there are occasions in the life of almost anyone when the worst side of his nature appears. The Frazers did bring out the worst in me, and I not only beat up Bobby—mainly by getting him down and sitting on him and thumping his head on the ground—but I outrageously sassed his family, and called his father a dirty old meany and accused him of cheating when he played ball with us (which he did) and I was a couple of times in a histrionic frenzy of invective at his mother when she ordered me out of the house and off the property. I can still hear my eight-year-old self screaming insults at her with uninhibited passion and relishing the experience as I never have since. And this too seemed to have no repercussions, no punishments or redress, though my eloquence did frighten me. But in time the Frazers accepted me again, and I came back to play with Bobby and Mary as though nothing had happened. But I was always uneasy with them, and their house was not as clean as ours and Dr. Frazer did cheat a little, and Mary seemed a little sly and a little dirty and poor Bobby was a slob—these are my memories as accurately as I can put them, and doubtless they represent simply the distortions of an eight-year-old.

But there may be a question as to what constitutes a slob. Both Bobby Frazer and George Cummings were clearly slobs, which means they were fat and slovenly, they couldn't run or fight, they were boastful and insensitive to the niceties of personal relationships—they brought out the worst in other boys, and were fair game for punitive attacks. Sometimes, though, slobs grow husky and dangerous, and eventually turn into football players and heavyweight wrestlers, and by then are left alone—but more often they merge with the general average of acquisitive citizenry and lead prosperous and successful lives. Many a political or business tycoon has begun life as a slob. I suppose inevitably it implies a me-first attack, and a lack of concern for the views and feelings of others; and it implies complacence even in the face of setbacks and failures. The slob generally gets what he thinks he wants, but he lacks grace and love. But of course it isn't fair to categorize so sweepingly. A boy's prejudices are hasty and often foolish.

If I had ever met such a boy as Samuel Johnson must have been, or perhaps Ford Maddox Ford, or Thomas Wolfe, or Oliver Goldsmith, I would have labeled him a hopeless slob.

There was nothing slobbish about the Forsythes. They were both modest and faithful, though they could be tough, as I have said, and profane, and proud. One day before the Fourth of July my father handed me two dollar bills to buy fireworks with—one for me, he said, and one for my friend Bob Forsythe. It was a large sum for the time and place, and I ran off eagerly to give Bob his dollar and to start off on our buying spree. He refused to take it. No sir, not a cent, not a penny. It was nice of my old man, but no—he couldn't accept a handout. He took his stand at once, without any prompt- ings—and the dollar fell to the ground between us. We faced each other in a tense moment of drama. I picked up the dollar, and together we went down to the store in the village and I bought two dollars worth of fireworks—an immense quan- tity—and we carried them back up to my house, and next day we all fired them off in a happy celebration, and Bob's honor and pride were preserved. But I couldn't forget his adaman- tine gesture as he let the dollar bill fall to the ground between us.

We lived then in a time of dreams and heroes. Boys still do, no doubt, but in that first decade of the century we all took for granted the wondrous destiny of our country and its triumphs in all areas. We knew our champions in war and sport and every human effort—we heard all about Admiral Dewey at Manila and Teddy Roosevelt and his Rough Riders and his Great White Fleet, and we assumed they were the wonders of the world. We said "Remember the *Maine!*" but hardly knew why, except that it was a matter of national pride and glory. We accepted the genius of Thomas Edison as the sort of brilliance to be expected in our countrymen—we were obviously the leaders in all mechanical and scientific progress. Buffalo Bill embodied for us the fable of the Wild West, which still so far as we knew existed out there like a great operatic drama continuously playing, and which we could still dream of taking part in—and we mixed our chivalric visions of King Arthur's knights with equally ideal visions of heroic gunmen, all remote and nebulous. But the great athletes were more palpable—their pictures came in cigarette packages and were precious collector's prizes: the fighters—Battling Nelson, Jim Jeffries, Jack Johnson—world's champions—and the ballplayers, Ty Cobb, Christy Mathewson, Chief Bender—supermen all, like classic heroes of the epics. And there was a tennis player named Larned who had never been beaten, and the greatest of all athletes was Jim Thorpe. All the superb champions confirmed our faith that our national destiny was to be first in all life's endeavors —it seemed quite self-evident, and we looked for daily confirmations of our success. It was a puzzling disgrace, we felt, when our marathon runners, a man named Hayes and a fabled Indian named Long Boat, were beaten by unheralded foreigners in the Olympics. But generally we were happily reassured that we did indeed live in the greatest country, and were proud to share in its triumphs.

My education in sporting events was of course due in large part to my big brother Charlie, and I began to absorb the experience precociously early. He always talked to me in man-to-man fashion. I remember when I was about nine walking with him to our mailbox in Maine to get the news of Marquard's nineteenth straight win when he was pitching for the New York Giants under Manager John McGraw. Charlie was always a hopeful pitcher, and late in his collegiate life, after the war, he pitched for a Yale junior varsity team against Harvard in Cambridge—and I was there and saw him get knocked all over the lot. Alas, alas, he took it very hard. He could never keep his cool under adversity; he was strong and erratic and temperamental. But never hostile or unfair. His anger was always directed against himself. He treated me magnanimously, even when I later beat him at his favorite game of tennis, but he castigated himself terribly. He lived in constant hope of proving himself a winner, and he kept himself in training and had visions of astonishing victories.

And the young are still hoping for heroes, but they are learning to be angry and cynical and to reject the simple success stories of that innocent earlier age. The battle for heroic triumph is still very fierce, though. Skill and prowess are admired and all but worshipped, now as then. Our cynicism, when it appears, arises from suspicions about the immense commercialism that controls all these profitable enterprises. We are taught to be more cynical about human activity of any sort.

I have a dim picture in my mind of my grandmother riding on a donkey, though I am not sure how much I saw and how much I heard about it. She lived with us, in what was really her own house, for part of the time, and with her two daughters and her younger son Rob in New York for the rest of the time, and I'm sorry to say that I remember her mainly as very old. There in our neighborhood, she was known as Madam Brace, and her donkey riding, which she of course did with a decorous side-saddle, was one of the sights of the village, as I was told much later. Her children were devoted to her, and called her "Mammy," and spoke of what a cool and courageous person she was, though in her old age she seemed to me full of anxieties. She had an Anglo-Irish accent, sharp and clear, and when she was annoyed with me she called me "child o'grace." Her big black pocketbook always had money in it, and I assumed that it held all she had in the world and I used to wonder where she got it and how much there was, though it seemed to be an endless supply. She was very severe about keeping my door shut when I went to bed at night and my mother had gone off downstairs after leaving it open a crack so that I wouldn't be scared in the dark. I listened for her to come across the hall from her room and the fearsome dark enveloped me and the door very quietly clicked shut. I must have feared her more than the dark, for I never complained.

What strains in the managing of affairs occurred between her and my mother I never knew, and apparently everything went on harmoniously, but since they were both women of decisive character I think there must inevitably have been conflicts. They were trained to be ladies, however, and could act with forebearance and mutual respect and devotion to an ideal of conduct. My mother had a heroic capacity for both duty and love—that much I am sure of. My grandmother very probably had a similar capacity, but of course I never knew her in her prime. The two of them got along, and the household happily flourished.

The one Irish relative we saw a good deal of was Cousin Larmour Neill, who seemed to live mostly in New York and came often to visit. I say "seemed" because his habit of life was something of a mystery; in fact, we regarded him as an adventurer of extraordinary fascination. He was, for one thing, a man of worldly elegance with the dress and manner of a grand duke—so at least we always said of him: he wore tailored black clothes, with wing collar and ample cravat, fur-lined overcoat and white silk scarf, and even on occasion a silk hat. He had courtly manners, and addressed all ladies with elaborate and charming compliments, and told endless stories about his wonderful adventures—I can still hear his Ulster accent of sixty years ago as he told of his conquests in the South, and invariably there was a climactic line that brought forth gales of laughter: "The most beautiful, the loveliest creature you ever saw!" He was, I gathered, a speculator in cotton, and incidentally had a job as a sort of field inspector for the Children's Aid Society and visited the boys they had farmed out in the South and West. But I think he lived a gambler's life, alternating poverty and prosperity—and since he had no wife and family he could follow his luck with a clear conscience. There were times, I am sure, when he was broke and miserable, and holed up in a cheap New York rooming house, but now and then he made a killing and emerged in worldly splendor with his ducal clothes and irresistible manner. After one such bonanza he invited all his relatives—fifteen or twenty or so—to dinner at the Astor Hotel followed by the theatre. We had just moved in to New York, and I had never been to an evening dinner or a theatre —I was about twelve at the time—and the splendor of the occasion seemed very impressive to me. Cousin Larmour was in his element as generous host and ducal gentleman, in full evening regalia—like all the men in his generation of my family he had a trimmed white beard, and I am sure was handsome and distinguished. He toasted the lovely ladies, and specially my mother, who I think was fond of him but somewhat embarrassed by his ardent praise of her beauty—I was even aware that she held him off, as it were—and what his private relations with the women he loved were I have no idea. For all his outward attachments, he seemed a lonesome and solitary man. But how he relished his splendid theatre party! We dined in state, and then sat in the best orchestra seats—and we saw none other than the first Douglas Fairbanks in a Graustarkian romance called *Hawthorne of the USA*, in which our hero rescues a European kingdom from its enemies and wins a princess for himself and demonstrates the sort of brash American complacence that has been such a trial to the rest of the world. The play still glows in my memory as part of that most glamorous of evening parties, and in later years I felt a proprietary attachment for Douglas Fairbanks in his career as a movie star.

For years Cousin Larmour came to us on ceremonial occasions—for Christmas dinners, or Easter, or weddings, and he always arrived with an effect of enthusiastic adventure, as though he had just seen the most enchanting of all lovely creatures or as though he were on the verge of making a fortune out of the cotton market, and he was warm and affectionate in his concern for our lives. He brought me Charles Lever's picaresque *Harry Lorrequer*, which astonished me by being so funny and human (I had assumed it was a stuffy adult classic). He was not much of a reader, I think, but he liked Irish comedy. He and my father compared notes on the stories of G.A. Birmingham—which I still recollect with wonderful pleasure.

But then he disappeared from my ken, and I fear he died alone and neglected, an old man in an alien land, with no wife or children of his own to stand by him. Yet he would never have demanded pity. I think he remained true to his somewhat theatrical image of himself as a gentleman and a gambler who was concerned also for the welfare of the outcasts from New York poverty seeking for a new life in the West. He lived with the kind of dramatic zeal for the immediate experience which is most characteristic of the Irish. His life, in fact, seemed to be a performance that was somehow not qute realistic, in the ordinary sense, as though he were acting out a predetermined role that required of him certain manners and clothes and attitudes—at least he always put on such a performance when he visited us. He must have had a private self too, which he took care to conceal.

My family for the most part are cautious and somewhat repressed Yankees who keep their emotions and desires under control, but the Scotch-Irish Neills did add some touches of spontaneous enthusiasm. My Aunt Emma, who in middle age became Mrs. Henry Donaldson, was the *grande dame* of the family, and terrified us all by her presence and manners, but she prided herself on her intensity of response to experience and her very theatrical enthusiasms which she attributed to the Irish heritage in her. And my Aunt Leta, her younger sister, was far less inhibited than most Yankees in expressing her affections and pleasures. My father and Uncle Rob were inclined to be very quiet and undemanding and were patiently amused at the histrionics of their sisters—I fear Freudian scientists would consider them repressed, though they both lived as well and happily as it is normally permitted.

As a family we lived with immense respectability and, I fear, some complacence. We considered ourselves as representing a plain-living and high-thinking tradition and we rejected pretentiousness and snobbishness, but at the same time

we scorned any manifestation of bad taste in manners and behavior. In 1910 the standards of what we considered acceptable behavior were uncompromising, and any deviation
into vulgarity could be detected like a bad smell. From our
beautiful hilltop we looked down on the village below and
were confident that our own habits and tastes were the standard by which all others should be judged. In all innocence we
assumed that the various social levels were arranged and fixed
by some natural law, and even though we were not rich like
the Rockefellers who lived across the road below us we were
in some mysterious and immeasurable fashion their betters.
Our grandfather had been a scholar and writer and a great
man, and so also in his day had our great-grandfather—and
even *his* father had published a book called *Scriptural Por-
traits*, which none of us had read, and we naturally took our
cultural superiority for granted. We were, I fear, naive about
these attitudes, and hardly aware that we had them. We were
certainly never taught to be snobs: on the contrary, we were
taught to be unpretentious and simple in our demands on life
and tolerant of others, and we lived without any of the osten-
tations of the socially ambitious. We were, in fact, always
amused at and a little resentful of the great-lady mannerisms
of our Auntie Emma, who talked and acted as though she
were in an Oscar Wilde play—though I suppose in a way we
relished the performances she put on. She had grown up as
her father's favorite—in her own view, at least—and she took
pride in sharing his worldly as well as his intellectual activities and she lived on in the bright memory of his career: she
kept us in touch with the great people he had known and
prided herself on her knowledge of their affairs and her ability to meet them on equal terms. The rest of the family operated with less assurance and more modesty.

My father took his social obligations quite casually, and
in fact as he grew older he abandoned most of the social connections he had and lived inside the bounds of his family. He
had little of his own father's extraordinary talent for finding

friends and companions wherever he went. But he—my father—was far from misanthropic. He took a kindly view of
mankind and got along well with his fellows; he was loved by
all his family, old and young, and was always generous and
concerned about them. But he made no demands or anyone
and never, so far as I know, punished or even scolded his children—though I recollect a time when he took me to Grand
Central to put me on a train for school and I had refused to
kiss my mother goodbye for some reason that I dimly realized was purely petulant, and I can still see my father's stiff
uncompromising back as he walked a little ahead of me to the
station. He mentioned my behavior briefly but memorably.
It was not a scolding, but merely an effective expression of
disapproval. This of course occurred after we had left Ches-
knoll, and I was twelve or so, and growing more difficult. In
my Dobbs Ferry days I never quarreled with my mother,
though at times she punished me for wrongdoing.

We had once had a horse and carriage there, and of course
the barn with stables and grain bins remained for us to play
in: my memory of the horse and Patrick driving it is as dim
as a dream. For important goings and comings later on we
hired a cab, of course, and I specially remember how my
mother would hire a carriage for a series of ritualistic afternoon calls in which the system, as I recall it, involved ringing
a doorbell and depositing cards in a silver tray held by the
maid-servant who answered and then departing with a sense
of duty accomplished. I went along simply for the ride and
generally stayed in the carriage while my mother did the
rounds, though it is possible that she may have at times actually entered a house and had speech with whatever lady
might have been at home there. I was chiefly concerned with
the carriage ride between calls. But whenever I read Elizabeth Gaskell's *Cranford*, as I occasionally do, I think of my
mother's ceremonial calls: the genteel rituals of the eighteen
forties continued still into the nineteen tens, and though we
were all quite aware of the artificiality and even the folly of

our behavior, and could laugh at ourselves as Mrs. Gaskell did—and as of course Gilbert and Sullivan did—we took satisfaction in playing by the rules. Anarchy of any sort was a remote absurdity.

In winter my father took us to skate on Ardsley Pond, and of course we walked both ways—a longish distance, it seemed to me. We wore ordinary high laced shoes with leather soles, and galoshes for walking in snow or slush, and we carried the old-time rocker skates that clamped on our shoes with a key-wound clamp and straps on the heel, and my ankles always seemed weak and wobbly though I tightened up my laces as tight as I could. I stumbled and slithered around the edges of the pond, avoiding the elegant fancy skaters and the fierce hockey players in the rink at one end, and I watched my father who delighted in his ability to do figure eights and the grapevine. The pond operated as a private club, I think, which maintained a warming hut and cleared and smoothed the ice, and only very nice people came there to skate—ladies in long skirts and nipped-in waists and muffs looking very pink and happy, and gentlemen in tight suits of knickers and wool stockings being graceful and gallant, as my father always was. He skated cross-handed with Cousin Alice Day who was wonderfully smart and vivacious. I think she came out from New York simply to enjoy the pleasures of skating, and was celebrated for her skill at it. In fact, skating was exceedingly popular among the gentlefolk of the time, even before the invention of the indoor rink and the efficient shoe-skates of later years, though it was during the twenties, I think, that the vogue of figure skating reached new levels of mass activity—encouraged specially by a show in New York. But in that earlier prewar age of innocence it was an art practiced mainly by ladies and gentlemen in the natural surroundings of outdoor ponds.

It was, of course, as I have said, a pre-ski age too, and we lacked the efficient winter equipment that is available today: we had to wear rather heavy woolen clothes with buttons

and buckles and stocking caps with tassles and knitted mittens
that soaked through and it took a major effort to get dressed
and undressed, but I suppose actually the experience of going
out into the intense bright cold of a morning after a big snow-
storm in the country will remain unchanged as long as northern winters endure. The place was a strange sea of curved
and crested drifts, still powder dry and icy cold, dazzling in
white sunlight, all landmarks lost or changed into mysterious
new shapes, bushes and trees heaped and bowed under their
loads, the barn far away across unknown depths. You dragged
your sled out into it and left it half buried and useless. You
began to help Patrick shovel out steps and paths—and presently the team of horses came jingling up the driveway hauling the primitive timber plow with the driver standing and
balancing on it and nodding a reserved greeting as he moved
steadily along. And afterward you could coast with your
Flexible Flyer down the steep driveway—not quite making
the sharp corner in it—and then on down the hill and across
Broadway and down the pitch of Tom's Hill, with no fear of
traffic other than an occasional horse-drawn sleigh.

There were in fact few fears of any sort. I remember
once playing on the ice floes on the banks of the Hudson and
being warned of the danger by a passer-by—and at first we
scorned his advice, and then suddenly it came over us that
we were precariously floating in deep black water on an un-
stable hunk of ice and we felt a few moments of terror until
we could jump back to the shore again. The man assured us
that we were on the verge of drowning ourselves, and I saw
that he was right. But in general, winter and summer, Dobbs
Ferry was a safe and peaceful village—or so at least it seemed
to us. We heard about city evils. The Forsythes were full of
tales about the crimes that went on in New York, and especially about a group of conspirators called the Black Hand
who menaced all decent folk—and we believed in their existence as we believed in the villainous robbers and murderers
in the story-books we were reading: that is, we accepted them

imaginatively and theoretically but not in actuality. Alone in darkness I could be afraid, I could feel the terror clutch at my spine as images of evil were magnified in my mind, but in the course of a day's ordinary activities all such fears seemed part of the half-pleasurable excitement of the story-book world. Once we heard a repeated hollow booming sound that came up from the south, where Hastings was, and for some reason we were afraid. Bob Forsythe and I were playing in his yard, and we both felt the mystery and the terror of the strange sound. We were sure it was a menace coming inexorably nearer, bringing some sort of danger and destruction. We told Mrs. Forsythe about it and she said maybe it would be safer if we stayed in the yard, which of course confirmed our suspicions that there was indeed an approaching danger. What the noise was I never found out—perhaps it came from a pile-driver at work—but I have never forgotten the conviction we had that an unknown force of evil was upon us. We lived among hobgoblins and chimeras, and what was reality and what was dream and fantasy cannot be told.

We of course believed in all the familiar miracles, in and out of the Bible. It was, we realized, immoral not to. Belief in Santa Claus was as essential to our lives as belief in the resurrection, and doubt in either case was not permitted. I suppose we were naive, young and old together, but the sense of immanent mystery above and beyond our ordinary affairs turned our lives into a drama of transcendent possibilities. There was no fixed creed that we were taught to subscribe to, but a general participation in the folklore of our earlier times —with an acceptance of all traditional attitudes about God and country and Santa Claus and our immortal destiny.

At Ches-knoll we had a parlor with rather stiff formal furniture and a Steinway piano, chiefly used for practicing and evening playing by my eldest sister Dorothy, and it was there that the Christmas tree was set up—and hidden from children's eyes until after breakfast on Christmas morning when the sliding doors to the dining room were opened and we crowded in to see the wondrous sight. Before the opening of the doors we had to wait with an almost frantic impatience while my father came very tardily to his breakfast, and then slipped alone into the closed parlor to confer with Santa Claus who was still busily arranging things, as my mother explained, and after an interval of very tense silence he flung back the doors—and there it was, the tree alight with real candles and adorned with wondrous golden and silver ornaments and angels and musicians and miniature Santa Clauses—and on the floor underneath and round about in chairs were the presents in bright tissue paper and ribbons. Santa himself had disappeared, presumably up the chimney, and my father hovered about the lighted candles with a jug of water—and after a few minutes he snuffed them out, but by then we plunged into the piled up presents in a state of pure ecstasy. I must add that we young ones had already had a preliminary little festival up in the bedroom we called the nursery, where I slept and where we all hung stockings on the mantelpiece of the fireplace—and no matter how I tried to stay awake and watch I never succeeded, and wakened by the blaze of the firelight in the dark early morning and the sight of bulging stockings silhouetted against the flames. I believed without the shadow of a single doubt that Santa Claus had been there in person while I slept and had filled our stockings with little toys and an orange in the toe.

Happiness could never in the world be more pure than it was for me and I think all of us on those Christmas mornings, not simply because we had new toys and surprises but because we believed in the myth and mystery of Christmas and lived for a while in a presence of a vast benevolence that cherished us with perfect love and generosity. The day passed with a strange timeless ecstasy. Nothing outside counted or even existed. It came as a surprise to realize that the weather was functioning as usual, that people were doing things: the world was as remote as a dream, it had no immediate reality, it was simply a sort of stage-like scene over which presided the spirits of Santa Claus and Jesus who made all good things happen.

We of course had a major dinner in the early afternoon, with turkey and plum pudding and all the fixings, and ate more than we could comfortably hold. It never occurred to me to wonder about the blessings and luxuries of our life or to contrast it with the life of the "poor" who inhabited the city slums. We assumed that we lived plainly and simply, and were reassured by the faith that our grandfather and his two sons had devoted their working lives to helping the poor children of New York. But obviously the contrast between their lives and our lives would have been staggering if we had actually realized it. Once I remember talking with a man who was painting the woodwork in an upstairs room. It was the day before Thanksgiving, and I asked him if he would be having turkey with his family and he turned on me with unexpected bitterness: "Turkey, for the likes of us? We'll be lucky to get a bit of salt fish." It was more than I could believe at the time, and I assumed he was simply annoyed with my questions. But the possibility that not everyone had a turkey dinner on Thanksgiving or Christmas haunted me for a long time, especially a man who was working as a professional painter with competence and self-respect. In general, though, the deprivations and inequalities seemed to us to be inevitable and even desirable in a highly competitive world where success was always possible for those Alger heroes of the times who won out by "pluck and luck." Some, especially the city masses and the foreign immigrants, had been caught in the trap of inescapable poverty, but the future of freedom and "success" for their deserving young was still an article of American faith—requiring will and enterprise and the helping hand of good citizens like my grandfather and his co-workers and heirs.

At any rate, we indulged ourselves in family festivity and security without the least nip of conscience. The house from

top to bottom was full of human warmth and good will: the
cook in the vast basement kitchen turned out perfect meals
and sent them up on a dumb-waiter, the two upstairs maids
did their duties cheerfully—my mother saw to it that we all
had little presents for them and treated them with special kindness and generosity.

Actually, we still inhabited the world of Charles Dickens,
where Christmas became the season of transcendent good will
and every household, no matter how down and out, depended
for its survival on its servant girls. As my Auntie Emma used
to say, the last thing she would give up was her "help"—if,
that is, it ever came to such an extremity of crisis—a sentiment
that Mrs. Micawber would certainly endorse. The sheer physical labor of running such a house as ours was obviously too
great for a Victorian lady to cope with—the dusting and
sweeping, the slop jars and chamber pots, the scrub-board
laundry and stove-heated irons, the coal-fed furnace and
cook-stove, the oil lamps. It took a staff of professionals, who
inhabited remote third-floor bedrooms and slipped down narrow back stairs to the dark regions of the kitchen in the cellar
where the big black coal range burned night and day. I think
of the little slavey of *The Old Curiosity Shop* called the
Marchioness dwelling in her underground dungeon, cut off
from light and air and freedom, until discovered and rescued
by the irrepressible Dick Swiveller, and though our girls were
not treated harshly or meanly, as the Marchioness was, they
did live a back-stairs and somewhat subterranean existence.
Some of them I loved very much, and depended on for simple
and affectionate responses in the small encounters of daily
life: I remember Erica, blonde and Swiss, and Frieda, and
Irish Maggie who later became our cook and made the best
rice pudding I ever had. I can just barely remember an elderly
and rather grim German who was called Fräulein, not an
ordinary servant but a governess who taught my older sisters
German and I think French too. By the time I belatedly came
along, language lessons as well as piano lessons seem to have

been abandoned and I grew up without accomplishments. I had no governess, though I think one of the house girls was supposed to look out for me and see that I had a bath and bring me my supper, which I had in the downstairs playroom an hour before the grown-ups had their dinner in the dining room. I remember resenting the ritual of being given a bath by a new girl under my mother's directions—I must have been very young and small then, but I was old enough to be aware of the indignity of being handled by a strange female, who was, I think, as embarrassed as I was. I was also old enough, I recollect, to ask her to say whether she was "for Yale or for Harvard"—a major commitment in my life then—and suddenly to realize what a fool I was to expect her to be "for" one or the other or even to know that they existed.

We as a family were wholly "for Yale." My father, grandfather, three uncles, and several cousins were all Yale men, and though they were not avid sportsmen or athletes they did create an atmosphere of serious dedication. My sister Betty always trained her dogs to lie down and die at the mention of the name of Harvard, and leap up joyously for Yale. Football was the great issue, of course, and to a lesser extent crew, and it is my impression that in that first decade Yale generally prevailed—at least I assumed it did. There was a fabulous backfield hero named Ted Coy whom we considered a superman—and one day he was seen in person at Miss Masters' School, surrounded by excited girls: the little glimpse remains in my consciousness like a fragment of an epic. My brother Charlie was of course a hopeful athlete and kept me up to the mark and saw that I followed the Yale teams with fervent devotion. It was a very grim period for us when a man named Percy Haughton came along and taught Harvard how to win— which it did for several years in a row with the assistance of its own supermen such as Charlie Brickley, Eddie Mahan, and Tacks Hardwick.

One of the great events of my young life was a trip to New Haven by motorcar to see the Game that inaugurated the Yale Bowl—a famous affair, and a thorough and almost humiliating defeat for Yale. Both Charlie and I were at a school called The Gunnery, in Washington in Connecticut, and he with characteristic generosity included his twelve-year-old brother in the party of big guys that made the trip, and we sat on the Yale side and were provided with blue silk handkerchiefs to wave on signal as a background for the white letters that were allotted to certain seat-holders to spell out YALE— a logistical scheme that seemed almost magical to me (I think I still have that same blue silk handkerchief stored among the relics of my life).

It was many years before my emotional involvement with Yale began to wear off: even as a graduate student at Harvard I felt the pull of the childish old loyalty at the time of the annual Game, and sat in conspicuous silence among the Harvard rooters as they yelled and sang for victory. That long-gone era of passionate amateur sportsmanship seems somewhat quaint and even irrelevant to me in my age and I can now look on the whole affair with the sort of detachment that I once would have scorned, but I see that I am merely noting the inevitable coming on of *ennui* and death. I suppose the amateur sport, the risk and the striving, are partly what make life seem worth living. Other things too, of course—like love, beauty, position, or food and sleep, but the game keeps people young.

DEER ISLE

IN THAT AGE of simplicity and peace the family left its Hudson River hilltop in the summer and went off to the coast of Maine—once, before I was born, to Northeast Harbor, then to North Haven in my first and second years, then to Deer Isle for most of the rest of our lives. My father's first and last love was for the forest and mountains, and he dreamed all his life of finding the perfect trout stream, as his father and grandfather had also dreamed, but there were no milk and vegetables for his children in the woods (he used to say) and he compromised on the coast of Maine with plenty of fresh milk and farm produce. The first memory of my life is a bright vignette of a morning at North Haven when I was two years old. It is like a little Dutch painting in my mind, quite isolated in time, unattached to anything before or after: I can perceive the still blue and white water of the morning, myself supposed to be taking a nap in a carriage beside a shingled building on a wharf, my stepcousin John Donaldson, later to be my brother-in-law, holding in his hand a new-painted toy boat and saying he intended to hang it on a string below the wharf so that it would dry. It is a scene I verified with him years later, and it has existed in my consciousness with a perfect sharp focus undimmed by time. I don't remember any such event as clearly for some years after.

At North Haven we rented a house that I think is

no longer there and my father taught his older children to sail, first in a tiny centerboard skiff named *Tripet*, then in a classic North Haven dinghy called *Dago*, owned I think by the Donaldson boys, and then in a twenty-eight-foot knocka-bout, *Bettina*, which lasted us for thirty-five years and which I inherited when I grew up. North Haven was and still is ded-icated to old Boston families, but my impression is that ours was made welcome: I remember many years later meeting one of the old-timers there and his eyes lit up with eager cor-diality as he held his hands about two feet apart and recol-lected when I was only so big. "There were girls," he said reminiscently. "They sailed." The place has not changed very much.

But the true paradise of my early life was a small quarter-mile-long island called Mill Island, semi-attached to the larger Deer Isle, a few miles to the east and north of North Haven. A shingled house had been built on a headland of gray igneous rock looking westward across the bay and southward to sea, but the lady who had it put there was more romantic than practical for she was never able to live in it. The problems of housekeeping were very great. From one end the island was approachable by a rough and rugged road that came first along a stony slanting long beach, then down over low-water mud flats, then up a narrow lane to the house—the trip, of course, negotiated by "horse and team," with buckboards and freight wagons, always mindful of the tide, and sometimes embarrassingly caught one way or the other. The other ap-proach was by boat across the channel from the point on the main shore that we called the Horn, where an actual foghorn hung on a fence-post and was blown by visitors who wanted to be fetched—except that at very low tide the strait was al-most impossible to launch a boat in, even the flat little punt we kept for the purpose. The tide rushed in and out in rapids through a rocky narrows, and at lowest water it was possible to skip across on foot from rock to rock—this tidal rush being of course the site of the long-gone mill that had been built by

FOUR

GWB   MILL ISLAND

the earliest settlers. So of course our life on the island was partly controlled by the tides: could we go or come by boat, or on foot—and what could we do in the half-tide stages when we could neither row nor walk? During the working day we had a hired boy whose job it was to answer the horn and ferry people back and forth, as well as the groceries and ice and supplies that were delivered there, but the complications of fetching and carrying, of boats left on the wrong side, of people stranded or stuck at odd hours, turned our life into a constant daily drama.

But the whole yearly cycle of our Mill Island venture was a pure delight for us young ones—perhaps specially for me, the youngest. My happiness began to expand inside me as soon as we departed from Ches-knoll with cabs and baggage wagon —except that I was a little embarrassed by my formal traveling clothes and hid from being seen by my friends and neighbors. Now that I can think back on the logistics of that annual journey I am amazed that my mother was able and willing to undertake it. There were five children, a cook and a maid, a dog, cat, and canary bird, a flock of trunks, and we proceeded by train to New York, by cabs (though I remember once taking a horse car) to the Fall River Line Wharf, where the romance really began and I could stand on the upper deck as the great ship moved out into the river and forged splendidly along round the Battery and up the East River among the tugs and barges and innumerable vessels of all sorts coming and going, under the bridges with rumbling traffic, past the narrow reach of Blackwell's Island and the dark barred prisons, through the strait of Hell Gate—and we noted a sailor standing watchfully in the bow as though he were ready to act in some emergency in the dangerous passage. We had supper in the grand dining saloon, with white clothed tables and napkins and black waiters, and I went to bed and sleep in an upper berth with the sound of the rushing water and the pounding throb of the paddle-wheels.

I was only faintly aware of all the crises that attended our journey, but I recognized the anxiety my mother did her best to conceal. She took it all pretty hard—the whole complex operation of a two-day-and-night journey of eight or nine people, with trunks and bags and dog, cat, and canary bird. I, being five or six or seven or so, was useless and helpless, and it seems to me that when we got to the South Station in Boston by train from Fall River early in the morning I was generally left alone in the waiting room amid the piled up baggage while everyone disappeared on some matter of essential business— and there I sat in fearful expectation that none of them would ever find me again. I know my father had to go and see about having our trunks sent to the Bangor boat as we called her, and my sister Betty led a party to fetch her dog from the baggage car, and Charlie probably wandered off to see the sights and our two patient maids took refuge in the ladies' room— and they all instructed me to watch out for our possessions, including the bird in its cage and the cat in its basket. But then in time they reassembled, were counted, and all moved upstairs to the station restaurant, where we had the best breakfast in the world. I can still remember the big sweet orange I ate with a spoon, and the nut-like taste of the oatmeal and cream, and the fresh poached eggs and bacon and the rolls and sweet butter: it sounds like ordinary fare, but the memory of it is still bright after sixty years. I have never since then tasted such good oatmeal.

So we had the day to spend in Boston, until the five o'clock sailing of the "Bangor Boat," and somehow we found our way to a couple of rented rooms—doubtless in a small hotel, though I don't know where it was. The June day was always hot. My mother took a nap. We rode on the open trolley cars. We walked to the Public Gardens and were wafted around the pond on the swan boats—a strangely dream-like venture for a small boy. The hours went slow. We must have had lunch somewhere, but I forget. Then at last the cab to Rowes Wharf and the boarding of our vessel, *The City of Rockland* or *The City of Bangor*—not quite as huge and splendid as the Fall River Liner, but somehow much more adventurous and much closer to our hearts. We had a strong affection for them, especially for the *Bangor* which was said to be wonderfully reliable and faithful, and we greeted her with a sense of renewed devotion as though we belonged to each other. We ran around the decks, and up and down the companionways, and hung over the rail to watch the loading process, with the infinitely varied freight rolling down the gangway on the hand-trucks piloted by stevedores some of whom slid behind like skiers in a schuss, so that the maneuver looked very expert and daring. There were countless barrels and boxes and trunks; we kept a sharp watch for ours, and now and then saw them, or thought we did. And horses, led one by one. And dogs—and Betty's Irish setter, behind a young stevedore and disappearing into the vast cavern of the hold, where she was allowed to greet him and renew his happiness and faith.

Then at last the cry of "All ashore that's going ashore" and the hauling in of the gangplanks and closing of the loading port and the casting off of the hawsers—and the long shattering blast of the whistle as the ship trembled and the wharf began to slide by and she forged out into the harbor. The great whistle seemed almost too much for me to withstand, especially if I were on the upper deck, and I had to clamp hands over ears until it ceased. But the event of our sailing was very splendid, and the blast of the whistle proclaimed it. The ship moved with pride out past the tugs and lighters and schooners, beyond the dust and smoke of the city, down past the harbor islands and the lighthouses shining in the late afternoon sun, meeting at last the long slow roll of the open sea. Maine was just ahead of us now, the wondrous coast down there in the dusky east, a world brighter, fresher, more beautiful, more like a dream of earthly paradise, than anything we knew back in the regions we came from.

My parents were glad to go to Deer Isle, of course, but I think they made the immense effort of getting us all there and settling for two or three months on Mill Island because their children were so perfectly happy. We all had the feeling that we were translated into a better life and time. We felt free and pure. Everything there was somehow pristine and perfect—the granite stones and ledges, the pointed spruces and firs, the cold water, the running tide, the surf, the sea winds, the channels and coves and islands all clean and fresh like brand new creations. When we arrived each June we felt at once the ecstasy of coming back to the promised land and rediscovering its perfect harmony of beauty and function, where everything seemed to fit into a natural design—wind and tide, cove and reach, rock and sand, forest and pasture and field, all somehow working together to achieve an ideal whole. The place, the people who lived there, and the creatures and the growing things and the weather, were all parts of the same kind of life.

The Bangor boat, as we called her, got us into Rockland between five and six in the morning, and we were roused up by sharp knockings on our stateroom doors. In later times I used to make a point of getting out on deck earlier, in time to see us pass Owl's Head and turn into the harbor and that first coming out into the cold of an early morning off the Maine coast was a sudden immersion in what felt like the arctic north with a rush of air that had blown down across fields of ice. I realized at once that we had been transported into a different world, far from the dust and heat we had left behind. We had come through a frontier into a clean cold region that shone with a celestial morning light brighter than anything we had seen before. It is always in my memory a pure summer morning with white sunlight glinting across the eastward bay, the waters all calm except for the long heave of the groundswell that reared and creamed along the rocky shores of the islands on our port hand, and the air is faintly redolent with the fragrance of fir and spruce, and up on Owl's Head the lighthouse shines as white as snow, and ahead the great harbor of Rockland opens up with its fleet of schooners lying in perfect stillness, three, four, even five masters, some with mizzens or spankers set without a tremor of motion in the morning air.

It was a busy port in those days, with its schooners and tugs and barges and fishermen, and three or four lines of coast-wise steamers all active in the early morning. We trans-shipped ourselves, bag, baggage and pets, into that famous old side-wheeler the *J.T. Morse* which every traveler in those waters still remembers with affection—and once again we could hang on the rail and watch the drama of loading the freight, hoping to see our own trunks in the long procession of mysterious objects that schussed the gangway—though here comes our dauntless sister Betty actually leading her Rory down the slippery planks into the hold below.

In early times the *Morse* ran to Bar Harbor round the northern side of Deer Isle, stopping at Dark Harbor and Bucks Harbor and Sargentville before getting to what was called the North Landing—at least she did it that way for a short time. Going and coming made a long day's trip. Later she went via North Haven and Stonington, on the south side of Deer Isle, a more direct route—and for thirty years she was a trust-worthy daily event in the summer season. She was a fast, use-ful, competently handled vessel with a strong tenor whistle that over the years became very familiar to us. When she fi-nally gave up and was taken off to New York to become an excursion boat, as we were told, we know that an era in coast-wise life had ended.

But meanwhile we had breakfast in her dining room—and those shipboard meals seemed wonderfully exotic to me, I suppose because of the adventure of it, and the ship's motion and the scenes passing the windows, as much as for the actual food. But it tasted specially good. Did we have hot blueberry muffins in the *Morse?* It must have been at some later time than June.

Deer Isle and the North Landing at last—and I felt myself to be a pale and conspicuous outsider in the eyes of the onlookers. There was always a bunch of local boys who attended the docking ceremonies of the steamer, even in that unpopulated north landing of Deer Isle, and some of them were allowed to catch the pennant lines flung from the ship's deck and to haul in the big hawsers and loop them over the bollards on the wharf—and I was conscious that they were privileged native old-timers who undoubtedly regarded me with well-deserved contempt. They were strong and free and confident and dressed in old gray clothes—and I, as far back as I can remember, at least, wore black shoes and black stockings with garters like a girl's on a sort of harness, and knickerbockers (short pants, we called them) and matching Norfolk jacket bought at Rogers Peet in New York. I even had to wear on all serious occasions an abomination called an Eton collar, a starched white affair that overlapped the jacket collar and came askew at the slightest activity; it was a symbol of pious respectability, worn in my day by nice little boys and by the high church choir boys, who by now have probably rebelled and abandoned them. My mother believed devoutly in the genteel formalities and saw to it that we looked and acted appropriately—and traveling in those times was always a formal activity, even arrival and departure in the rural setting of the Maine coast. It wasn't until trunks and suitcases were broached that I was allowed the blessed freedom of sneakers and khaki pants and open collars and sweaters, though even those seemed at the start too conspicuously new and clean, and made me what I assumed to be an object of scorn to all honest natives.

But—we arrived with expectations of delight, and were never disappointed. Benny Raynes was there with his four-seat buckboard and team, and another wagon for the baggage, and everyone greeted us with courtesy and kindness and seemed to take it for granted that we had a right to be there with all our confusion of possessions and pets and the two patient and dutiful maid-servants—who went off, I think, in the wagon with the trunks.

Country roads over open mowings and pastures with cows and flocks of sheep, neat white farm houses and shingled barns, truck gardens, plantings of potatoes and corn, stone walls and dark spruce trees—on our right the blue waters of Penobscot Bay still calm in the morning sun with innumerable islands and ledges folding away to the far western shore and the range of the Camden mountains. Countryside at that time was cleared and open, and distances seemed almost park-like, trimmed as they were by generations of grazing sheep: even the wild islands in the bay were once partly bare of trees, though they are now solidly forested. Four miles to Deer Isle village, the Harbor, along an upland road, with sweeping views all the way, then down across a milldam where tide flooded and ebbed with a rush, then two miles more through the village of Sunset, with store and post office and white church on a hill looking westward across the bay.

My mother's strategy for getting us settled on Mill Island was quite complicated. The house had to be opened and made ready—the big solid shutters removed and stored, the wood-burning water pump set going—as well as the wood-burning kitchen stove, ice ferried over from the Horn and loaded into the icebox—and boats to use for the ferrying—and of course immense supplies of provender including half a dozen barrels sent by freight from S.S. Pierce in Boston. George Dodge was the caretaker—a profane, erratic, often angry man, at times difficult, but a bundle of energy who saw to the cleaning of the house and the launching of the boats and the moorings and out-hauls. I have a memory of him pole-vaulting across the tidal rapids, very spry and quick on his feet. He was always driven by his undertakings—"d-d-druv," as he put it with characteristic stammer, or "r-right out s-straight," and it took tact to get him to finish what he started. Anyway, while the Mill Island house was being opened and swept and stocked, some of us boarded for a few days at Kate Sylvester's, and my mother went back and forth to the island to see to its settling. I think also that my father, after seeing us safely there, returned to Dobbs Ferry and then came down later for a six weeks vacation through August, though I am not very sure about the details.

It was still the era of *The Country of the Pointed Firs* and Kate as well as her neighbors could have been created by Sarah Orne Jewett. Kate—inevitably Aunt Kate to most of the neighborhood—was a clean, sharp, frugal spinster, and her house had the same qualities. It was cold, I remember, with gray painted woodwork and floors and straw matting and uncomfortable chairs and iron beds—not that any such austerities bothered me in the least: I was constantly filled with happiness at being there, at the miraculous natural felicity of the whole place, the pastures and spruce woods, the rocks and beaches, the tides and coves, the boats and vessels—the schooner *Etta Davis* at her wharf, the *Hattie L. Gray* hauled up in the hay field, and all the kindly and neighborly people who seemed actually glad that I existed—even the austere Aunt Kate who forgave me for spilling the two-quart pail of milk when I stumbled and fell on her front steps after the evening milking, though I realized that the loss seemed quite excruciating to her and I have never forgotten my guilt and humiliation at the disaster. But as I said, she was willing to forgive and forget, though she remained suspicious of erratic small boys like me.

At that time the little community of Sylvester's Cove still carried along the old ways of self-sufficient indigenous life, and while we summer folk added to its prosperity we were not the major influence we have become since then. The native Sylvesters, as well as the Eatons and Dodges and Becks and Haskells and Howards and Browns, represented four or five generations of farming and fishing and seafaring with little dependence on outside aid. They lived with confidence that they could personally cope with any problem that might arise; they had no doubts at all about their function or competence, or the direction of their lives or their past and future. Whatever had to be done they set about to do themselves—

whether building a house or a vessel, or digging a well, or planting and raising and preserving their produce, or catching fish and lobsters. That half-legendary pioneer time did exist in my early days there at the Cove and elsewhere on the coast. And I remember the encompassing simple-hearted kindness of the people—for all their crotchets and the sharpness of their ironic humor that so wryly faced the odds they were up against. Some are still there, a few whose experience goes back farther than mine, and some of the younger folk are still competent and strong, but they no longer live quite in the same self-sustaining world and are troubled about their chances for the future. There is even an edge of despair and decadence among some of them that reflects the larger tendencies of our time—though less evident, I think, than it may be in other more worldly places. They are still held by the old dream of living their own life on their own natural ground and they try to maintain the traditions of competence and responsibility they inherited from their fathers. But the times are somehow against them.

Actually the era of the summer people had already begun a decade or more before we first came to Deer Isle. At first they had come to board with the native families, or in such a house as Kate Sylvester's—and the boarding house era lasted for many years. Then in the nineties and after they bought land at picturesque sites and built the shingly "cottages" that are still there—many of them large and ungainly, with gables and porches of remote gothic ancestry: the Mill Island house is such a one, though it is well weathered and partly hides among its trees behind the great igneous bedrock it is built on. There was actually a boom in such houses at the turn of the century, and a dozen or so went up in the Sylvester's Cove region, after which the place seemed to settle down and remain unchanged for years. In the community of Eggemoggin on Little Deer Isle you can still see a whole row of "gingerbread" houses all put up in the same era. There has been no such building boom since then, though one by one new and modern houses do appear. Luckily our cove area was spared the ugly and even absurd effect of the Eggemoggin development, and even the worst of the houses have become part of the land-scape.

We originally came to Mill Island because my Aunt Leta and Uncle Jim Croswell had bought land near there, at Dun-ham's Point, and had built a house on it in 1903. They had first come to Deer Isle to visit their friends the Olmsteds and then they came as summer boarders and rented a native house in Sunset and then bought a piece of land on Dunham's Point from Eben Eaton, who had parceled off six or seven lots there and was selling them for summer cottages (any house of any size, even a palace or a castle, built for summer folk in Maine is locally called a cottage). And actually the Croswells had rented the Mill Island house the summer their own house was being built on Dunham's Point, and my parents sailed over from North Haven to see them there. When I was old enough to be aware of them they had settled in their new house, a mile walk from Mill Island—and since they were such a large part of our lives, in Deer Isle as well as in New York, I want to try to introduce them.

I used to tell my children that Uncle Jim Croswell, who died in 1915, many years before they were born, was the nicest man who ever lived. And I know that now, sixty-one years after his death, there are many, perhaps hundreds, who would agree without the slightest hesitation or doubt. No man was more purely and unaffectedly loved, and no man better deserved it. For the last twenty-seven years of his life he was the headmaster of the Brearley School for Girls in New York, and whoever knew him—his girls, his teachers, his Harvard classmates, his many friends—were united in their devotion to him and their grief at his death. Whatever qualities one might specify in the perfectly civilized man he seemed to possess: wisdom, humor, conscience, love, competence—the list could go much longer. There was a sweetness in him that won ev-eryone's heart, young and old, male and female alike. When I

met Dean Briggs in 1923 at Harvard I was astonished at the
intensity of his feeling about Uncle Jim and the tremor of his
voice as he spoke of him. They were two very similar New
Englanders, lifelong friends—Brahmins, as Oliver Wendell
Holmes somewhat facetiously named them; thoroughbreds,
we might better put it—men of great learning and infinite
modesty.

Uncle Jim was a graduate of Harvard in 1873, an instructor of Greek there and then a graduate student for three years
at Leipsig and Bonn in Germany, then an Assistant Professor
at Harvard until 1887 when he took over the headmastership
of the Brearley School. The next year he married my father's
younger sister Leta—and family rumor has it that it was assumed by all that such an eligible and brilliant young bachelor
would of course propose for the elder sister Emma, who was
herself conspicuously eligible and brilliant: they were all staying at the Crawford House in New Hampshire, and it came as
a stunning sensation when he picked instead the uninhibited
and unpretentious Leta. And they got along together with
wonderful felicity, she with her high and eager spirits, he with
his warm-hearted ironic humor—but by a tragic twist of fate
their only child was hopelessly retarded and insane, a heredi-
tary disaster, I fear, since Uncle Jim's brother and sister both
were unbalanced. His own extraordinary sanity stands out
more poignantly in comparison. Dean Briggs used to say that
he was the best talker he had ever heard—he told me that
when I first met him—and indeed he has said so in print. "He
talked as no man has talked before or since. I believe there was
never a more charming impromptu talker, whimsical, witty
always with an underlying seriousness, adventurous always;
yet never foolish or cynical or unrefined, never anything but
his natural, spontaneous self. . . . He was unlike any man we
have known or shall know." It would be easy to assume that
a man of such unique brilliance was himself close to an edge of
madness, but I have never known anyone more warmly and

lovingly human than he was, or more possessed of self-effacing wisdom and balance.

So the Croswells gave depth and dimension to our early Deer Isle summers. They occupied their new house on Dunham's Point and we went over very often to visit and arrange picnics together. The biggest delights of our summers were the picnics on the wild islands in the bay—an inexhaustible choice, as it seemed, of anchorages and coves and beaches where we were free to explore and discover. Uncle Jim had a little catboat that he called the *Tureen*—she being somewhat round and fat (we still have her blue pennant with a white soup tureen appliquéd on it)—and we would make plans to meet at one of the Porcupines or Crow or Pickering Island, and often we delegated my sister Eleanor, as an unusually able sailor, to go along with the Croswells and see that they were properly taken care of—they being in our view innocent in the ways of boats. There is a high rock that juts out over the water off the idyllic beach of Crow Island that we still call Uncle Jim's Rock because I remember him there in a clown's conical hat striking absurd attitudes for the entertainment of the children. He loved laughter, especially the laughter of children, and could share their follies. "Everything is funny," he wrote once to my sister Betty from Italy. "Naples was funnier than a flock of goats. Capri was beyond its reputation. . . ."

Many of our friends and family came to Deer Isle in that early time, some to stay with us, some to board either with Kate Sylvester or at her brother Ed's farm. There were the Donaldson boys, John and Norman, whose father married my Auntie Emma and thereby made life difficult for them—she being, as I have said, a lady who made formidable demands on all her associates—and later John and my sister Dorothy fell in love and married very happily. Their mother was Julia Vaux, daughter of the architect Calvert Vaux who was associated with Frederick Law Olmsted in designing Central Park,

THE HORN - MILL ISLAND

GWB

as well as Ches-knoll, and their aunt was Marion Vaux Hendrickson who came with her husband Lincoln and daughter Little Marion to board with one or the other Sylvester. Uncle Lincoln, I should add, was Professor of Classics at Yale and a man of enormous charm and natural dignity—not my real uncle in any literal sense but very closely allied. His wife and my mother were girlhood friends, and she, Marion Vaux, was celebrated in her younger days for her beauty and wit—along with her sisters Julia and Agnes—though as she grew older her neurotic nature took more and more control of her and she ended her life in an asylum. Those brilliant and famous families, like the Olmsteds and Vauxes and Croswells, did seem to have their fateful obverse sides, but their human achievements shine out more strongly because of them.

We all lived there on the island and round about the cove with a felicity that seems ideal and idyllic as I look back at it. There was no darkness or roughness in our lives, no sin or wrong, no miseries—except the minor scolding I got when I was caught swimming against orders with some of the bigger boys, and naked at that. Nearly everyone was older than I was, and I was a nuisance and a trial in my insistence on doing what the others all did, but they were always tactful and even kind in putting up with me. It may seem that I am looking back too sentimentally, but I know that for us young ones the early Deer Isle summers were as purely happy as life could possibly be. There was no sorrow for us, no loss, no failure of hope, no concern about anything—except the passing of the lovely days.

FIVE

KENNEBAGO

M Y FATHER, as I have said, had a primary love for the wilderness of our northern country, especially for the Adirondacks where he had spent his boyhood summers in the Lake Placid country, and for northwestern Maine, where he had once gone on a canoe trip with my mother and his brother Rob on the upper waters of the East Branch of the Penobscot. When he got a sailboat at North Haven and cruised in her with my mother he was always seeking out the small channels and estuaries and taking his boat into the most secluded inland waters—she originally had a centerboard and drew only two and a half feet. At Mill Island he had a canoe, and paddled round through the mill pond at high water, and I remember two occasions when he was out with my sister Eleanor on moonlight evenings they tipped over and swam ashore and came in all soaked and cold. He was good with canoes, and I never found out why they tipped over—except that the canoe was said to be a very tippy one.

But—he did dream of that wildness, and he taught me to dream of it too. It is an old and peculiarly American dream of a country beyond the frontier, undefiled by roads or wheels or even the axes and saws of woodsmen. In my young days it was already mostly gone—the virgin part of it—but the memory and spirit of it still remained as a palpable experience, as perhaps it does to this day in a few northern regions. And certainly there is something about pure wilderness that appeals uniquely to the human spirit—the beautiful on-going harmony and self-sufficiency of it, perhaps, as though it had achieved an ultimate perfection which could be discovered and shared. The loss of our primeval forest lands is somehow a spiritual tragedy.

So he arranged trips to the woods, sometimes with the family, sometimes with me alone, and his arrangements were major operations. When I was very little I used to hear of his Adirondack ventures—in fact he told tales of them all his life, and the names of Marcy and McIntyre and Avalanche Pass are part of my earliest memories. And later I went with him back to some of that country. But my first experience of the great forest happened when I was about twelve and he took us up to what he hoped was a trout-fishing paradise at a place called Kennebago Lake—and indeed in those days it was. My father was wonderfully eager about his fishing and very pure and fastidious in his methods. He fished only for brook trout and landlocked salmon, and only with flies and the lightest possible tackle; he had no interest in salt-water fishing of any sort, and any bait fishing or even trolling with a spinner seemed somehow vulgar. He was very reluctant to admit that the largest brook trout he had ever caught was an eight pounder on a "plug" as he called it in Lake Mooselookmeguntic many years earlier. He relished the delicacy of the fly-fishing apparatus and technique—which he had learned from his father and passed on to me, beginning with that Kennebago trip.

At that time the Maine Central had built a track all the way in to Kennebago Lake, and I remember being astonished to see the name posted on the bulletin board in the North Station of Boston—a night train called The Kennebago Express boldly proclaimed itself, and it was felt that the wild country up there was now at last being "opened." Up to then the only access had been by buckboard and horses over a wood road from Rangeley. So we got there before the inevitable exploitation and ruination of the region could get started, and the place still existed in a state of frontier innocence—an old time fishing camp with log cabins and a central dining room and that mysterious atmosphere of story-book woodsmanship that seemed more operatic than real. Except for the fact that lumbermen had been working in the region for years, it was all still wild and could be penetrated only by canoe or on foot over blazed trails. And by a remarkable exercise of legislative power, only fly fishing was permitted in the ponds and streams of the region—and it was even decreed that fishing in the Kennebago Stream below the falls could be done only in the company of a licensed guide, with a daily limit of two fish—trout or salmon. It was, I quickly realized, one of the most notable fly-fishing streams in the country, and when we hired a guide and went down to its pools our expectations were immense.

My father had taught me all the dramatics of a fly fisherman's experiences—from the delicate dropping of the flies in the chosen spot to the swirling rise of a fish that seemed to strike my arm like a galvanic charge—and then the snatch, the miss, the new cast with prayerful eagerness, perhaps another rise and a real strike—a big one perhaps, a threequarter-pounder, big enough to take line out, to play with care, to bring in with a landing net—a triumph, a glorious success after hours of patient effort. But down there in the big pools of the Kennebago Stream lived the giants of our fly-fishing visions—the four and five pound brook trout, the six pound landlocked salmon, and the very thought of them made my heart thud in my chest. All trout embodied the wonder and mystery of that wild northern country, and the bigger they were the more wonderful and mysterious they seemed. In my romantic innocence I thought of them as somehow challenging me to outwit them, as though they were players in a subtle game, opponents of supreme beauty and godlike excellence. That I should catch them and kill them was part of a ritual that I took for granted—it seemed inevitable, as long, that is, as it was done with a certain style, according to the codes established by generations of fly fishermen. So I suppose all true sportsmen feel and think. But it is a matter about which we seldom reflected—in those days, at least.

Actually we got very few fish out of the Kennebago Stream. My father caught one big trout and one bigger salmon in the few days we fished there; I caught nothing—had not even a rise, and as a novice I hardly deserved anything, but what I remember is the expectation and the conviction that the big ones were there, waiting for the right moment to strike. And indeed I saw some of them trying to leap up the Falls—emerging like ghosts from the foaming pool at the base and disappearing in the smother of white water that swept them back—and the flashing glimpses of those sleek long bodies remain bright in my mind's eye. But for the most part they rejected our hopeful efforts to catch them.

But one excellence of our days down on the Stream was the lunch provided by the guide. Ordinarily on our day's expeditions we had no guide, and were therefore forbidden to build a fire—a decree designed at once to save the forests from burning and to provide employment for the licensed guides. So our lunches were cold and rather meager. But the guide's lunch seemed like a masterpiece of outdoor cookery, with broiled steak and fried potatoes as the basic substance—and he conjured up his fire and all the fixings with an effect of professional magic that was purely delightful.

But of course the guide was much more than a good camp cook. He was, for me, at least, the embodiment of all the wisdom and skills related to life in the forest and I watched him with extraordinary intentness—the way he handled a canoe or stepped along a rough trail or chopped and split a dry log for firewood and laid and lighted his cooking fire. He possessed, I was sure, secret knowledge of birds and beasts and all the mysteries of the wilderness. He always knew where he was and what he had to do—and he always did it right. He was in

my mind the perfect old pro who operated with the sort of
certainty that made him seem almost preternaturally attuned
to forest life, as though he had a share in what I devoutly believed were its divine harmonies. And actually, so far as my
experience goes, I think this idealized view of the old-time
Maine guide is mostly sound and just—though whether the
tradition of perfect frontier competence is still being maintained I can't say.

Except when we fished down the Stream, however, we
never hired a guide—and were for that reason quite conspicuous among the serious fishing gentry. As a family we were
never all there at once, but on day trips up the Stream to Little Kennebago Lake we went in two canoes—my father and
mother in one, perhaps, and Charlie and Betty and I in another: it was my place nearly always to paddle bow, and
watch for the hidden rocks as the man in the stern poled up
through the wild rapids we encountered in the river. My father took special delight in poling, and got quite skillful at it.
And the adventure of the trip always seemed new and somehow mysterious, with the wildness of the region and the rushing little river and the sight of white-tailed deer and beaver
and even once a black bear. In one cut-off channel we went
through, the beavers had built a dam which we had to drag
the canoes across. Little Kennebago lay always in primeval
solitude—and there were wonderful big trout in the deep
pool with the lily pads at the upper end—several times I
caught two-pounders there, especially in the late summer
when they began to gather for their spawning season. We
fished occasionally in the dusk of early evening, and ran the
stream homeward in moonlight, and when we paddled in the
quiet places were startled by the crashing thump of a beaver
as it dove close to our canoe.

The drama of September in that north country seemed
very intense, with the cold northwest winds and the chance
to catch the big trout that headed for the spawning beds. One
arctic day I vividly remember when my mother offered to

paddle for me and we went off in the canoe to a deep place near the outlet of the lake where the fish were said to be. Several canoes were already there, with guides and a few eminent fishermen—one the well-known author of a book on trout fishing—all intently engaged in casting their flies. The expert, I noticed, always cast a very long line—and once I had seen him land what I thought was a good-sized trout and toss it back disdainfully with the remark that it was nothing but a half-pounder. It was a lordly attitude, I thought. At any rate, he was out there with the others on that cold and windy evening, throwing out his long line with considerable difficulty. His guide, like the others, worked hard to hold his canoe in position. My mother found a spot on the margin of the pool where she could thrust our pole into the bottom firmly enough to hold us in the wind and allow me to cast into the deep waters to leeward of us, and there we sat shivering in the gathering dusk while I tried first one fly and then another —large ones, small ones—Royal Coachman, Parmacheenee Belle, Silver Doctor, Professor, Montreal—the names make a sort of litany of my youthful hopes. And all around the pool those other silent fishermen patiently cast their lines and caught nothing—but suddenly I saw a swirl where my fly was, heard a thump of a big tail, and I jerked my rod with galvanic speed and hooked what I believed to be a monster trout—and in full view of that silent audience of experts I played him as patiently as I could, letting him take out line from the singing reel, gathering him little by little closer, at last bringing him to the net carefully, carefully, dipping him up tail first, not missing him or knocking him off the hook. Yes—a triumph. With witnesses. Not quite a five pounder, as I expected—but a three pounder of splendid form and beauty.

My father never tired of retelling that story—with embellishments: how his thirteen-year-old son, with his mother as guide and paddler, caught the largest trout of the season right under the noses of a group of fishing celebrities—and using at that a quaint old-fashioned lemon-wood fly-rod given

him by his Uncle Rob as suitable for a boy who was just
learning.

That was the summer of 1914 and the world war began,
and my elders were full of incredulity and anxiety. To me it
was a storybook event—and in a way I think it seemed so to
them too. From our camp in the northern wilderness a war in
Europe was too far away to seem real; it was a piece of melodrama not to be taken seriously—at least that's how it struck
me at age twelve going on thirteen. But my two older sisters,
Dorothy and Eleanor, were in Switzerland with the Croswells
and my parents were more concerned about them than I realized. They stayed on there at one of the big hotels in St.
Moritz into September, living on credit, enjoying the beauty
of the mountains—and John Donaldson was there with them
and he and Dorothy agreed they were in love and would
marry when they got home, which they did. I think they all
lived an enchanted sort of life in that magnificent place for a
month or more while Germany and France and Italy plunged
into full-scale war. It was when they climbed a mountain
called Piz Nair, I believe, that John and Dorothy happily settled their fate—and continued so to the end of their days.
Neither one was much of a mountain climber, and their ascent
of the minor Piz Nair was a triumph they never forgot. I
must later try to say what manner of man John was—my
brother-in-law, stepcousin, and lifelong friend and companion.

At all events, they escaped to Genoa, raised enough money
to pay the hotel in St. Moritz and buy a passage home in the
Adriatic—while I innocently returned from Kennebago and
went off to boarding school. I considered myself by then an
experienced woodsman and trout fisherman—as well of
course as a sailor.

SIX

CAMPING

M Y FATHER'S LOVE for the forest was very deep and persistent and he kept returning to it, during and between our Maine coast summers. Along about 1916, while we were all staying at the Stanley House in Southwest Harbor, he worked out a scheme for taking me off to a place called Grand Lake Stream, in northeastern Maine, which he had heard about as the ideal wilderness fishing country. We got there by devious one-track railroad trains, driving the last part from Princeton in what was probably a Model T and putting up at one of the characteristic Maine fishing "camps" at the Stream which was the outlet at the foot of Grand Lake. It was then—and may still be—a great and wild region of many interconnected lakes and streams, with the same traditions of frontier skills and ancient natural mystery that I had found at Kennebago. My father had arranged for two guides, with canoes and basic camping equipment, and we took off into the unknown with high hopes for glorious fishing and adventure.

My guide, Tom Avery, paddled of course in the stern and surprised me by whistling the tune of "The Old Fall River Line"—which I knew well, but wondered how it had penetrated so far into the Maine wilderness. At times he even said the words of it:

You could make that trip
In a battleship
On the old Fall River Line.

He had had a Victrola record of it, but at that time and place it struck me as incongruous.

He also discoursed on his technique with the paddle, which he described as the Grand Lake method. The canoe, a local product he assured me to be the best ever made, had a leather strip along the gunwale near the stern seat—on the right side, which was the side he always paddled on, and on each stroke he brought his paddle up against the leather strip and exerted the leverage that kept the canoe straight on its course. His right hand gripped the shaft of the paddle above the level of the gunwale, and the main force of his stroke came from the leverage or prying action of the paddle against the gunwale. He was eloquent in explaining the unique virtue of the technique, and indeed he operated it very efficiently and tirelessly. But it made a somewhat jerky motion, unlike the smooth flow of the normal method, and when I tried it later in a wind on salt water I broke the paddle in two. But Tom Avery felt that he and his Grand Lake fellows were the best in the world.

The other guide was a dark Scotsman named Dugal who worked in the lumber camps in winter and was famous, as he said, for his singing—he was hired and paid partly as a singer, in fact. And in the evening, after supper, by the campfire in the midst of that lonesome region of forest and lake, he lifted his voice in the wailing laments of ancient border ballads that had come down to him through generations of his forebears. Without hesitation, with no accompaniment and no discernible tune or melody, he plunged into tragic recitals of battles long ago, of a fair haired boy breathing his last among his enemies while his old mother and his betrothed wept at home. I was shocked at the wild and primitive appeal of the performance, and the anachronism that made it seem so remote and, as I thought, naive—but as time went on I began to re-

KENNEBAGO 1914

G.W.B.

alize that Dugal represented a wholly authentic folk tradition, untouched by anything literary or scholastic, and it was for me a unique experience. I was only about fifteen at the time, and I perceived this extraordinary event quite carelessly and ignorantly—in fact, I felt a bit superior to what I conceived as a display of backwoods absurdity—but it came to me little by little that Dugal's was a true voice of a long-lost human experience. He was of course proud of his professional success as both woodsman and minstrel.

I suppose we spent a week paddling and camping round the linked lakes of the region, but we caught very few fish. It seemed to be the wrong season, as it nearly always is for hopeful fishermen. We each caught a five pound salmon in Grand Lake—by trolling with a small spinner, which justified our efforts. I remember the exasperating sight of the big salmon that lay all day in a pool in the Stream and paid no attention whatever to the flies we so carefully drew past their noses.

Another Maine woods venture took us up to a place called Round Mountain Pond, some miles north of Kennebago, but reached by a buckboard road from Eustis, farther to the east. Since then the Arnold Trail motor road has been built through the region. Again my father took me as his most likely disciple in trout fishing and woodsmanship, and we ventured into the wilds with high hopes—and reveled in that wondrous world of trackless forests and pristine streams and ponds, but inevitably as it seemed we were disappointed in the fishing. One day we followed a trail to fish in the north branch of the Dead River, along which I was told Benedict Arnold and his army had struggled on their march to Quebec. It seemed to be a small and sluggish stream, choked with alders and brush, with no trout in it. I may be unjust in my recollections, but I am sure we felt frustrated in that venture. Doubtless we needed a guide to show us where and how to fish there, but my father in general was a do-it-yourself fisherman and he was happy enough simply to be at large in the wild country with his familiar rod and reel and flies all ready for the action and the expectations he specially relished. He rejoiced in the song of the reel as the line zipped off or wound in, and the swish and whistle of the line and leader and flies as they whipped before a cast. He hoped always for the miracle of the swirling rise and strike of a big trout, but his true delight was in the present moment of his time and place with all its harmonies and memories and promises. I think in those moments he identified himself with his father and grandfather and somehow gathered in his son in a small family epiphany.

He was a very gentle and unassuming man, as I have intimated, but he could plan and organize larger enterprises quite boldly. As chief executive of the New York Children's Aid Society he had to handle many administrative problems in the running of its schools and convalescent homes, but I was always a little bit surprised that he could operate so efficiently. I think the high point in his family enterprises, for him at least, came in the two summers he took us camping in the Adirondacks—first to a misnamed Salmon Lake, then to a little river called the Oswegatchie, both located in a wild state-owned virgin forest more or less in the western part of the region. Whether the forest has remained virgin I don't know, but even then there were rumors that it was doomed—and of course it was surrounded by cut-over country. But at that time it was a magnificent territory of first-growth spruce and white pine, hilly rather than mountainous, with many ponds and small streams. It was of course the forest that attracted him, and he had found out that we were allowed to camp on public lands—I don't know how he had made his arrangements, but he had hired a guide and sent in a load of equipment by train to the flag station Beaver River where we got off. It was, I think, on the main New York to Montreal line, and we took a sleeping car and arrived, he and I as an advance party, in the early morning, and somehow we got ourselves and our baggage from the station and its neighborhood store and post office down a little dirt road to the edge of a wide river or flow backed up from a dam—and there we met a man in a canoe who turned out to be our guide, Bert Dobson. And we paddled with him across the flow, and took a trail into the wonderful forest there.

It was the forest you dream of, with monumental pines six or eight feet in diameter, the kind that might in their youth have had the king's mark blazed on them and so have been preserved for masts for the royal navy. Or so, at least, we imagined. They seemed immeasurably ancient and splendid to me—along with their companion spruces—and we walked among them with reverence. The spaces under the trees were quite open and unencumbered by new growth, and the ground was a bed of needles and moss. Old Leatherstocking, the Deerslayer himself, would have been at home in that forest.

The trail led upward for a couple of miles along the outlet stream to Salmon Lake, where Bert had begun to make camp for us. It seemed to be all wild country, and for the six weeks or so we were there we saw almost no one—except of course for the times we came out to Beaver River to get mail and supplies. The lake, a mile or so long, lay untouched among its forest hills, and the camp was set up on a grassy space near the outlet. But Bert had no idea of what he was getting in for, with a family of five or six to take care of with tents, and equipment and canoes and food supplies—all to be packed in over the trail. Later my Uncle Rob and Aunt Bessie turned up with another guide named Gus—and of course we all carried pack-loads of stuff. I was fifteen, and full of the vanity of youthful muscle. But even so, it was an extraordinary problem in the logistics of family camping, and Bert and my father coped with it with very great ingenuity. I can't remember what food we ate except for oatmeal and the pancakes Bert made a specialty of. I know we caught very few trout—though I did at last find some in the pools of the outlet stream. There seemed to be no fish at all in Salmon Lake or the two lakes above it, but they were beautiful places to explore—especially Lake Clear, which was wholly pristine and pure, with water that was both translucent and blue in its depths, like a great spring. There must surely have been trout in those wild lakes, but we never found the secret of catching them.

One day my father and I went with Bert by trail a long way through the forest and came to a place called High Falls on the Oswegatchie River, where we camped for the night. Bert hadn't taken much food with him, and assured us we would catch plenty of trout. We tried our flies in the pool below the falls—with no expectations and no luck, and I was of course ravenously hungry and somewhat despondent. So Bert took my rod, baited a hook with a big angleworm and slipped down over the rocks to a spot he seemed to know—and at once hooked and landed a pound and a half trout. "I keep him handy there," he said with a dry sort of smile. "Just in case. I figgered we'd need him tonight." It was the only fish we saw on that trip, but it restored our bodies, and gave my father something to laugh about. He relished Bert's ingenuities and whimsies, and was amused at the way he had gone after his trout.

Next day we took the trail back by Lake Clear again, and to where we had left the canoe on Lake Witchhoppel, above our Salmon Lake, but my father was greatly taken by the Oswegatchie River and that pound and a half trout and he began then to plan on his next summer's trip there.

Other events of the Salmon Lake summer come back to me—especially the cat and the visit of my brother-in-law-to-be, Huntington Gilchrist. We were at war, that year, nineteen seventeen, and Huntington was a captain, I think, attached to the general staff in Washington—an impressive rank and job for a young man paying serious attention to my sister Betty. It seemed remarkably enterprising of him to find his way to our flag station and by canoe and trail to Salmon Lake in the remote Adirondacks, but *amor vincit omnia* and he came. It is his departure a day or two later that I recollect most vividly, because when we went with him back to the station the agent there said under no circumstances could he flag the New York train—which was due to pass in a few minutes—for some technical reason he was forbidden to do such a thing. A tense argument followed. We heard the far-off thunder of the approaching train. Huntington pulled rank very strongly. He was a member of the general staff. He had to be in Washington. It was a matter of national importance. The agent shook his head—no, no, he couldn't do it. The thunder grew louder, the rails trembled, the ground shook. Huntington gave orders, he spoke out so impressively that the agent began to weaken. And then just as the great steam engine came down the straightaway full speed, doing seventy miles an hour with all twelve cars of the Montreal-New York limited, the agent in a convulsive leap grabbed the signal handle and pulled it. I saw the engineer up in his cab jump as though he had been shot at, and he registered anger and astonishment together.

It took nearly a mile to stop the train. I was dancing about in an ecstasy of excitement, and I grabbed up Huntington's bags and started sprinting down the tracks—but the train backed and backed all the way to the station—and I ran back with it and when it finally stopped put Huntington aboard its one coach on the end. But alas for our vacillating agent—he was cursed up and down by the angriest engineer I ever heard. Huntington, I think, never had any repercussions at all, and got to Washington on time.

As for the cat, it came mysteriously out of the forest and haunted us at night. We thought it was a wild one, and caught the shine of its eyes and had glimpses of its dark silhouette, but little by little it revealed itself as a black and white house cat. It watched us with deep suspicion and vanished at the slightest gesture on our part. We spent several days trying to entice it with dishes of evaporated milk—which it didn't care for—and scraps of food—and very slowly it agreed to make friends. It was evidently a free and self-sustaining creature of the forest—and we assumed it must have been abandoned somewhere by lumbermen. There was no way it could have got across the wide river flow from the community at Beaver River. But in time it took to us with enormous affection and was a constant delight in its display of hunting skill and agility. At the end of our stay we debated anxiously about what to do with her, and decided she probably couldn't survive a winter alone in the woods and had best be taken in to the little village of Beaver River—and so along with our load of packs we carried a frantic and obstreperous cat that fought and yowled in a cloth bag all the way. An angry cat must be the most irrepressible of all creatures, but we got her there in the end, and let her go, and of course she vanished. We told the people in the little store about her, and we were almost tearful at the parting. She could go wild again if she wanted to, we thought, or she could make some new human friends. But we, Betty and I specially, had come to feel an almost mystical attachment to the little creature. I still wonder how she fared, and whether we did right to carry her from the open forest back to the settlement. I have never since then forgotten the sorrow of our parting with her, or the idyllic life we led together at Salmon Lake, but we realized that we couldn't take her back with us to a Park Avenue New York apartment on the fourteenth floor.

And actually we didn't go straight back to New York: some of us, at least, spent a September week or so at a "boarding camp" at Big Moose Lake, which was the next station southward on the railroad. No trout, as far as I can recollect. My father left us there and went back to town. I remember climbing with Betty the little mountains round Big Moose Lake in the bright September weather.

But the Oswegatchie River was much on my father's mind that winter, and he and Bert Dobson conspired to set us up at a camp on the edge of the great forest on a low cliff overlooking the river. I don't think I appreciated even then the immense planning that underlay such an enterprise: the equipment had to be assembled and transported—the tents and sleeping bags and fishing gear and housekeeping equipment and food supplies. He even had our old Mill Island canoe, the one he had twice tipped over with Eleanor, sent by freight all the way from Deer Isle—and it came through intact, via Watertown, New York, and thence by truck (I think) to the river.

About mid-July we set forth. I had just graduated from Loomis School, and was accepted as a fall freshman at Amherst—and in the three or four weeks between graduation and our trip to camp I had worked on the Children's Aid Society farm school in Valhalla, in Westchester County, doing everything from pitching hay to shoveling coal. As the son of the New York boss I felt conspicuous and so had to prove myself among the city boys, and I worked harder than I had ever worked before. The head man there was adept at the kind of flattery that kept me at it, and I was pleased that he admired my muscles and my persistence. At any rate, by the time we got up to the Oswegatchie I was ready for the carrying and paddling and was proud to show off my abilities.

The river is the chief inlet of Cranberry Lake, and we embarked on it several miles above the lake at a place called Wanakena, where there was a boarding camp and supplies. From there it was an eight mile paddle up the meandering slow flowing stream, mostly through scrubby alder regions—until at last we came to the edge of the first-growth forest where Bert had made our camp. He had teamed up with Gus, the guide my Uncle Rob had brought in to Salmon Lake the previous summer, and the two had managed to assemble quite a lot of useful equipment—some of it from abandoned lumber camps, as they assured us, such as a piece of sheet iron for a stove top, and boards to make a table and benches, and actually a few bedsprings—though I scorned such artificial comfort and insisted on a bed of fir boughs. We had several tents and a lean-to with a tarpaulin over it—and after we settled in, my father and I as the advance party, the others came and were met and paddled up the winding eight miles—my mother and my sister Betty (Huntington came later) and my brother

Charlie, who came toward the end of our stay there on leave from the Air Force, where he was about to be commissioned as a pilot and second lieutenant.

And at last, after a good deal of frustration, we began to catch trout. At first we used small flies, suitable as we thought for midsummer weather, with no luck at all. The water in the river was deep and amber colored, and one day my father tried a big Parmacheenee Belle, a bright red and white show-piece of a fly—he tried it as a sort of last-chance stunt—and almost at once hooked a two pound trout. The water there was a very deep channel among alder bushes, and it was a problem to handle so big a trout, but we found out how to do it, and from then on we had good luck. We used big bright flies. And it gave my father wonderful happiness. All his plans and hopes and dreams had at last been fulfilled. Even one two-pounder, caught on a fly, would have seemed to him a summer's triumph, but to be able to go off any day with the expectation of getting a fine trout was a pure delight to him. I think nothing in the world can match the intense dedication of a fly fisherman—his almost mystical concentration on the rituals of his effort, his devotion to the apparatus he uses, the delicate rod, the ungeared reel, the light coated line and filament leader and the beautiful and improbable flies, and all the half-supernatural lore surrounding the trout itself—the most elusive and pristine of all living creatures, the symbol of the purity and wildness of our forests and mountains, and somehow the challenger who invites us to a test of wits and skill. In the cold light of reason and old age I am opposed to the killing of all free and beautiful creatures, but there are many seasons in my early life of passionate devotion to catching trout.

It does seem to me amazing that we got along so well on these Adirondack camping enterprises. It was all wild country then—we hardly saw any strangers for the weeks we were there, and we had to pack and paddle all goods and supplies, and how we managed the housekeeping problems is more than

I can now understand—but Bert and Gus always came through with good and various meals, and we kept warm and dry and were not devoured by mosquitoes; in fact our only problem in the Oswegatchie camp was a hive of ground wasps that for a time almost took over our living space and had to be smoked and burned out by desperate means. I think our guides were somewhat frustrated by their duties, because instead of the exercise of their skills as woodsmen they were mainly occupied by cooking and housekeeping chores. In times of wet weather they were specially apt to seem disgruntled. But they kept things going to the end, and occasionally restored their self-esteem by paddling us on our trout-catching forays which they felt justified them in their office as guides. My impression is that the going rate for a trained guide in those days was three dollars a day, and even that seemed to my frugal mind rather extravagant.

When we broke camp at last, it was decided that my mother and Betty would go back to New York, and that my father and my brother Charlie and I would embark on a complicated canoe trip to the Raquette River. Charlie had arrived on leave full of immense vigor. He never cared much for fly fishing, but he loved to paddle and climb and carry weights. So the three of us set off down the river to Cranberry Lake in the two canoes, the one from Deer Isle and the other bought probably from Bert Dobson. We were loaded with tent, sleeping bags, cooking equipment, and the other minimum essentials.

But getting ourselves to our destination of Tupper Lake was a catch-as-catch-can sort of adventure, involved with trains and junctions and very hostile baggage handlers. We first paddled across the six miles or so of Cranberry Lake to the town of the same name, and there toted our junk and canoes to the railroad station where we hopefully checked them to Tupper Lake via a junction on the main line. There was some grumbling about the two canoes, but they and our duffel bags were taken on as baggage—this being, after all, canoe

RAQUETTE RIVER
1918

country. I think we must have spent the night at an inn in Cranberry Lake, and gone on in the train the next morning. It was at the main line junction that the hostility showed itself. The agent said those baggage cars on the limited wouldn't want to bother with a couple of canoes to Tupper Lake, though we could maybe try them and see. So my father asked him whereabouts the baggage car would come to a stop, and he stationed us there with the canoes and duffel all ready and waiting, and when the great train came steaming in and stopped and the big door of the car slid open we flung in one canoe after the other along with our duffel bags and packs before the opposition could rally to prevent us—and we called out "Tupper Lake" and ran all the way to the coach at the far end of the train where my father was chatting with the conductor in order to delay the "all aboard" signal. The trainmen were all annoyed with us that day, but we got our stuff and ourselves to Tupper Lake intact—and were on hand to unload the canoes and lug them and everything else down to the shore of the lake.

It all sounds like a series of unrehearsed comic scenes, and my father was delighted at our success, especially with what he considered his own little part in holding up the train until we could get ourselves aboard. We were in a euphoric mood —we had won through, by luck and nerve, as we thought, and were ready to set forth into the unknown. We launched our canoes and paddled off eastward to the Raquette River and up the river where we made camp for the night.

It was, I must say, a complicated operation to find a site, put up the tent, unpack our rolls of bedding, assemble our food and utensils, build a fire, and cook a meal—we hardly knew what we had or where we had put anything, and we seemed to have brought along a great deal of junk, and we were not organized to work efficiently together. Because I was the hungriest I did most of the cooking—which consisted mostly of warming up canned food like beans and hash. And

I had got Bert Dobson to teach me how he made flapjacks, which he did by mixing flour and an egg and a dollop of water and another big dollop of condensed (not evaporated) milk and a dollop of maple syrup and finally a spoonful of baking powder, and with good luck and a hot polished greased pan they came out as delicious as pancakes can be—though I must say that my luck with them was uneven. There were always variables—probably in the size of the dollops—but in time I became in a small way famous for them. My father always liked to boast of my abilities as a camp cook—he took, as a have said, great pleasure in his children's little accomplishments. For many years thereafter, in camping and cruising, I made Bert Dobson's pancakes—and when they were good they were very, very good. I think the special secret was in that dollop of condensed milk.

At any rate, on the first morning on the Raquette River we had pancakes and maple syrup. We also had oatmeal which I had simmered in a two-pail double boiler over the campfire the previous evening—another Bert Dobson trick that produced a delectable smoky-flavored porridge.

So we cruised up the river, taking turns paddling alone—and I remember how my arms ached as I tried to keep up with the other two—and we camped again and then came to Raquette Falls, where my Uncle Rob and Aunt Bessie were part owners of a camp that provided food and lodging for voyagers up and down the river. There was a carry of a mile or so past the falls, and a horse and wagon for the heavier boats and loads. In this last summer of the war in Europe there were few voyagers of any sort, and when we went on up the river to camp out on Long Lake and Cold River we met no one except a man camping with his wife on Cold River, who carried a gun in a holster to protect them, he said, against bad men and wild animals. It was in his view dangerous country up there, but he was the only dangerous creature we saw. But how beautiful was that region, with the high Adirondacks looming to the east of us, especially Mount Seward and Santanoni Peak! No trout, though—none at least that we could catch.

We stayed during our coming and going of course at Uncle Rob's camp, and after my father went back to New York, Charlie and I took off in one canoe for a trip through the Saranac Lakes. We first paddled down the Raquette River to a small stream that led us up to a carry across to the shore of Lower Saranac at a place called Corey's, where a post office and store were. But we carelessly missed the carry and kept on up that stream, which had a succession of high beaver dams across it—and it wasn't until we had unloaded and carried our canoe and junk past four or five of the dams, reloading each time, that it occurred to us that we had gone wrong and would have to reverse the process of unloading and carrying over the beaver dams. We did it with intense frustration —and then having found the right carry we had to make two trips to get the canoe and all the duffel across to the shore of Upper Saranac. Charlie was angry with himself—as he often was in his times of frustration—but the hard physical work restored our balance, and we pushed off cheerfully enough for a three-day exploration of the lakes. And we made out very well. We found a store and bought some fresh corn, among other things, and we camped on an island in the lake and boiled the corn for supper and afterwards sat by our fire and sang as many of the current popular songs as we could think of— such as "Over There," "Pack up Your Troubles," and "When You Wore a Tulip" and "Smiles" and "Tell Me Why You're So Wonderful to Me." The next day we paddled through Middle Saranac, and it is my impression that we climbed Ampersand Mountain, though I can't remember the details. We felt very happy and pleased with ourselves, and I cooked oatmeal and made pancakes for breakfast each morning. Charlie, as I have said, could be impatient and made reckless by ill temper, but we worked and played together with great harmony. When he got mad it was always at himself, never at me. He was eager for adventure, and full of the romance of being young and strong and courageous. He saw himself always as the champion, the one who came through in the crisis—I think he was very like Conrad's Lord Jim, a true hero in his visions, an ideal fighter and lover and adventurer, who was often baffled in the very crux of decisions. Even as a young boy I always had the feeling that it was my task to act as a balance against his romantic impulses. His end at last was heroic and tragic.

We got ourselves safely back over the carry and up to Raquette Falls again, where my Uncle Rob demanded an account of our ventures. He was a younger, slighter edition of my father and was even more dedicated to trout fishing—and since he had no family but a wife he could devote himself to it with all his heart; he had taught Aunt Bessie, who was a perfect Helen Hokinson image with a city background, to be his companion in the woods, and even to handle a canoe for him while he fished. I remember her pudgy little figure with an inappropriate hat perched on top of her head, and how she struggled to be the competent outdoorswoman she thought he wanted her to be. They were quite middle-aged when they were married, and up to then she had lived a timid and cloistered life in an ancestral brownstone house on East Eighteenth Street in New York, and then suddenly she found herself taking to canoes in the north woods and even once a packing trip on horseback in the Rocky Mountains, where she rode I am sure on a ladylike side-saddle. Her husband had made her feel free and useful, and she was ready to face any adventure with him. In later years she even learned to drive a Model T Ford, and if ever there was the original "woman driver" of legend it was she, who drove about regardless of consequences in perfect innocence—he, of course, like my father would have nothing to do with driving a car himself, though he was happy enough to ride with her.

We left our canoes at Raquette Falls—and for all I know they may still be there, though I recollect that Uncle Rob told me that our old Deer Isle canoe was chewed by porcupines who may have had a taste for the traces of salt water that must have inhered. I used to dream of going back, but I never did.

SEVEN

THE DONALDSONS

I T IS EVIDENT of course that country freedom was the best part of my young life. My idea of happiness was to be out of doors in the north country, either forest or sea coast, and urban life seemed no better than purgatory. When we went to live in New York City when I was nine I made a nuisance of myself by pining for my old happy home in Dobbs Ferry. My mother used to weep at my complaints, and I actually had spells of sickness which were brought on, she was sure, by city life. I had hollow croupy coughs and sore throats and tonsils.

I was sent to a private school for boys called the Allen-Stevenson School, in a brownstone house somewhere about Fifty-sixth Street, between Park and Madison Avenues—and of course I roller-skated to and from our apartment on Sixty-first Street and Park Avenue. It was considered a good school, and I am sure was conscientiously administered, and was full of the kind of boys my mother designated as "nice"—meaning that their parents were respectable and well-to-do, but none the less it closed on me like a prison house every school day and I was overwhelmed by misery. I was a poor scholar and my homework was always hopelessly smudged and wrong and my classes were so dreary I wished I were dead, and on top of the daily morning suffering there was a system of demerits that required the victim to come back to school after lunch and expiate his sins by memorizing and reciting poems—short or long as the weight of the sin seemed to require. In the sixty-odd years since then I haven't forgotten the jingly lines of Robert Southey's "After Blenheim." Demerits, I think, were accumulated for all sorts of faults, major or minor, and discipline was old-fashioned and stern. I was not naturally rebellious, but I resisted discipline and yearned for freedom and to be imprisoned in the afternoon hours seemed to me cruel and inhuman. I was of course spoiled, and always have been.

I remember several of my schoolmates fairly vividly: there was Pruyne, for one, a waxy, white-skinned prodigy whose homework was always as perfect as a copper-plate engraving—I think he must have been a genius, though I have no idea what became of him. There was a Morgan Morgan, whose name reflected ancestral pride. There was a pugnacious boy named Ransome who tolerated me because my clothes came from Rogers Peet—which he always called Rogers and Peet. There was a son of a well-known lady novelist. There was a fiercely energetic boy whose mother invited a group of us to go with him to the Barnum and Bailey Circus for two years running at their spring appearance, and many years later I saw his name and picture in an F.B.I. notice of the Ten Most Wanted Criminals as a robber and extortionist—we used to call him the Cyclone Kid because of his reckless speed on roller skates. I dimly realized at the time that there was something queer about his home life, with his mother's rather pathetic effort to propitiate him by giving a large circus party. But we thought he was a fine boy.

I had a few other friends—my mother was always on the lookout for "nice" boys, and encouraged me to play with children of her friends. In the afternoons I skated over to Central Park and joined furious games of tag in the Mall—I was vain about my skating, and considered myself a speed champion. I used to skate all over town, east side, west side, through the Park, to the dentist, down to my father's office on Twenty-second Street, block after block at high speed, dodging in and out of pedestrians—but of all the skating I did the time I remember most vividly is when Fifth Avenue had been resurfaced and was closed to traffic, and I came on it about Seventy-second Street and discovered a pure, untouched, velvet-like surface stretching away downtown—and I skated like one in a euphoric dream, floating right down the middle of the empty avenue, carving out smooth and luscious strokes on the virgin tarmac all the way to the Plaza. No one interrupted my flight, no one else seemed to have set foot there—I did it with the freedom of a gliding bird.

My best friend of those two New York winters was a boy named Edward Janeway, who lived in a brownstone house on East Sixtieth, and we got along together with perfect accord —so much so that it troubled me when we grew apart in later years and I lost touch with him. I haven't seen him since we were twelve years old, but I remember him with affection. I think we encouraged each other in mischief. I can see us busily folding sheets of paper into cleverly fashioned little bags, filling them with water, and aiming them from his third-story windows at the shiny roofs of the four-wheel cabs that came tooling along Sixtieth Street. Usually we missed, but once in a while we scored a direct smack on a cab top—and of course we ducked out of sight and closed the windows and waited in suspense for what might happen next. And though we were never really caught in the act, I think Edward's mother suspected that we were up to no good and put an end to our game. It is true that boys of ten have no sense. We even thought of tossing our water bombs from the roof of the fourteen-story apartment building where I lived, but were scared of the dizzy height of it: we did make an implacable enemy of the superintendent by dropping pebbles down the mail chute. We did not, in the end, manage to kill anyone, as he predicted.

I lived in those days in a summer dream of sailboats, and Edward did too; he had cousins out on the Connecticut shore at Rowayton who were notable sailors and racers, and we spoke of them with reverence. We read *Yachting* together, and knew all about the famous yachts of the era, the legendary cup defenders like the *Reliance*, the greatest racing machine ever built, and those beautiful big schooners like the *Irolita* and the *Elena*, and the *Enchantress* that seemed to us more like splendid myths than real vessels. When a few years later I found I could actually take a five-cent subway ride out toward City Island and walk on to where many of the great yachts could be seen and touched in the yards and buildings there, I could hardly believe in their actuality. I saw them always as visions, charging along under their lofty spars and press of great white sails. Though in later years, as I have said, my father introduced me to the world of inland forests and streams, my true love remained the life of the seacoast, especially of course in the state of Maine.

But it was during this New York interval, when I was nine and ten, that the family deserted our Mill Island paradise and instead settled for one summer in a rented cottage at Vineyard Haven and for another summer at Woods Hole, at a hotel called the Breakwater. I can't claim to have been unhappy in either place, but I did have a low opinion of both those regions—particularly of course of Woods Hole, which had none of the fresh and free beauties I looked for in a summer place. My mother's idea, I think, was to give us more social life, as well as warmer water for swimming, and it is true that we met people and did a great deal of swimming, but the damp warm climate and the level sandy scrubby vegetation seemed quite oppressive to me.

We chose Woods Hole because the Donaldsons, Uncle Harry and Auntie Emma, had bought a house there—he being a research scientist of great eminence who carried on his work at the Marine Biological Laboratories. Auntie Emma always insisted that Woods Hole in summer was the sort of place we young ones needed, and she made a point of introducing us to her proper circle of acquaintances. For a good

many summers it was arranged that I should visit her for a
few weeks in June and early July so that she could oversee my
social education, and while I think I actually admired her efforts for myself, I always set myself against her plans and
hopes. I remained pretty much a loner.

We had boats in those summers, including a little class
knockabout at Vineyard Haven that my father rented, along
with a mooring, an outhaul for the rowboat, and a raft for
swimming. The older ones, Charlie and Betty and my father,
raced in the weekly races, and did very badly, I think—which
is what often happens in a rented boat. The Donaldson boys
had acquired a small sloop called *Scorpion* from their uncle
Lincoln Hendrickson, and I am reminded of what my father
always used to say about it: when their widowed father,
Uncle Harry Donaldson, asked his advice on what he had
best do about his two growing boys, my father urged him to
get them a boat to sail and cruise in. So they bought *Scorpion*
from Uncle Lincoln—who had himself sailed her from North
Haven in Maine, where she had been built by Ozzie Brown,
around Cape Cod to New Haven in an epic struggle against
heavy southwesterlies. Uncle Lincoln, in his turn, had bought
a new 37-foot overall cruising sloop, built by Lawley, whose
name in boat building in those days was comparable to Steinway's in pianos. And after long delays and expectations they
both arrived at Vineyard Haven—first the Donaldson boys
and my brother Charlie in *Scorpion* with a dramatic tale of
an eighty-mile day's run from Sachem's Head, I think, to
Sakonet, and then later the Hendricksons in *Vega*—he rather
worn and worried at having to handle his heavy sloop with a
frail wife and daughter for a crew. He was an able sailor, with
great poise and confidence, and owning a splendid vessel like
Vega was the dream of half a lifetime—I can hear the relish
in the words "Lawley-built" as he often uttered them—but
alas I fear he was too often frustrated by her. He along with
Charlie started to bring her from New Haven to Maine a few
years later, but gave up before rounding the Cape—I don't

know why, except that he had a motorized tender that
wouldn't work and he was delayed too long. She had no aux-
iliary power in her, and the idea was to make use of the tender
as a tow-boat, but the thing was much too primitive. Marine
engines in 1911 were still in the embryonic stage, and the
heavy tender was an awkward boat to tow, and it never did
work very well.

But the Hendricksons came in *Vega* to Vineyard Haven
the summer we were there, and they took me with them for a
one-night cruise to Woods Hole—my first "cruise" in a small
boat of any kind. I had the greatest respect as well as affection
for Uncle Lincoln, as we all called him though he was not our
real uncle (except that his wife was the real aunt of the Donaldson boys)—and as I look back on his very long life he
seems to me a veritable palladin of the scholarly and gentle-
manly world he inhabited. He was a classical scholar, had
done his graduate study in Germany, had been one of G.
Lowes Dickinson's young scholars at the brilliant beginning of
Clark University, had gone from there to Chicago, and then
to Yale where in time he lived and worked actively into his
nineties as a figure of almost legendary distinction. He was
celebrated for his wit and charm and his beautiful voice and
his competence as a scholar and sailor—and he was surely one
of the kindest and pleasantest men who ever lived. But on
board his boats he could be a no-nonsense skipper, as I found
when he once tossed me bodily into *Scorpion*'s cabin for getting in his way when he was making a mooring in Sylvester's
Cove at Deer Isle—an indignity he soon erased for me by giving me the honor of being hauled in a bosun's chair to the
mast-head to reeve a new peak halyard through its blocks.
That morning of our cruise to Woods Hole he gave me the
first mug of coffee (diluted) I ever had, as a suitable drink for
a sea-going hand, and I took it as a foretaste of manhood.

Vineyard Haven in 1910 or so was a famous harbor of
refuge for the coastwise schooners that voyaged through the
Sounds and round the Cape, and by day and night it was full

of great vessels, including a few five and even six masters, but
there is a wide exposure to the northeast, and we heard stories
of the wild northeast storms that blasted straight in from open
water—and once or twice that summer such a storm did blow
up and we watched the embattled fleet with eager anticipation of wrecks. But aside from some dragging, I think nothing
went really wrong. The vessels, though, made a daily drama
for us as they came and went under sail, maneuvering in the
fierce running tides of Vineyard Sound, out past Hedge
Fence Shoal, and L'Homme Dieu (Lummy Do) Shoal, and on
through the treacherous channels of Pollock Rip Slue to the
eastward out of sight. Those strong tidal currents and the sinister shallow waters and low sand shores lost in haze seemed
always dangerous to me—or at least alien, or hostile. I felt
much more at home in Maine, where the waters were deep
and sheltered harbors were plentiful. My mind's eye still vividly sees the five canted masts rising from a sunken hull on
Stone Horse Shoal, where she had been stranded and abandoned in a winter northeaster—and lay there like a ghost ship
in the midst of miles of open waters—an apparition I encountered in the summer of 1923 when my brother and I were
heading down east with John Donaldson in his sloop *Bufo*.

After those summers of 1910 and 1911 we returned to Mill
Island for our last time there in 1912, but I think the effort of
running the place seemed too strenuous for my mother—and
as I said, my father yearned for the woods. For the next two
years we went up to Kennebago Lake. But before we did so,
for a few weeks in late June and early July, I was sent off to
visit my Auntie Emma and Uncle Harry Donaldson at Woods
Hole, where an effort was made to improve my manners and
give me more social confidence. Auntie Emma was a blue-
stocking of the old school—that is, she was both socially and
intellectually formidable, and expected others to take note of
her distinction. Before she was married she was addressed by
the world as Miss Brace, as though the bare phrase were a
title, and when she became Mrs. Donaldson she formally con-

ferred the title on my sister Dorothy as the eldest unmarried
Brace female; now she was simply Mrs. Donaldson, and
sounded out the name as if it had overtones of royalty. She
was very pleased with her eminence as the admired elder
daughter of a great man and the wife of another—for we all
agreed without question that Uncle Harry was indeed one of
the great ones.

And actually he played the part of a great man with relish
and perfect dignity. He seemed to live and move according to
a prearranged pattern, with ritualistic formalities in all daily
affairs—and of course his wife devoted herself to the same
aim and end. It is not much of an exaggeration to say that she
worshipped him, but her devotion was an aspect of the immense and theatrical complacence that she relished in her role
as the chosen mate of so eminent a character. But I hasten to
add that though Uncle Harry had all the makings of a stuffed
shirt, he was in fact not one at all—certainly not to his young
nephew. It is true that he terrified my mother, as she often
said, by his very presence—and I used to hear other ladies of
the family remarking on his alarming manner, but to me he
was a spring of kindness and marvelous wisdom. He did look
like a grandee, with a splendid head of wavy white hair and
white trimmed beard and mustache, and he walked with a
limp and a cane—a result of an early bout with bone T.B.—
and he spoke with measured dignity; I could certainly recognize that he was a scholar and a gentleman to be treated with
perfect respect—as everyone of course did; but I shall never
forget the warmth of his interest in my little affairs and the
intelligence and authority with which he talked of the world
we lived in—the birds and beasts and the weather and all natural events. He was a biologist and neurologist by profession,
but I thought he knew everything worth knowing. There
seemed to be no limit to his understanding of man and nature,
or of his willingness to share it with me in terms that I could
appreciate. In his day he was one of the foremost authorities
on the rat, and even now Donaldson's book on the rat is con-

sidered a classic in its field, but on top of that eminence, and in addition to his immense dignity of look and action, he could glow with an almost poetic eagerness at the beauty he perceived in his world. He even wrote an occasional sonnet to express his very controlled sentiments on what he believed to be the true and logical harmony of all things. Like the other great research scientists of his day, he was filled with perfect faith in the infinite worth of the knowledge they were bit by bit uncovering—he had a priestlike devotion to his calling, and I think considered himself to be in the service of a Darwinian universe which was little by little revealing its divine secrets through the trained and dedicated methods of objective science. He represented what might be called the romantic age of scientific discovery when everything opened up at once into new wonders of apprehension and knowledge and all the possibilities seemed infinite.

But although he was wonderfully kind and patient with curious young boys, like me—and like his sons John and Norman—he could cloak himself in splendid austerity in the presence of the sort of ordinary mortal he didn't quite approve of. His limp, his cane, his noble head with white hair and trimmed Vandyke, his measured and literate speech, his bright searching eyes, all combined to give him an aspect that could be quite intimidating. Everything he did was rigorously controlled. He seemed to live according to a formal pattern that governed his coming and going, his meals and his work and his leisure. He behaved in a way as one might suppose royalty might behave, with expectations of perfect attendance on his needs—which is the way his wife, Auntie Emma, behaved too, so that together they made a formidable pair, but were very solicitous about each other's demands, and in case of conflict it was she who gave way and catered respectfully to him. What battles they may have fought in private none of us ever knew; outwardly they behaved with a dignity that was almost theatrical.

I should add also that this performance of theirs was quite

often interrupted by ironic minor catastrophes, the sort of ba-
nana-peel slips that afflict the progress of people of great dignity. Whenever Auntie Emma and Uncle Harry came to visit
us, we expected trouble, and prepared for it, and it nearly always occurred. If we took them for a sail, a squall would
come up, with bursting wind and rain. Or we'd be stuck in
calms and hot sun. Or we'd come ashore on a shallow beach
in rough water. Or there'd be a cloud of mosquitoes. It got
to be a recognized hoodoo among us. If we drove them—
especially to catch a train—we counted on a flat tire. In our
efforts to maintain decent quiet and decorum, something was
bound to go wrong—a squalling child, or a yapping dog at
five in the morning, or a rattling milk-wagon, or a passing
lobster boat with no muffler. Auntie Emma had supersensitive
hearing, and was roused up by every thump and squeak. But
their struggle with all these Shandy-like misfortunes seemed
to go on regardless of who was responsible: we used to hear
tales of the troubles they seemed to collect in spite of their
best efforts to avoid them. There was the time, for example,
when they were enjoying a gondola trip in the Venetian la-
goon and a squall rushed upon them and swept the helpless
gondola before it while the gondolier called upon his favorite
saints for help, so that at last they were shipwrecked on a
small island with a monastery on it and rescued and sheltered
by the inmates. It was, we said, the sort of thing anyone who
knew them would naturally expect. Another time they were
taking the night boat from New Bedford to New York to be
at my sister Betty's wedding in Grace Church at two o'clock,
and a great storm delayed the ship and eventually caused her
to put into New Haven, where they proceeded by train and
arrived at the church in their traveling clothes, breathless and
a bit bedraggled, just as the ceremony was getting going.
They made, of course, a sensational entrance.

    With all her histrionic great-lady ways, my Auntie Emma
lived an eager and active life. She did make a genuine drama of
herself. She was full of hope and high-minded concern for the

human state. She read the liberal journals and discussed the affairs of the world with fierce earnestness and emotion. After her father's death she had set herself to write his biography, and had done so with extraordinary discipline and tact, and she considered herself the chosen heir of his intellectual estate —though in fact she was unable to share in his profound concern for the children of poverty. She could properly be called a snob, I suppose, but the word is hardly adequate to convey the strength of her intelligence and the vigor of her life-style. She had, in common parlance, more brains than any of us, but like many brilliant people she also had delusions of self-importance. She dramatized her speech, her manners, her social connections—and she expected others to play up to her, to respond with at least a show of wit and wisdom as well as respect. I remember once at dinner at Deer Isle she was conversing on a serious high-minded level when I spotted through the window a big steam yacht forging along down the bay— whereupon we at once rushed to the porch to admire the sight, and Auntie Emma in a fury of disgust at our frivolity retired upstairs to her room for the evening. She made us feel like naughty children, though we did think she was taking herself far too seriously—and have never since then sighted a passing yacht without recalling Auntie Emma's tantrum.

But I fear she made life almost hopelessly difficult for her two stepsons. Her expectations and demands were incessant, though of course she was sure that she was wholly devoted to their best interests. She lived with a vision in her mind of social and professional greatness, and measured all achievement in the scale of her father and husband. She constantly tested us all by that measure, and urged us onward and upward in our quest for the success she so clearly perceived and understood. She may have been a snob, as I said, but she was a romantic idealist as well, and counted herself unquestionably on the side of the angels. Nor was her snobbery merely social: what she sought was great achievement such as might be found in the family friend of her youth, James Bryce, or in people such as Sarah Orne Jewett and John Masefield and S. Weir Mitchell and John Morley—all of whom she had been proud to know and correspond with. I remember how she read aloud with deepest emotion Masefield's poem *The Dauber*, the story of a poor artist, a painter, who sailed before the mast in a Cape Horner and was persecuted by the harsh seamen who scorned him for being a futile artist—and how she eyed me with a little testing smile to see whether I was reacting properly and recognized the significance of the sensitive esthete in the presence of brutal humanity and the grandeur and rage of the wildest seas. I did feel sorry for the poor devil, and have had an image in my mind of that Cape Horn passage ever since, but I did not have the strong identification with his plight that she seemed to have—at least for reasons of perversity I resisted her exalted and romantic view of it. What I objected to was the theatrical insistence of her idealizations, her voicing of profound certainties and perceptions in tones of extraordinary significance as though she alone knew what beauty and grandeur really were. She spoke always, even of ordinary things, with resonant eloquence and strong emphasis: she expressed her great hopes and visions histrionically, watching the impact with her little probing smile. Once when she was staying at the Somesville House at Mount Desert, after Uncle Harry's death, I stopped to visit her on a cruise in my small sloop, along with my young son and younger daughter, and she welcomed us and escorted us into the dining room with cries of pride and pleasure, looking about to see that everyone heard and admired. She demanded a table by the window "for these brave mariners who have come so far to see their aged aunt." My children were astonished and embarrassed at the time, but they still quote her words with relish.

But this Somesville scene occurred long after our Woods Hole days. There, when I was twelve, I fell in love with a girl named Marjorie Paddock, who was twenty-four—and I knew that because she was twice as old as I was my case was hopeless. But I persisted, none the less—and I am still sure that no sweeter and lovelier girl ever lived. What I couldn't understand was why my step-cousin Norman, who was her age, didn't marry her. After all there she was, a prize for an eligible man, and Norman was as eligible as any man could be— and like all of us he found her very lovely indeed. And he was the sort of irresistibly charming man who could have won any girl he wanted—in fact, he had more genuine and natural charm than any man I have ever known. But Marjorie was his stepmother's protegée who had come to Woods Hole as a piano teacher somewhat under her auspices, and I think Norman simply resisted her on principle. He treated his stepmother with infinite tact, but he kept as clear as he could of her dominion. I never saw Marjorie in later years, but Auntie Emma used to refer to her as "poor Marjorie" or "poor dear," and implied a sadness as to her fate, but I don't know why. I still have a luminous vision of her in white, as beautiful as an angel, playing Chopin in the little backyard barn she had made into a music studio.

Norman and John were, as I have said, a close part of our family and were often with us in winter as well as summer, and in our last summer at Mill Island they lived in a tent there, and I was so fascinated by them and their life in the tent that I made a pest of myself and had to be restrained from visiting them at awkward times—like early morning. But during all the years of our lives together they were as kind and brotherly as it was possible to be—and in their different but oddly similar ways as charming. Norman, the younger, was the perfect pattern of a gentleman of Yale University—where he spent all his adult life—and I say it without the slightest invidious irony. He was very worldly in his experiences, very polished and even stylish in his manner, with a wonderfully suave and merry wit and infinite tact and a great store of kindness. It is quite probable that he was more genuinely liked by more people than any Yale man of his time: in his student days he was the most popular member of his class, and continued so throughout his career as head of the Yale University Press—right up to the time of his sudden heart attack and death as he was driving his car on a Sunday morning. The sense of loss among his family and his innumerable friends was overwhelming—that anyone so altogether delightful and spirited and just in all his dealings should be cut off abruptly seemed cruel indeed.

I find it difficult to write about John, who became my brother-in-law, because he was so very close to me for so much of my life, and because he was in a way a more complicated and remarkable character even than Norman. Their mother was Julia Vaux, and they both inherited a marvelous lightsome wit from her, an eager and youthful humor that played around all their affairs. John positively burbled with outrageous puns and conceits—he couldn't help turning the simplest statement into absurd paradox, as when he translated the mast-head slogan of the *New York Times* into "All the Fits that's News to Print," or remarked of the head of Procter and Gamble when he unsuccessfully entered politics that "if he had used more soap and less ivory it would have been less of a Gamble." He invented or picked up an infinite succession of ironies, familiar enough to his friends and family but almost incomprehensible to slow-witted strangers. And he spoke always in the literate voice of the academic lecturer and seemed quite out of touch with vulgarities of the ordinary world—though in actual fact he was one of the kindest and most generous-hearted people I have ever known. In his humor and humanity he had much in common with his brother Norman, but his style of life was wholly different. Where Norman was a polished and even elegant man of the world who delighted in the society of his equals, John felt himself to be socially awkward, and he took refuge in his ironies and humorous obfuscations. Norman always wore the right clothes and said the right things and was perfectly easy and unaffected in any company. His laugh was one of the sweetest of all human sounds. But John even at his best looked like a char-

ity case, and at the sight of any well-dressed company he began to snort and breathe hard and make oblique remarks
about cocktail hounds and sideboard cruisers—not bitterly or
disagreeably, but always with his characteristic good-natured
sense of the absurd. He wanted to be kind and fair, but he
lived in a different world from that of what he considered the
slightly alcoholic social sophisticates of his brother's; he had
always had a sort of ugly duckling view of himself in comparison, as the nonathlete and nonvarsity and nonsociety one;
he didn't drink, he didn't play around, he didn't make Skull
and Bones. He was wholly the amateur individualist, the lover
of home-made gadgets and hobbies, the inventor of innumerable ploys that delighted children of all ages: my earliest memory is of him whittling little boats, and he spent his life at it.
But in the midst of his inventions and devices, how awkward
he could be, what a mess he could make with materials and
tools and gadgets scattered about—and how warm and funny
his running comments were as he burbled along!

At Woods Hole, with his new wife Dorothy—and after a
time a new daughter Julia—he lived in the shadow of his distinguished father. With immense effort and dedication he had
earned an M.D. at Johns Hopkins, and was beginning a career
as a teacher of anatomy at the University of Cincinnati Medical School, and between his father and his conscience—not to
mention his stepmother—he agreed to settle in at the Belfry
in Woods Hole to devote himself to "serious research" in the
laboratories there. And for a few summers they tried to keep
to that arrangement. But of course the Auntie Emma regime
was very hard on them, patient and infinitely good-natured as
they were—and I think his research seemed profitless to him:
though he was a born putterer and gadgeteer, with an inventive faculty comparable to Rube Goldberg's, his laboratory
efforts so far as I ever knew generally ended up in a state of
hopeful confusion. But he made life delightful for me while I
was there. We played golf together, and he was probably the
worst golfer ever seen—and the most amusing and good-na-

tured and persistent; he stroked his ball very slowly and gently, as though he were playing croquet, and rolled it along little by little toward the hole—quoting with ironic pleasure the instructions in the how-to-play manual he had been reading. "My form is not quite *de rigueur*," he said. "At this point I am playing ten, I believe. . . ."

And he took me cruising in his boat *Scorpion*, which for a time had been hauled out at Willis Phinney's yard in Falmouth. He delighted in all things nautical, and was in fact an amateur authority on ships past and present—so much so that in later years he made up an exhibition of little models of old ships and used them as the basis of an informal lecture at small gatherings. And in our lifetime of sailing and cruising together I found him always the pleasantest and most entertaining of companions. We cruised first to Nantucket—it must have been in June of 1920—and we were both astonished at that lovely little city rising from the sea on its sandy isle, with its old and beautiful clapboard mansions and big shade trees and its air of isolation and peace. It seemed to lie still in its nineteenth-century sleep, as though time and change had passed it by. I had a romantic vision in those days of a classic New England past, the time of my forefathers who lived the good life in just such serene and perfect houses, on quiet village streets under great elms and maples. I believed devoutly in their virtue and worth and the harmony of their inner and outer life, and whenever I discovered such a setting as Nantucket was, or Concord or Kennebunkport or Wiscasset or Litchfield, I felt that I had once again glimpsed a felicity that was native to me—even as it slipped away into the unrecoverable past. It is an illusion I am still reluctant to give up.

By 1920, Nantucket was still unexploited, though its new life as a modern resort was about to begin. On the outer shore, along by Tom Nevers' Head, we came on an abandoned real estate development where a grid of streets had been laid out in the sandy scrub, with signs such as Sea Breeze Avenue and Beau View Road canted by the winds; but no houses as yet. I have never been back to see what has happened to the area, but I fear the worst. We walked on, wearily in the sun and sand, to Sconset, which was a small resort community of gray shingled cottages—and from there I think we must have found a bus to take us back to Nantucket town. John was never a rugged walker, though I was—it was my vanity and pride.

Scorpion was then about twenty-five years old, and had begun to leak. John had been to North Haven, in Maine, a couple of years before and had talked with her builder, Ozzie Brown, who seemed glad to have news of her but was mildly surprised that she was still afloat: "These old boats do seem to hang on," he cheerily said, and John used the sentence like a refrain. We had to pump and pump to keep her from sinking. But in Nantucket we bought a big galvanized fisherman's pump that gave us much relief in comparison with the little yachtsman's pump we had been working with. It seems to me that much of my boating life has been given over to manning bilge pumps—and remembering how these old boats do hang on.

After our Nantucket venture we waited at Woods Hole for a heavy southwester to blow itself out and then took off on a week's cruise to New Haven—and thanks to our new bilge pump we had a successful voyage. We anchored in Cuttyhunk and Point Judith and Fisher's Island, and ran from there to New Haven in a strong easterly rain storm, with two reefs in our sail and poor visibility—and as we came on the wind to beat into the harbor our towing tender swamped and took a planing dive far under water—and we had much ado to heave-to and haul our boat alongside and get it bailed out in the teeth of wind and driving small waves. I don't in fact know quite how we managed it, since there is nothing more hopeless to handle than a swamped boat in rough water—and I think we must have lost the oars, but by main strength and persistence we got the water out of her and went on to the shelter of the anchorage. That tender was a beautiful little model, also built at North Haven in Maine, and ordinarily remained buoyant in any kind of sea, but the heavy rain had filled her up. We had an extra pair of short oars for an emergency. So we got there, more or less intact, and spent a night with Norman and his wife Hildegarde and their new baby, Harry—Norman I think was beginning his career at the Yale Press, which he carried on for the rest of his life. And next day a clearing northwester blew in, and we took off and ran back to Fisher's Island with a rush of speed, seeing all the sights we had missed in the fog and rain of yesterday. We carried two reefs in the sail both ways.

It was a couple of years later that John finally gave up on *Scorpion*, in spite of the potent bilge pump, and bought a thirty-five footer which he renamed *Bufo Agua* because he thought she looked like a water toad when seen head on. Not, in other words, a pretty boat. And I remember my first shock at seeing her—I was at Harvard that year, at the School of Architecture, and he wrote and suggested that he'd like some accurate measurements of his boat and her rig, and perhaps I might run down by train to Falmouth and see to it for him— he had gone to the University of Pittsburgh Medical School by then, I think—and he said he had at last made the fateful decision to abandon his Woods Hole researches and to take his new boat, and his family, to Deer Isle where they could live in unprofessional freedom and let his career go hang. So of course I was delighted, and got a measuring tape and a notebook and went off to see his new boat—which, by the way, cost him $300. Crosby built, he said, copper fastened, with a lot of cat blood in her. A flat, enormously wide sloop, with a shoal fin keel and a huge centerboard going through it, and eight hundred feet of sail, mostly in a mainsail with a long gaff and a boom that reached six feet or so beyond the end of the stern. John always refused to believe the figures I sent him— her twelve-foot beam and that seven hundred square feet of mainsail. She seemed positively monstrous to me. Yet she was well and stoutly built, with copper fastening and strong timbers—and once afloat and under way she behaved much better than I had expected.

I had gone to Deer Isle in June of that summer—1923, it was—and the family had taken over our Aunt Leta's place. I had put my father's boat *Bettina* in commission at North Haven, where Ozzie Brown had hauled her out, and had moored her off the house at Dunham's Point, and one day I was sailing her back across the bay from Cape Rosier, where I had been to visit the Fairleys, and I saw from afar someone shaking a white blanket on the porch of our house—a continual shaking that seemed to go on and on. It turned out to be a desperate signal from my sister Dorothy—though of course I couldn't make the boat go any faster than it was going anyway. But at last she could call by megaphone that John was ready to start and expected a crew, and I must come at once. So I hurried ashore, packed my gear, and along with my brother Charlie, who happened to be there too, was driven in the Model T to Stonington just in time to catch the *Morse* for Rockland and the Boston boat. Travel in those days was dependable as well as cheap.

So Woods Hole in the morning, and Auntie Emma graciously receiving these two "stalwart mariners," and John in the midst of confused and somehow hilarious preparations, with long quotations from his favorite poem, W. S. Gilbert's "I am the cook and the captain bold and the mate of the *Nancy* brig," which he produced on all occasions with marked emphasis. *Bufo* in the water looked more manageable than she had on land, but when we got under way at Falmouth in a whistling sou'wester and had to beat out the narrow channel between the jetties I was still appalled at the size of the mainsail and what seemed to me the awkwardness of her great beam. But nothing went wrong, she stood up to it and answered the helm and charged back and forth across the channel and out into Vineyard Sound, crashing hard into the choppy waters. She had a solid feel to her, though I could see that she would pound heavily in a steep head sea. But we felt good about her as we reached into Woods Hole Harbor and anchored. We loaded *Scorpion*'s old cruising gear aboard— pots and plates and utensils and bedding and a primus stove and water jugs and a set of mason jars in a wooden box which John treasured because he had inherited them from his Uncle Boyer Vaux; they held matches and sugar and salt and tea and coffee and anything that had to be kept dry, and were awkward to handle and always in the way—but Uncle Bo had been a famous yachtsman in his day and John treated his relics with respect.

Actually, he was a hopeless cook and housekeeper, and could hardly be trusted to heat up a can of beans properly. Charlie was not much good at it either, so it was up to me to see to supplies. But of course John was wonderfully generous in providing everything we might want or need—and I think we made out very well. We were young enough and hungry enough to be satisfied with any sort of fare, provided only there was enough of it. Our equipment was really pretty primitive, though—with few of the gadgets and conveniences the present-day cruiser expects: no running water, no sink or plumbing of any sort, no stainless countertops, no springs to sleep on, no power. And though the cabin was very wide, there was only sitting headroom and barely crawling space before the mast. As John pointed out, *Bufo* was designed to take large parties for day sails—the cockpit was big enough to seat a dozen people.

And at last we set sail for Maine, with a fresh sou'wester blowing and a lumpy sea in the Sound and two reefs in the mainsail. John was usually in favor of close-reefing on all windy occasions—which meant four reefs in that big sail. Charlie was all for carrying full sail to the last extremity. It was left to me to compromise between the two, which is the sort of position I have been in all my life. But actually our two reefs seemed about right as we pounded through the rips toward Edgartown and John, still stowing gear in the cabin, intoned the opening lines of "Rose Alymer" with eloquent feeling: "Ah, what avails the sceptered race! Ah, what the form divine!" and then as an overflow, as it were, of his euphoric delight in being at last off and away he offered up one of his favorite riddles: question, what is the difference between a barber and a sculptor; answer, one curls up and dyes, the other makes faces and busts—the question and answer to be rendered with the resonant articulation of a lecturer after a preliminary moment of eager sniffs and snorts. As a seasoned raconteur he never laughed at his own jokes, but he kept them coming with wonderful energy and pleasure. I think I never knew any grown man who got more fun out of life than he did—and perhaps I should add more innocent fun, because he seemed to live in a world as sinless as the world of Alice in Wonderland.

We anchored early in the afternoon at Edgartown, near Chappaquidick, where my friend and Harvard roommate Lincoln Fairley had a summer job as a family handyman, and I went ashore and scouted around till I came bursting through a jungle of undergrowth and found him sitting in a garden hammock quite unaware that I was not at Deer Isle, where I belonged. It is a small event in a lifetime, but I have never seen anyone as astonished as he was at the sight of me coming out of that tangle of bushes in the wilderness of Chappaquidick Island: he had not the slightest inkling that I might be turning up—he had, in fact, just been writing me an account of his life there, and regretting that he couldn't be back with his family in Penobscot Bay. But he made me welcome, and presently we were playing a couple of sets of hard tennis, which we loved to do on any possible occasion, and then he took the family motorboat, which he was in charge of, and powered back to *Bufo* with me, picking up my tender on the beach a half mile or so along where I had left it to plunge into the island jungle. And we had supper of baked beans and brown bread together, and felt young and adventurous and very happy. And in the morning the three of us, John and Charlie and I, sailed on to Nantucket with a light and very hazy southwest breeze—and that lovely little city in the sea was still there, half asleep with its shaded streets and cobblestones and white clapboard mansions.

On our third day out we were up and away early with a light morning southerly and eased along northeastward, waiting for the day's wind to come in stronger—which little by little it did as we ran past Great Round Shoal where the five-master lay foundered—a fearsome sight in that lonely expanse—and on past Monomoy and Malabar and through Pollock Rip Slue where we could see the color of underwater sands, and then by noon the wind we hoped for came in stronger and stronger, quartering a little from the port side, and as we ran the Cape's outer shore, heading north, we had enough lee to give us smooth water. *Bufo*, as I said, had a flat, scow-like hull, and with her big mainsail and running free in untroubled water she could plane along faster than any boat of her size I ever sailed. That day we did thirty nautical miles in exactly three hours—and kept pace all the way with a big Gloucester fishing sloop running under both sail and power. But then as we little by little turned the rounded end of the Cape we came on the wind, and presently were beating into a steep head sea from across Massachusetts Bay, and the little vessel thumped and shuddered and the going was slow. We tied in a couple of reefs, and kept a wary eye out for the fish traps that seemed to be set quite far off shore, almost invisible in the dusk. It had turned cloudy, fog was coming, we were relieved at last to get in past Wood End Lighthouse and anchor in ten feet or so of water—quite forgetting that we were now in a region of a nine-foot rise and fall of tide. When in the small hours we thumped and settled on the bottom and slowly canted over we were thankful for smooth water and sand under us and were glad it was still dark so that no one would witness our ignominy. But nothing was damaged, and when we floated in the morning a clearing northwester came in with a new weather front and we got in our anchor and beat up to a better lee off the wharves of Provincetown and there rode out a strong day-long breeze. There was argument, of course. Charlie was all for making a northward passage, John pointed out that we'd be slamming into a tough sea—and we felt very snug in our harbor lee. So we waited for the norther to blow itself out, and got under way in the early quiet of the next morning—and drifted along northeasterly in light airs, with the Boston Custom's House tower standing like a dim finger on the western horizon, and then gradually the south wind came in again with its white haze and we held on through the dusk and dark, and saw the lights of Thacher's Island and later the Isle of Shoals, and so on through the night and by morning a powerful southerly was blowing and we hove to and tied in three reefs, and then in early morning we caught and passed a tug towing three barges, and off Cape Elizabeth a big following sea kicked up against the tide ebbing out of Casco Bay and it took all our strength to hold her off before the wind. It was coming in to Harpswell Sound that we almost put her ashore. Our boom was out on the port side, and we couldn't hold her off to keep from closing in on the rocks of Bailey's Island on our starboard hand—so as we got in fairly close we decided to come about, and when John gave the word I put the helm down and Charlie hauled in the main sheet. But she wouldn't come, she wallowed and lost way and payed off again and headed for the breakers on the shore of Bailey's Island. We got speed on her and tried again, with the same result. She was unmanageable, and though it was blowing too hard for it the only thing left seemed to be to risk a jibe. Then John cried out, "The board, the board!" and leaped to release the pennant of our centerboard, which had been hauled in ever since we had left Provincetown early in the previous morning. So once more we gathered way and this time came round in style, just short, as John said, of scraping barnacles from the steep rocks of Bailey's Island where the slanting breakers were foaming and churning.

So we made the quiet lee of Harpswell Harbor, and anchored there in rain and fog two nights and a day, lying in the cabin in the suspension of time that comes most pleasantly in a small boat in a strange place, when you can do nothing and go nowhere and are enclosed as it were in the cocoon of your warm cuddy. You snooze and dream and read and rouse up long enough to cook and eat some basic food. You look out at the gray waters and the falling lines of rain and the fog-shrouded shores and you feel perfectly free of all responsibility and you resign yourself to your existential captivity as though you were forever safe from the world outside. It is one of the primary pleasures of cruising—this riding out a spell of weather in a snug cabin in a sheltered anchorage while time and the world seem far off and somehow motionless.

But in the afternoon, when it stopped raining, I roused up and bailed out the tender and rowed ashore and walked up across fields to a store and filled a water jug and bought some eggs and a loaf of bread and a can of ground coffee. The storekeeper wanted to know if I was from the "yacht" down there, and I brooded a bit about his designation, thinking of a yacht as a large and resplendent affair. But I had to admit that he was technically right. *Bufo* looked small and almost humble all alone out in the gray water of Harpswell; there was no other boat of any sort in sight. All this happened more than fifty years ago but it comes back to me as an experience of poignant happiness—the whole adventure of our little voyage around the Cape and down east and the safe anchorage after the stormy seas and the close call on the rocky shore of Bailey's Island, and then the rain and fog closing in and the long sleep in our quiet cabin and the walk up over the wet fields to the old-fashioned country store and the storekeeper's query about the yacht and the accent and look and feel of the Maine coast again.

EIGHT

THE GUNNERY

Fter two winters in New York, back when I was ten
and eleven, it was decided that I should go off to boarding school. It seemed evident that my life at the Allen-
Stevenson school was full of misery, and I kept having
dreadful colds, as well as chickenpox and measles, and I still
yearned for my happy home in the country. So The Gunnery
was selected—a name derived, I was told, from its founder, a
very eminent man named Gunn who lived in the middle years
of the last century and had been well known to my grandfather. It was in the village of Washington in Connecticut, not
far from our ancestral town of Litchfield, in a region of very
beautiful hills and streams, and back in what seemed to me the
dim past my Uncle Rob had gone there—and all he could remember about it was that he fished for trout in Bee Brook,
where his father had fished in his own youth. He urged me to
seek out Bee Brook and try for some trout, but I never did. I
hadn't actually learned about trout at that stage of my life.

But, like many hopeful enterprises, The Gunnery when I
encountered it had grown somewhat tired and worn. It
seemed to be run almost entirely as a family operation by Mr.
Gunn's son-in-law and daughter and their offspring, and there
was a faintly Dickensian air of hopelessness about the place.
Since then, I believe, a thorough rehabilitation has occurred,
and its spirit and methods are quite up-to-date and filled with

the best expectations. But in my day there it even struck me in my innocence as old-fashioned—with its quaint mansard-roofed main building and its "school house," and the rather futile disciplines of its teachings. And I was made aware of a pervasive traditional corruption among my fellow students, whose habits seemed evil in ways I had never encountered. I was almost as innocent as it was possible for a boy of twelve to be, and was shocked into helpless silence by the pornographic interests of some of the older worldlings there, the big guys who talked familiarly of sex and sin. From what I have heard about boys' schools their behavior was quite mild and even relatively innocuous, but at the time it seemed to me too wicked to believe and I tried to pretend that it was all simply a ceremony of initiation and didn't really "count"—and actually I think that is what it partly was. And such as it was, the evil was very young and foolish. Question: why is the Hudson River like a woman's leg? Answer: because the farther up you go the more interesting the scenery is. Yet I remember a set of professionally pornographic pictures which shocked me like an electric charge.

My schooling that first year was entirely in the hands of a grim martinet of a man we all addressed as Pa—one of those school fixtures who had become a tradition. He presided over what I suppose was the equivalent of an eighth grade and held us in absolute subjection. His authority seemed to operate on an inhuman level: he never laughed or jested, he never altered his countenance or spoke one word more than was essential. According to his own standards, he was perfectly just—and of course he was always right. I lived in fear of him, though I knew if I obeyed his orders I would be safe. It was known that he occasionally administered an old-fashioned spanking or caning, but ordinarily his punishment consisted of an after-school study session (a torture to me) or more whimsically a trip off into the country of a couple of miles to pick up a note he had previously concealed—say, in the structure of the suspension bridge over the Shepaug River. He was a great walker himself and planted little clues here and there for such future use. He thought country walks were good for us—and of course he was right, and I have remembered ever since how much I enjoyed those expeditions he sent me on. But in the two years I was there I never saw him really loosen up and behave spontaneously—even though I lived for the second year almost next door to his rooms, and he saw to our getting to bed at night and out of bed in the morning. He revealed nothing of himself except the image of the old-fashioned schoolmaster in perfect control of himself and everyone he dealt with. It astonished me in later years to meet someone who knew him in his home community of Windsor who remarked on what a nice man he was and what a fine teacher he must have been. It had never occurred to me up to then that he could be judged either as "nice" or "not nice," or that he was in any normal way a fellow human being. As for his being a fine teacher, it is true that he preserved order and won awesome respect, and he did it mainly by dint of a perfectly controlled and understated certainty that allowed no question to be raised or doubt to be hinted at. The only occasion when I saw him even slightly ruffled was once when we were all assembled in the study hall of the upper school, listening to our headmaster scolding us for our lax and slovenly ways—and in came Pa with a couple of young miscreants whom he had literally collared and propelled ahead of him, one in each hand, exactly like a Cruikshank illustration for *Nicholas Nickleby*. "These young gentlemen," he said with unruffled aplomb, "have been exercising in the cellar." A lock of hair had fallen out of place, but otherwise he retained his accustomed quiet and cool. The two boys, we realized, had been caught fighting, and they looked it—and we were all shocked and delighted at the spectacle, and watched intently while our irascible and troubled little headmaster tried to cope with the public crisis Pa had so righteously precipitated. They all retired for a judicial session to an office room, and what happened in the end I never knew.

Our headmaster, the great Mr. Gunn's son-in-law, seemed always a bit bewildered by the responsibilities of his job, and ordinarily spoke in dry and somewhat laconic terms, but now and then he worked himself up into a frenzy of dramatic eloquence and excoriated us for our sinful ways. "It's all humbug!" he would shout. "It's nonsense—it's a will-o'-the-wisp —and I won't stand for it!" We had actually no idea what he was talking about, but waited in respectful silence for that climactic "will-o'-the-wisp" which came out in a desperate sort of sputter. We half realized that his act was put on in deference to his morally formidable wife, the founder's daughter, who often stood beside him on the schoolroom platform and represented to us the highest ideal of virtue. Their son and daughter were also part of the teaching staff, so the Gunn influence was pervasive.

The founder, by the way, in whose lengthening shadow we had our existence there, has been given literary life as a character—together with his school—in a minor classic of fiction called *Arthur Bonnicastle*, by Josiah Gilbert Holland, a writer well known through the middle years of the nineteenth century, and an editor of the *Springfield Republican* and of *Scribner's* and the *Century* magazines. It is a long time since I read it, but I recollect it as something of an imitation of Dickens's *Great Expectations* more subdued and more literally didactic; our hero, filled with vanity and self-esteem from expectations of inherited wealth, is sent to a boarding school called the Bird's Nest where he learns about humility and virtue from the wise headmaster—and it is well known that the Gunnery was the model for these school scenes; in fact, in my day there reference was made to the novel in the school's public announcements—and as living witness of the connection one of my classmates turned out to be the eminent author's grandson and namesake.

The school, as I said, seemed at that time to have lost the educational vitality it had once had but it went in strongly for athletics, and even arranged a few games of football and base-

ball with other schools on the level of what it called its Fourth
Teams—which referred to boys of twelve or thirteen. So all
of us who were at all active could compete, since there were
hardly enough of us at that age to make up a football squad.
And of course we played with the utmost dedication—and
more often than not were disastrously beaten. I was usually an
obscure lineman, down among the mass of bodies, though I
yearned to be a heroic running back; but with all my resolves
to be a fierce fighter in whatever position I played I never
achieved very much glory. I remember how soundly we were
trounced by a team of very tough youngsters from a school
for city delinquents called the George Junior Republic who
seemed to take a lot of pleasure in running over and through
us. I can still see with some astonishment how their center
mounted himself over the ball with his back towards us, the
opposing team, facing his own backfield, his hands between
his legs and grasping the ball all ready to hand it to whichever
runner he chose and then run interference ahead of him.
Whether it is a legal ploy or not I have never known, but it
worked wonders for them and quite demoralized us.

Our Fourth Teams were not actually much good and
were badly equipped and prepared—though I must say we had
an exciting time of it, but our First Teams, which of course I
couldn't aspire to, were quite successful and even heroic. This
was the era of Stover at Yale and the Rover Boys, and we
looked up to our stars with pure worshipful adulation—particularly, I vividly recollect, to our school champion at whatever sport he took up, a youthful god of speed and grace
named Norman Lyman, who once did me the honor of firing
a snowball at me—which I ducked as it shot past but which
filled me with pride at being so chosen and admiration for the
power of his throw. He was magnanimous in not following it
up with another, and good-naturedly granted me his amnesty,
but I had much to say to my young friends about my narrow
but very honorable escape. In our schoolboy world, performance was very uneven, and the brilliance of such a natural ath-

lete as Norman Lyman always stood out; while ordinary
players stumbled and fumbled he performed with ease and
poise, and we all looked upon him as one who could do no
wrong. Even in defeat he was never the responsible one—he
remained always beautiful and powerful.

In the spring of my first year my brother Charlie came to
the school, and since I hadn't seen him for nearly two years I
had the extraordinary experience of greeting him as a grown
man, with a man's voice and manner. He must have been nineteen, and had been out West for all that time. When I had
last seen him he had just come from a well-known school in
Rhode Island called St. George's where he had contracted a
dangerous sinus infection and was in a precarious state of
health. He went off to the Evans School in Mesa, Arizona,
and turned himself into a Zane Grey hero who owned a forty-
dollar horse named Red Wing and rode the trails into the
Superstition Mountains and even up to the Grand Canyon.
I can still recall his passionately eloquent letters about the glory
of the West and the Western adventure, and can hear his
voice as he told about the grandeur of the country and the
brightness of the stars at night and the romantic mystery of
those vast horizons. He had discovered and reveled in the
legendary West of his dreams—just in time, actually, before
modern progress killed it all off, and he had learned to carry
himself with Western assurance, and even to speak with a
slower Western intonation as though he were to be recognized and treated as a veteran ranger with a good deal of
hard-riding experience behind him.

I overflowed with pride and delight and followed him
with adulation and boasted unforgivably, but I must testify
that he put up with me quite patiently. He lived in a dormitory with the other older ones, and I haunted his room and
made a nuisance of myself—I even used him to go over my
arithmetic homework for me, though I knew I was evading
my duty and taking unfair advantage. But he was always a
generous big brother. I felt that he gave me status among my

fellows, and I was proud that he was accepted and liked—and that spring he made the baseball team as pitcher and out-fielder and in one game against our big rival Kent he got five hits—all singles, but none the less glorious. I realized that he was one of the school heroes, and next fall when we came back he made the football team.

He also very quickly found himself a girl—a girl and a horse. I don't know how he did it—probably there was a school dance which I was too young for (though my group did have a "dancing school" along with a group of very sub-dued and very young girls from a neighboring girls' school called Wykham Rise). Anyway, Charlie began to disappear in the afternoons, and pretty soon everybody knew he had a girl named Buzzie because when he came in a little late for the evening meal the school all set up a subdued buzz—a small event that my father never got over being delighted by when he heard about it. When I met her I saw her at once as one of those mysterious and enchanting Zane Grey heroines. She was seventeen, and lived on a country estate a couple of miles away, guarded by fierce airedale dogs, and she rode horse-back, and I was overwhelmed with yearning for all she seemed to represent. Once in the spring when I went back to New York for a weekend, probably to visit the orthodontist, I encountered her on the train, and she blithely sat beside me all the way down and agreed to meet me for the Sunday after-noon trip all the way back, which she did with wonderful good nature. We were very merry together, and I have never forgotten her, though I think neither Charlie nor I ever saw her again after we left school. She is still in my mind my brother's heroine, forever bright and young, living up there in her country place with her horses and dogs.

In my second year I was promoted from Pa's one-room elementary grade to what I suppose was a high school level, which meant a desk in the general study hall and separate classes in the various subjects such as English, Latin, French, history, and algebra. I discovered that I was a poor and reluctant student, easily lost in the devious obscurities of learning. I seem to remember, after nearly sixty years, that *utor, fruor, fungor, poteor, vescor,* and their compounds *a* or *ab* take the ablative, and that when I faltered after naming the first three and our teacher (a Gunn granddaughter) brightly encouraged me with a "two more" I responded on cue, "Yes, that's it. *Two more!*" It was a cold winter morning and we were all shivering in our classroom, but we laughed aloud. I took Latin for five years in all, and got so I could read Caesar's *Commentaries* (as I discovered later when I was hired to tutor a boy who was worse at it than I was) but I could never get anywhere with Vergil. But the truth was that something about the Gunnery at that time made me feel like a hopelessly incompetent scholar—or at least a reluctant and backward one. What I chiefly did was to read stories of adventure and romance, including the Complete Sherlock Holmes, which I found in the village library—and I think I was at the age when I could read the same stories again and again with increasing pleasure. It must have been about then that I discovered Zane Grey and merged his visions of the romantic dream world of the West with my brother's. We all lived in those days, young and old, with that epic motive sounding in our ears and shining in our minds' eyes; we believed it was all still going on out there in the great open space—Charlie had even borne witness to it, and here was Zane Grey setting it forth with the eloquence of passionate conviction. I never went beyond the Pecos until I was old, I haven't read a Zane Grey in forty years, but that youthful dream of Western stars and purple sage and a stallion named Wildfire still lives in my imagination.

But romantic readers made poor scholars. I used to smuggle my novels into the study hall in disguise as textbooks and read them in such a way that they could be concealed in a flash. I did badly in my studies, and when taken to task by my parents I had the nerve to blame the school—the teachers were no good, I said. I felt almost as hopeless there as I had felt at the Allen-Stevenson in New York. I must say, though, that I

enjoyed the rather easygoing amenities of The Gunnery—
most of all the country pleasures, the hills and streams, and
the coasting in the snow season among the many steep hills on
the country roads where no automobiles ventured. Coasting
seemed to be a major activity, and it was an ideal region for it:
we could take off for a half-day tour with our sleds, up and
down the hills—Aspenwall's Hill and Popensic's Hill. When
my sister Eleanor and her friend Muriel Postlethwaite came
to see me once in winter I coasted them by sled back down to
the railroad station in Washington Depot—an adventure they
told about for years afterward. And I explored among the
hills in spring and fall—I especially remember the days of Indian summer when we could visit an ancient shingled cider
mill in a ittle hollow beside a stream and drink fresh cider out
of a tin cup. The scene is as sharp in my mind's eye as a Currier and Ives lithograph, and belongs to the same era. Once a
fellow named Grizwold Roche and I found a pair of big
wagon wheels in a barn in a high field, and some irresistible
impulse led us to set them rolling free down the open hillside
until they crashed into the woods at the bottom—and I was
amazed afterwards to find we had done wrong. We assumed
they were abandoned old wheels that nobody cared about, but
it turned out to be a serious crime, there were angry repercussions and a bill for damages—not very large, actually, but my
father paid up, with good humor, I must say: he was more
often amused than angry at the antics of his children.

During most of the first of my two years at The Gunnery,
my parents and sisters were abroad, chiefly in Rome, I think
—and my vacation time was spent either with my Aunt Bessie's parents or my Auntie Emma and Uncle Harry in Philadelphia. In early December we had had some fine coasting
weather, and in a smash-up I managed to break my right arm,
which made my traveling rather awkward. But for reasons of
tact the doctor and nurse didn't tell me it was broken, though
they bound it up in splints and put it in a sling and for many
nights it hurt terribly, so that all I could tell the world was

that I had *hurt* it when I was coasting—and it wasn't until my Auntie Emma took me to have it looked at by her doctor that I realized that it was plainly *broken* and that I had every right to be proud of it. To say I had hurt it was a matter of no moment at all, but an honest break seemed almost heroic to me. The tactful school doctor deprived me of a couple of weeeks of glory.

At that time Aunt Bessie's parents were still living in the family brownstone on East Nineteenth Street, somewhere between Second and Third Avenues, I think—and the house seemed to me as venerable as the Ark. It was darkly ancestral, a repository of the heaviest and most ornate Victorian furnishings, smothered in drapes and tassels and carved whatnots —a scene that I later saw rather dimly reproduced in the setting for *Life with Father*, which might have made literal use of the Hyde drawing room. I often see the place in my dreams, looming in the darkness of the past with its weight of mahogany and walnut, its marble table tops and glass-fronted cases and cupboards, its majolica vases and gilded clocks, and the Steinway concert grand where Aunt Bessie still played her little practice pieces. Her father and mother were bent and shrunken and ancient, and they padded about in the shadowy silences of their possessions as quietly and secretly as a pair of moles.

Her brother lived there too, a middle-aged bachelor who devoted himself to two activities: visiting the Bronx zoo and riding on railroad trains—and when I took the train to Philadelphia he eagerly came with me as far as Trenton, where he could skip across the platform just in time for the trip back to New York again. He had some sort of ticket or pass that allowed him to ride at will, I think, and he knew all about the schedules and the operations. He spoke always in a hoarse whisper. He often took this trip, he said; it was a very convenient sort of trip to take. He spoke about such matters very soberly and earnestly as though he were engaged in an affair of great importance, and he kept an eye on his watch to make

sure things were going properly on schedule. He had a large
gold Hamilton watch, just like a railroad man's. He seemed to
like being with me, and was kind, but I thought he was odd—
I realized there was something pathetic about him. Aunt Bessie treated him with tolerant humor, though I don't believe
she was willing to realize how simpleminded he really was. I
think he later fell into the hands of a professional parasite who
moved in on him after his aged parents died and robbed him
of most of his inheritance—though what became of the house
and all its elaborate furnishings I don't know. Aunt Bessie
and Uncle Rob had an old-fashioned apartment around the
corner on East Seventeenth Street with room for my grandmother, who lived to be ninety-four—she is the one who used
to ride the donkey in Dobbs Ferry and was said to be full of
life and spunk, though alas to me she always seemed infinitely
old. "Child o' grace" is what she called me—I can still hear her
voice.

I could see how Aunt Bessie needed to be rescued from
that haunted old tomb of a mansion, though she was one who
never let ghosts bother her. She was not arrested in a per-
petually childlike state, like her brother, but her nature was a
very simple one and she took life as it came whether in the
dark and airless world of her aged parents or out on the trout
waters of the Adirondacks. All her life she was one of the absurdly innocent and hopeful ones who never knowingly did
anything wrong and lived with serene trust that everything
was working out for the best. She and Uncle Rob were not
young when they married, and never had a child.

It seems incongruous that I should have been dumped on
the Hydes, but for the few days I was there I found them and
their house as fascinating as a play. The dining room was in
the basement, I think, with no windows—like the hold of a
ship, with solid mahogany furniture and darkly seen steel en-
gravings of classical ruins on the walls, and the two elderly
Hydes spoke only in muted tones—and their son Harry in his
spooky whisper, and the servants shuffled slowly about with

the dishes and disappeared into the kitchen where I never went. But how kind they tried to be! They plied me with milk and cream and butter and eggs and bacon and whatever they thought a boy would like, and they treated me with a polite respect as though I were a visiting prince. Once some years earlier, when I was about eight and still living at Dobbs Ferry, Mr. Hyde had invited me to go with him to see the Hudson-Fulton Centennial affair, which involved my taking the train to Spuyten Duyvil and meeting him and continuing with him on an observation train along the river and seeing the ships, the replicas of Hudson's *Half Moon* and Fulton's steamship *Clermont*, and visiting one of the battleships in the fleet that was anchored in a long line down the middle of the river. There were crowds of people, and I remember following the tails of Mr. Hyde's gray frock coat as he dodged along ahead of me, full of eagerness and energy. It puzzled me that he had asked me since I didn't really know him at all, and had probably met him only at Aunt Bessie's wedding a couple of years before, and I wondered why he was doing all this for me —but I realize that like his daughter he had a sweet and simple nature, and enjoyed celebrations and being kind to little boys. I have no idea what he "did" in the world, and it may be that he simply lived in his old family brownstone among his heavy family possessions. I often think of them there, the two rather small and stooped old ones puttering about among their shadows, and their son coming and going on mysterious trips to the zoo and the railroad trains, speaking always in his sepulchral whisper.

My arm at that time was still in a sling, but it had stopped aching and was merely a nuisance, especially in getting about with a suitcase, but I must have managed well enough because I arrived and was met in Philadelphia by Norman Donaldson. It was just before Christmas and he and John were both there at home, he being still at Yale, and John I think at Johns Hopkins medical school, and I was happy to be with them because they treated me with wonderful good nature and I loved them both. We made together a little conspiracy against the austerities of Auntie Emma, who had become their stepmother several years earlier and had no understanding of how to deal with boys. I must say that we tried hard to respect her concept of desirable social and intellectual behavior, and I for one was full of admiration for what seemed to me her brilliance and energy—she had more *brains* I used to say, as though I knew all about it, than any other member of the family, but gradually I realized how in time she blighted the lives of both her stepsons, especially after they were married and she tried to run their lives and wives. Norman's Hildegarde was very strong-minded, and openly rebelled, with Norman's collaboration. Even John, the kindest person I ever knew, couldn't in the end endure her effort to manage him and fled Woods Hole with his wife and daughter. In her last years, after Uncle Harry's death, she grew more and more difficult, though to the end she kept alive the image of herself as exalted by her status as the daughter of one great man and wife of another.

But for that Christmas time in Philadelphia we made out very cheerily, and they took me to my first Gilbert and Sullivan, *The Mikado*, with De Wolfe Hopper, who I was told had been a family friend in his young days—and he had to sing so many encores of "The Flowers that Bloom in the Spring" that he was reduced in the end to a humorous croak and finally flapped his kimono sleeves over a wall at the back of the stage as a sign that he could do no more. Auntie Emma called him Will Hopper, and remembered him at Lake Placid, but it was a long time ago and she didn't try to renew the acquaintance. In his day he was the most eminent of all the Gilbert and Sullivan players.

Uncle Harry was at this time the head research man at the Wistar Institute of Anatomy, and was about to publish his book on the rat. He carried on his daily life with ritualistic dignity, but as I have said I found him extraordinarily alert and responsive, and his intelligence on all manner of questions was a revelation and a delight to me. With all the careful formality of his speeches and behavior his face would brighten and his eyes sparkle as he spoke, and everything he said added new facets of understanding and truth. He seemed infinitely patient and responsive to a young boy's curiosity, and I was always surprised at the fearful respect which others seemed to have for him, almost as though he were a royal personage: he seemed to cast a spell over all the ladies of his family, even over his formidable wife who was always alert to satisfy his least desire. If something ever went amiss with her arrangements—if a meal were served late or the potatoes were underdone, for example—she made a half-suppressed tragic case out of it, almost as though she and her servants had failed in their primary duty of seeing to his perfect comfort and well-being. Any hint of his displeasure, or even the least excuse for it, became at once cause for a household crisis—though it made itself felt more in the silent charged ambience than in immediate speech. She did like to make "scenes," she performed theatrically on all occasions, but her part was always that of a lady—perhaps too consciously that of a great lady. And although her devotion to her husband was at times almost ostentatious, it was the role she could play with profound and genuine enthusiasm. She had made it her life.

There were several such vacation visits to Philadelphia in my young days, and I was always happy when John or Norman was there too. They were both wonderfully merry, and John especially had a magical way with youngsters; he loved little gadgets of all sorts, and was always making miniature boats, particularly batteships complete with tiny turrets and guns. I felt that he was somehow my own age, but of course much cleverer. But Norman, who was equally nice to me, was more mysteriously a man of the world, and tutored me in polite behavior—always with a light and ironic touch, as though he recognized how much of a charade it was. But none the less he believed devoutly in good manners, and practiced them as a lovely and genuine art. He lived in a world of invitations and parties and dances, and wore evening clothes and came home late at night—he had an allowance from his father of a hundred dollars a month, as I discovered somewhat inadvertently, which seemed princely to me. I pictured him wining and dining in elegant company and having chivalric affairs with beautiful girls—and often he talked quite candidly with me about life and love, though he did it lightly with an affectionate sort of humor. He was small of stature, but very muscular and upright—he was a coxswain on the Yale varsity crew and a lightweight wrestler—and he involved me in an elaborate game of taking measurements of our limbs and chests to see who would grow the most during the coming year, with the loser to take the winner to a vaudeville show, and since I was still growing rapidly and he wasn't the outcome was a certainty—though at the time I didn't realize it and devoted myself to a vigorous drill of setting-up exercises to enlarge my muscles. I remember that he wrote me from Saranac Lake, where he went to visit his Uncle Alfred, that he was getting in a lot of ice skating which would do wonders for his legs—and it was then I began to realize how much of a charade he had been playing with me. But of course I kept on with my setting-up exercises with unabated zeal so that when we got together for the reckoning I was clearly a big winner. We never did get to our vaudeville show, which disappointed me because at that stage of my life it seemed like a pretty daring adventure.

Old times have no sequence, and events come to mind in isolated flashes. I remember once visiting Yale when both John and Norman were there, and going to Norman's rooms and meeting some of the famous footballers with him there—and thinking of them as Olympian gods and seeing them sitting about and talking like mortals—and then I remember how

John and Norman went into a bedroom and took the mat-
tresses from two beds and put them on the floor and then set
to in a very earnest wrestling match—which Norman won, as
befitted a varsity wrestler, and which John lost with great
good humor, as though he were naturally used to it.

I actually visited New Haven quite often in those days because we were very close to the Hendricksons and they welcomed me like their own child. "Auntie" Marion—whose
maiden name was Vaux—had been a girlhood friend of my
mother's (she was John's and Norman's real aunt) and was
overflowing with devotion and good will for all the family.
She was in fact so intensely eager that in the end she over-bal-
anced herself and lost her reason; but in her early days she
was famous in New York and New Haven for her beauty
and vivacity—she and her sister Julia, who was Uncle Harry
Donaldson's first wife, were equally beautiful and vivacious—
and I fear equally vulnerable to psychological disorder. Julia,
it was sorrowfully intimated, had committed suicide when
her two sons were still very young. A third sister, called always A'ntie Agnes, lived out her life in Philadelphia as a sad
and very sweet spinster under the dutiful patronage of Auntie
Emma Donaldson. I never met their brother, the redoubtable
sailor Uncle Bo, who left some of his relics to John, but my
father spoke of him often and had cruised with him in his
plank-on-edge English cutter and knew him also as an avid
racer of sailing canoes.

The New Haven Hendricksons were very much a part of
our family, and I spent many holidays with them. Their only
child was called Little Marion and was a few months younger
than I, and her mother regarded our companionship with such
dramatic sentimentality that although we were only eleven or
twelve I was convinced that she was already plotting and arranging marriage for us, and much as I liked my faithful little companion I used to resolve to myself that I would never,
never agree to any such destiny. At night as I waited for sleep

I was troubled in mind as to what I could do to avoid what I was sure would be regarded as an inescapable duty by all the family. And though Little Marion's mother was certainly not taking her game seriously, she did none the less play at it with the kind of sentimentality that embarrassed and even scared me. She seemed to regard us as two lovely children who were destined for each other, like a couple of figures on a Valentine—and she thought it was a delightful notion. With all her bright charm, she lacked common sense. All the necessary practical duties of daily living, I recollect, were performed by her staff and especially by her patient husband, Uncle Lincoln, the eminent and learned classical scholar who was also on occasion cook and housekeeper as well as ardent sailor. One of the often quoted family recollections is of her calling out to him in times of frustrating calms under sail, "Lincoln, *do* something!"

As I said, I came down from The Gunnery with Charlie and other older boys in a hired automobile to see the first Yale-Harvard football game in the Yale Bowl—it must have been in 1914, and was carried on with fervor and pageantry, despite the world war in Europe that still seemed remote and shadowy—to us younger ones, at least. Driving any distance in a car in those days was a risky adventure, what with unmarked country roads to navigate and the considerable risks of engine breakdown and flat tires, but we made it in time to see Yale's humiliating defeat and returned the same evening with an adventurous stop in Waterbury to "take in a show"— which I think was my first introduction to the vaudeville I had been hearing about for so long. I had been to the movies— I had seen Fatty Arbuckle and John Bunny, though I can't now remember when the famous names like Chaplin and Pickford first appeared—but my family considered vaudeville as a vulgar entertainment, not suitable for a genteel child, so of course I was agog at this initiation, and I can still see the brightly lit stage and the couple in bathing suits—the striped and voluminous kind seen today only in old cartoons—who sang with immense enthusiasm the song that has not yet been altogether forgotten:

> By the sea, by the sea, by the beautiful sea,
> You and I, you and I,
> Oh how happy we'll be—

And there were jugglers and jesters and a man who could drive nails into a board with a hammer held in the toes of his left foot, and I felt I had seen and heard wonders.

It was two years later, when Charlie was a student at Yale and I was at Loomis School in Windsor, that I came to New Haven again and stayed with the Hendricksons in their new house on Humphry Street, and went to the Game in the Bowl and once again saw Yale sadly beaten—but after evening dinner Charlie bravely announced that he and I thought we would go down town, and take in a show, and there was a curious pause and silence, and the elders glanced sideways at each other, and before the objections could be uttered we were up and off for an evening on the town. The show was at Poli's Theatre, and its most sensational act was a girl in black tights doing slow cartwheels across the stage—a sight that evoked half-suppressed exclamations from my brother. We felt that our night of pleasure was a great success.

NINE

THE STANLEY HOUSE

Y SECOND AND LAST year at The Gunnery went very pleasantly—with country rambles and winter coasting and occasional Fourth Team games and hours devoted to half-surreptitious reading of adventurous stories. Nothing sinister happened to me—no enemies or depravities, except for a vague intellectual helplessness that somehow afflicted me. I grubbed along through my classes and homework without much conviction or pride, and put in a minimum amount of effort. The idea that I might be a passably good scholar never occurred to me, and I was almost resigned to a life of academic failure. But none of that seemed very seriously important—not when I could play first base on our Fourth Team, or watch my brother pitch and hit on a winning First Team. I had joined a secret fraternity called Beta Theta—referred to always as B-O—with a very small clubhouse on the school grounds, and our chief function was to hold a meeting once a week. There were other fraternities for the older boys, but ours was the only one for the younger ones—and how or why it got started I don't know. All we ever did was to meet every week, except when the weather was too cold—though I think we had a fireplace—and we must have had some sort of ritual to act out and we tried to pretend that we were doing something important. I guess the big thing was the ordeal of initiation, which involved a few

days of ingenious torture for the victims, who were humili-
ated and beaten with paddles and burdened with senseless
tasks. It was all a routine we took for granted as a time-honored essential of our education. When I was securely in and
anointed as a brother, I naturally applied the same treatment
to the next batch of neophytes. I remember we were perse-
cuting a local boy named Goodrich, who was the son of a
prominent storekeeper in the village, and a passing citizen
stopped a moment and observed the proceedings and then
asked him with some anxiety, "Be you sufferin' much, Goodrich?" We were, of course, somewhat taken aback, but then it
struck us as funny and we used it thereafter as a refrain. "Sufferin' much, Goodrich?" He did suffer, I am sure, and he did
it quietly without appealing for special sympathy—and I had
only faint intimations of how stupid and cruel we were. The
ceremony of the initiation gave us dictatorial power, and we
hardly spared a thought to the consequences—though I was
really shocked to be told that one of the school's well-known
older boys, who seemed to me a strong and reliant grown-up,
had been seen to break down and weep in public at the torture
he was made to undergo during his fraternal ordeal. "You
mean a guy like that *cried?*" It seemed almost unimaginable.
My notion was that only children cried—as I had done to my
everlasting shame when I was beaten in a silly game at a party
given by Miss Sigsby, the school nurse, where for some reason
I found myself in a state of hysteria. I knew I was being
a baby, and went to my room in disgrace with myself—but
that a big grown-up guy could be made to shed tears in front
of his fellows was frightening and wicked.

I was not actually given to tantrums, and led a fairly even
sort of existence, but there was another time when I embarrassed myself by blowing up. I took pride in being a good
wrestler, and one evening in the common room I was having a
bout with two opponents at once, and in my own view was
coping quite effectively with them. I was feeling heroic, in
fact, when a newcomer to the school, a large stout fellow—

from my point of view one of the big guys—stepped in and officiously rescued me from my two attackers. He thought he was doing right, I am sure, but I turned on him in a fury of fists and invective and had to be restrained by other bystanders. He was wholly astonished, and so afterward was I, but for a minute or so I was mad for revenge at his interference.

But though I was happy in the pleasant country life in and about the school, and got on with my fellows and enjoyed the sports, I did actually complain that I wasn't getting anywhere in my studies. It is not that I was intellectually ambitious, but somehow I felt baffled and stupid, and I had too little will to do the work I should have done. I loafed and evaded and backslid—and was encouraged in wayward indolence by my mates. So my parents took counsel and agreed that a change of school was desirable. In early June, at the end of the school year, my mother took me to Windsor in Connecticut to visit a new school called Loomis, just finishing its first year of life—and right away I was aware of an atmosphere of buoyancy and hope. It may have been that the buildings were all new and neat, or that I had been told of the splendid endowment that had been stored up and was now put to use—and certainly I felt disdainful of the flat and drab country where it was located—but there was a palpable spirit of spontaneous enthusiasm among both teachers and boys. I was startled to hear a boy carelessly whistling for all to hear a *last year's tune*—I think it was *When You Wore a Tulip*—which would have been unthinkable to any ordinarily sophisticated prep schooler of the era; I at once recognized it as a *faux pas*, and then took it as an indication of a naive but pleasant disregard for the normal youthful obligations. I couldn't at the time have let myself be caught whistling an out-of-date tune, and I may have felt a touch of scorn for so ignorant a display, but it did suggest a sort of relaxed innocence that might be quite likable. There was certainly no pretentiousness about it.

I shouldn't imply that I was ever a particularly sophisticated type, but I was naturally aware of the habits and customs of my fellows and inevitably I took example from them. Somehow we all learned the new show tunes as they came along, and it was a part of our vanity to be up on the latest ones and to scorn the old ones—an attitude, I found in time, as much in vogue at Loomis as it had been at The Gunnery—or almost as much. But I think back there in its first year of life Loomis did really sustain some of the natural and unworldly enthusiasms appropriate to its very hopeful beginnings.

On that visit I took some placement exams, which were apparently acceptable, though I knew I did pretty badly in algebra—and I was even a bit scared by the severity of the man who administered it, whose name was Ulric Mather, a very formidable teacher whom everyone called Hook. I took the test in his rooms in one of the dormitories, under his cold and watchful eyes, and I am sure I messed it up pretty badly, but it seemed to be about what he expected. I was admitted, anyway, as a student on the second-year or "sophomore" level—and in the fall began my three-year stint.

That was in 1915, and I was thirteen going on fourteen years old. And that summer, after my Loomis visit, we went off to stay at a big old-time hotel called the Stanley House, at Manset on Mount Desert Island in Maine—exactly the sort of place depicted in some of William Dean Howells's novels. I don't know how we happened to hear about it, but it was the traditional haunt of professorial types, many from Harvard, who brought their families and settled down to a life of simple-hearted fun and games and outdoor activity. The hotel was a vast wooden barracks standing starkly on a point of land overlooking the harbor and the islands and the whole range of mountains—the finest view, we told each other with complacence, on the Atlantic coast.

We got there, my mother and sisters and brother and I, by night train from New York to a terminus at the head of Frenchman's Bay called Mount Desert Ferry, where a steamer took us via the celebrated ports of Bar Harbor, and Seal and Northeast Harbors, to Southwest Harbor and across to Manset, where we took a buckboard to the hotel. At first it seemed quite empty and cheerless, and we hardly knew what to do with ourselves. The few oldtimers treated us with cool indifference. No one was there to promote social togetherness. We felt like beginners at a new school. The others all seemed to have intimate connections and backgrounds, and knew what to do and expect. But gradually we made a secure place for ourselves, and I must say we led a very happy life there. I suppose it was partly just luck that we fell among so many interesting and remarkable people, especially the ones from Harvard—the Websters and Sheldons and Bierleys and Lanmans and Brownings, who had all been coming there with their young ones for many years and were by now old and interrelated friends. After a short period of apprenticeship we were accepted and included in the activities of boating and picnicking on the islands and climbing the mountains. It was a great asset for us to have boats—we brought our knockabout *Bettina* from North Haven, where she had been stored, and our North Haven dinghy from Deer Isle, where she was loaded on a wagon and put aboard the steamer *J.T. Morse*, along with three hundred pounds of lead ballast and her mast and rig. It was my brother Charlie, with an enterprising landlubber named Jack Warburton, who saw to those operations —and they made an epic event out of it. The summers of our youth were timeless and free—and the days seemed to be crowded with adventures without end or limit, and everything was possible and our energies were inexhaustible.

Jack Warburton and his beautiful young wife Ellen made quite a splash in the Stanley House social waters in those times, mainly because he owned an automobile—a very sporty and powerful machine called a Mercer—and rented a motorboat, and was wonderfully generous in sharing them. He was a sharp businessman and seemed at first a bit vulgar in comparison with the very academic gentry there, but he was so eager and active in enjoying the out-of-door pleasures, and so full of plans and projects, that he became a central fig-

ure in our enterprises. He took us off on picnics to the islands
and climbs in the mountains, and was nearly always ready and
willing to be counted on. He seemed to be able to leave his
business for most of the summer, and I gathered it was a fam-
ily-run affair in charge of an older brother. He was a genuinely warm-hearted man, and naturally popular, but I was
told that he drank too much, and now and then I saw little evi-
dences of it in bits of unexpected ill temper. I was a child of
innocence, but I dimly realized that he was making his lovely
wife miserable and that she and my brother were falling in
love. It seemed to me a thrilling little drama, but scary too. I
knew that Charlie could be impulsive and quixotic, and I
couldn't imagine what the outcome might be, but I knew how
he felt about Ellen because I felt it too. She was altogether
lovable, and was troubled in spirit by her popular and wayward husband, and both Charlie and I (he being twenty-one
and I fourteen) felt impelled to be her champions. Charlie, as
I have said, was a fantastically chivalric person, and full of
powerful yearnings for a life of romantic glory—and he
might easily have got himself into a theatrical catastrophe
with the Warburtons. They did visibly yearn for each other,
he and Ellen—they went sailing together in the fog and
walked in the mountains, but Jack Warburton for all his alcoholic and rather crude habits was a man of good will and
fundamental restraint and he seemed to enjoy my brother's
romantic youthfulness, and treated him always cheerily. How
he treated Ellen I can't say, but I think he must have been severe in private, because at times she was clearly unhappy. And
I am sure she renounced any dreams she might have had for a
different sort of life and did her best to remain faithful to her
marriage—it was, after all, still a time of strong moral restraint. She was the daughter of Christian missionaries to
China, and had been brought up there in old-fashioned innocence and virtue and a sense of duty.

It was later, when I lived in Cambridge and went to graduate school, that I realized the tragedy that was inexorably

destroying the lovely Ellen Warburton—she had contracted sleeping sickness and was being slowly reduced to physical helplessness. It was an agony to see her trying to get through the motions of normal living, remembering her affection for us and her pleasure in our youthful activities—she could hardly move herself or speak simple words, she had to be fed like a baby, yet her mind seemed to function like a separate mechanism and her fumbling speech signaled a concealed awareness of her past and present. Little by little youth and beauty and life itself were drained away from her, and all the time she was fully conscious of the process and its inevitable end. She was always poignantly glad to see me and my wife, Huldah—we were married in 1927—and right to the last she remembered me and my family with extraordinary affection. I know she never forgot her summertime love for Charlie though she had long ago renounced him—and he in his turn had tragically died in a mine accident in Peru in 1925 when he too recklessly entered a shaft full of carbon monoxide—he at the time being recently and happily married and expecting the child that he never saw. I must add that Ellen's husband Jack had overcome his habits of excessive drinking and in the years of her helpless decline into death treated her with patience and tenderness, though his nature had earlier seemed at times neither patient nor tender. But when the poet Robinson speaks of

> . . . Each racked empty day
> That leads one more last human hope away,
> As quiet fiends would lead past our crazed eyes
> Our children to an unseen sacrifice,

the fates of those two good and hopeful characters, Charlie and Ellen, come inevitably to my mind. The quiet fiends are occasionally at work among us—or should I say always?

We spent most of three summers at the Stanley House, with before and after stays at Deer Isle (a thirty-mile sail away) and occasional forays into the north woods for trout fishing. It was in these years that I began to go cruising with Charlie in *Bettina*, whose cabin was about the size of a dog kennel—though in earlier times my very dignified parents had done a lot of cruising in the same cabin—and it seems to me that we were constantly pounding and crashing into strong head winds and getting soaked outside in spray and inside in sloshing bilge water. My father used to say that when the boat was new he could dry out the bilges with a sponge each morning, but it was hard for me ever to believe it: she was the sort of lightly built wooden craft that pounded and worked in a head sea, and in the twenty-five years I sailed her she always copiously leaked, and required all sorts of strata-gems to keep the contents of the cabin even moderately dry. We had at first a big double-sized air mattress, made of heavy rubber and blown up by plain lung power, and by piling all our bedding and clothes on it, on the flat floor of the cabin, and wedging them with a long oar on one side and a spinaker pole on the other, we could let the bilge water slosh back and forth under it without damage to what was on top. Charlie, as I have said, was a great one for making a passage, regard-less of weather, and our poor little boat was constantly half awash. For several years we did our cruising at the end of the season, in September when the autumn winds blow and the nights are cold and we felt adventurous and brave.

As I try to count up the old summer times it doesn't seem possible that I could have done all these things I remember so well. I think always of Deer Isle as the great good place of my life—at Mill Island, which is still an Eden-like dream of felic-ity, later at my Aunt Leta Croswell's house at Dunham's Point, which we took over in the years after Uncle Jim's death and which my sister Eleanor inherited and still uses, and finally at my own place and house which I bought in 1935—but it seems extraordinary that I could have also spent large parts of many summers in the forests of northern Maine and the Adirondacks, and at Woods Hole and Vineyard Haven, and at the Stanley House in Mount Desert: time today offers no such room and scope—at least it seems to hold me on a narrowing track and impels me onward at increasing speed. I was once a scholar and teacher, a writer of novels, a painter of pictures, a sailor and boat designer, a trout fisherman, a skier and climber, a carpenter, and handyman, a father and husband—and there seemed to be no end to the hours and days and years at my disposal, or to the effort I could spend on them. Yet actually my enterprises are not comparable to those of the great ones of the world—of my grandfather, for example—and seem to me quite desultory and self-indulgent. I had on the whole very good luck, more than I ever really deserved.

TEN

LOOMIS

A S I SAID EARLIER, my new school was filled with the eagerness of spirit that belongs to fresh and very hopeful ventures. We were partners in establishing the ways and styles that would become traditions and enlist our intensest loyalties—and teachers and boys alike shared in this heady sense of good will and potential achievement. Everything was still being created, and we had a good deal of rather self-conscious pioneer enthusiasm for our activities. We went into our games against older and larger schools, for example, with the naive courage of a David tackling the Philistine champion—and chanted newly devised cheers and sang new alma-mater songs (words and music composed by Mr. Howard Morse, the school's business manager) as though we were perpetuating a sacred ritual. In that second year of its life, the school had hardly succumbed to the sort of complacence that little by little accumulates in long-term establishments. And some provisions in its original charter by the Loomis family gave it a special quality and character which I remember as working very successfully, though they may not have endured in subsequent years. There was, for example, a surrounding farm, which some of the boys worked at as part of their schooling —and which any of us could work at on special projects at fifteen cents an hour—and many were the weary stints I put in with a buck saw or a hand-pushed lawnmower to accumulate a little pocket money to spend on ice cream sodas or the *Adventure Magazine* that was running the newest Zane Grey serial. And we also were required to assist in housekeeping chores—without pay—such as keeping our rooms and the dormitory halls clean and waiting on tables in the dining room. The original founders had had a vision of a plain and useful life style, and the virtues of old-fashioned work on the farm and in the house were to be encouraged.

Since then, I believe, the style has changed. The farm has gone, and the life of the farm—the potatoes and corn and vegetables and fruit and the Jersey cows and the pigs, and boys no longer take agriculture as part of their schooling. Where the big barns used to be are now science laboratories and the buildings of the girls' school, Chaffee, which used to be discreetly isolated in another part of town—though I think its original founding was part of a quite modernistic coeducational intention by the Loomis family. Possibly that coming together is to be commended—it at least seems to be an inevitability in our times. The loss of the old farm and its ways may be inevitable too, but I can hardly think it is commendable. The founders had had a vision of an indigenous New England school, encouraging local boys and girls and even stressing practical training in farm and business affairs, but more and more as the original capital accumulated and the project eventually took shape the school tended to emulate the older established prep schools with genteel habits—Hotchkiss and Taft and Choate, for examples. It is now well known as one of that somewhat exclusive fraternity. But, as I said, when I first came there it still retained its air of original innocence and its concern for simple household and bucolic duties.

One job I volunteered for was to fetch the school mail from the Windsor post office at seven o'clock every morning —and I never reasoned why I should be doing it or expected any pay for it, though much later I realized that my successor was getting paid, and finally of course the job was done by a man in a truck. At any rate, for one winter I got up in the dark at six-thirty and set out with a large canvas shoulder bag to walk the mile to the village—and neither rain nor sleet nor driving snow ever stayed me on my rounds. It was a heroic morning event, and I felt strong and virtuous and I rejoiced to be out in the cold air doing what no one else did—and of course I knew that I was essential to the very life of the school. The load of morning mail was often heavy, and the going in untrammeled snow before the plows came made the trip seem like a pioneering venture, but I was very pleasantly conscious of my status as special and trusted operator. And I enjoyed the pleasure of a late breakfast in the dining hall after the others had gone, with the rare perquisite of using up the cream that was provided for the headmaster's coffee—and then being permitted to be absent from the morning chapel service which followed the regular breakfast time. I never succeeded in being a hero in the Merriwell or Stover tradition, but I relished my minor successes and distinctions—the free breakfast cream and the authorized exemption from the chapel requirement. I was disappointed when the operation was put on a professional basis the next year and my volunteer service was no longer required.

We all competed constantly for higher places in the general pecking order, but the order was determined by all sorts of attributes, from pure athletic prowess to those mysterious qualities of personality that give some otherwise useless individuals distinction in the eyes of their fellows. The good athlete was always admired, and nearly always liked, but others won popularity by their wit or nerve or worldliness, or by some sort of secret knowledge that the rest of us didn't seem to have. Success or failure in this constant quest for recognition and esteem in a competitive group of more or less isolated boys can turn into a pathological ordeal, but I think in those early years of Loomis we kept hold of some of the innocence and good will of our hopeful beginnings. I never won very much glory, but I never felt smothered by those who did. I tried to be an athlete, but failed to achieve more than second-team status—though I used to run great distances by myself and dreamed of being a famous marathoner. Once in spring I ran all the way to Simsbury, fifteen or so miles away, to see us play Westminster School in baseball, and then ran back in time for supper—and was given the only formal cheer of my life. I have always been somewhat of a lone operator, and distance running is a lonesome affair, but some sort of temperamental tension seemed to keep me out of the competition I really aspired to. Later in college I put a lot of effort into being a runner, and in spite of intensive training and enormous feats of endurance I never won any glory—except a third-place medal once in a cross country meet.

What glory I won at Loomis was chiefly as editor of the weekly newspaper, *The Log*, which I used to put together every Sunday night and send off by mail to the printer in Hartford—after first taking it down to be inspected by the headmaster, Mr. Batchelder, who I think never made any objections to my innocent items of news and editorial comment. My co-editor was Owen Hart, and between us we composed the whole four-page—occasionally six-page—affair, with accounts of the games played, concerts and lectures and other events. As editors, we endorsed the virtues and encouraged school spirit and loyalty to all authority. I half realized at the time that the advice I gave out in weekly editorials was quite complacent and childlike, though it never seriously occurred to me to question the basic conventionalism of my attitude. I think I did take a somewhat Thoreauvian position of disdain for the urban habits of my fellows, and kept scolding them for what I arrogantly assumed was their blindness to the transcendental harmonies and beauties of the natural world. We had in fact been reading *Walden* in our English course, with Mr. Louis Clough as our teacher, and though the self-righteousness of it annoyed me I found myself very much a part of the life and world it created—as I did also with the similarly complacent poetry of Wordsworth, with its rejections of the life of "getting and spending" and its primary faith and trust in "nature." At any rate, my editorial policy took its direction from these romantic poets and prophets, and in my simplemindedness I fear I was even more complacent than my masters.

In contrast to my naive concept of the natural virtues, the world war raged in Europe, and the consequences were of course too vast to be comprehended. It seemed to me like a simple contest between the good guys (our side) and the bad guys (their side), and we cheered the successes we scored and had no doubt as to the ultimate outcome. It was like a temporary plague that had swept over Europe—and had touched our own lives on the fringes, but it would soon run its course and the good old traditions would reassert themselves and we could return to the free and natural life that would go on harmoniously for evermore. I at least believed devoutly in the permanent divine order of man and his world, in which all things could be arranged in a vast concert of complicated beauty and meaning with some sort of grand ultimate goal which encouraged us always onward. We still had a vision of a place and time called "the kingdom of God," whether in this world or some other we were not sure—though at our age I think we assumed that we would discover a life of everlasting prosperity and pleasure and love. Our own world and time seemed then infinite to us, and everything was possible.

I say "we" with some confidence because most of us were brought up with the sort of Christian hope that has since been largely lost, and we respectfully heeded the pious teachings of our clerical elders. If we professed faith and devotion our future would be the more secure and comfortable, and we would be recognized as naturally worthy. The stern Calvinism of our forefathers had tried to avoid this simple *quid pro quo* formula—not very successfully, I think—but we were still imbued with the sentimental romantic Protestantism of the Victorian era which held that pious virtue was the safest route to success. Not for us the existentialism or the nihilism

or even the general cynicism that have marked our later times
—though then as always there were a few individual rebels
who stood out wickedly against the prevailing pieties. Social
and moral revolt was still a somewhat absurd activity associated with foreign anarchists, who appeared in cartoons
as stout bearded Russians carrying bombs like small black bas-
ketballs—and of course it wasn't possible to take all that alien
radical stuff seriously. In our native pride and self-esteem we
were full of ignorant scorn for the ideas and ways of all foreigners, who we assumed were naturally inferior and unen-
lightened and backward in the cultural race. The good
American, by which we meant the white Anglo-Saxon
Protestant, was the ideal citizen of the future, and must inevitably be so recognized in the world and given the power
and glory he deserved.

These attitudes belong more actively to the period that
followed the First World War, but they came in before the
war—I remember the jingoistic novels of Rex Beach as an example—and of course during the war our patriotic fervor was
naturally very strong. At school we even went in for a sort of
semiprofessional military training, and learned how to march
in formation and do the manual of arms drill with wooden
rifles—an activity we took mainly with a fun-and-games attitude, to the annoyance of our soldierly instructors. I remember being convicted of some sort of military delinquency and
required to march back and forth across the quadrangle for a
couple of hours in expiation—and also I remember how we
had to dress in our "good suits," with white shirts and ties, as
representing a proper uniform, and go through a final drill in
the presence of some upper level army officials. At one point
we were ordered to "deploy," which meant flinging ourselves
on the ground with rifles at the ready—and our good suits
came out the worse for it. That was the only military activity
I ever engaged in. At Amherst the next fall, two months before the Armistice, I had the choice of joining a company of
under-eighteen-year-olds as a part of a regular Student Army

Training Corps [S.A.T.C.] or of going on as an unregulated outsider—and acting partly on the advice of my Uncle Harry Donaldson, who happened to be in Amherst at the time of decision, I chose the latter alternative. I had at the time no philosophical position on pacifism, but merely a natural desire to avoid any kind of group activity. I thought quite seriously about patriotic duty, but Uncle Harry convinced me that the army didn't yet need a seventeen-year-old.

It had troubled my conscience a little that during the war I had been having such a joyous time of it during the summers —in the woods of Maine and the Adirondacks, at Mount Desert and Deer Isle. At school we were constantly exhorted to "do our bit," which meant unspecified useful service—chiefly, I think, as farm workers, and many of my fellows there seemed to perform tremendous labors for the common good, and were publicly commended. I had little to boast of. It is probably fair to say that I have always avoided group duties and commitments; I am no good even as a committee member, and would have been a poor recruit for any sort of army. I used to think I had courage enough to stand up to the dangers and hostilities of the world, but my life-long habit of doing things as a lone and unregulated amateur is probably partly a manifestation of social fear. At any rate, notwithstanding a troublesome conscience, I mounted no bandwagons, either for the cause of school and college spirit or for saving the nation from its enemies—and it was not that I was averse to any of these aims but that I felt unable to contribute to them, or at least unwilling to try. A few years later a candid and angry girlfriend turned on me for no reason that I could then perceive and bitterly accused me of bland self-esteem and evasion of reality, and now that I can look back with a half-century perspective I can understand why she felt that way. But at the time I was simply bewildered. What had I ever said or done, I wondered, to deserve such an attack?

A few more scraps of my life at Loomis still stay fresh in

my mind. The formidable Hook Mather, whom I met when I took a preliminary exam in algebra, taught not only math but a class in what was called manual training, which meant woodworking. I enlisted in it with eager anticipation of making a model sailboat—for years it was my dream to make ideal sailing models, and I assumed that a good manual training class was what I needed. We met on Saturday mornings for an hour, and were each given a piece of inch pine board and told to make a "cutting board" out of it, which meant that all edges and corners had to be perfectly rectangular. That was a preliminary exercise with saw and plane—and once we had properly done it we could then advance to making a small bookcase or even a box. At first, though, we were taught how to sharpen the plane blade on an oil stone—which took up the first hour. Then, the next week, came the careful planing and testing by tri-square—and Hook Mather came and inspected and shook his head and noted the inaccuracies in my angles. It had to be perfect, he pointed out with characteristic severity. So I continued on my pine board the next week, and the week after, and so through the whole school year, planing (and sharpening the plane blade) and continually testing with the tri-square, but never achieving the perfection demanded by my teacher. At times I looked at him with despair and even hatred, and he certainly regarded me with grim disgust. We carried on a year-long frustrating duel, but it seemed impossible for me to come up to his expectations, and equally impossible for him to be in the slightest degree less than absolute in his demands. That was for me the end of my manual training course, and it at least made me aware of my natural ability to be inaccurate which has plagued me ever since. But I did in time make some pretty good boat models, and I have built a house with fireplace and chimney and have done innumerable jobs of repair and painting—and have maintained a small summertime fleet of boats with moorings and outhauls and fairly complicated gear. I believe devoutly in the ideal of perfect workmanship, as manifested in such craftsmen as Hook Mather, but I generally seem to operate on a more pragmatic and even makeshift level.

But at Loomis I did manage to achieve a more competent sort of scholarship—not by any means brilliant but good enough to win honorable grades and to give me respectable standing in the college board exams. What we were supposed to learn in those days was clearly prescribed, and we got the notion that essential knowledge was to be found in certain limited areas—for example, one elementary science, such as physics, one foreign language, preferably French, and of course classical Latin with the inevitable sequence of Caesar, Cicero, and Virgil, and American history, and literature, which meant *Macbeth*, *L'Allegro* and *Il Penseroso*, *The Spectator*, Burke's *Speech*, Lamb's *Essays*, Carlyle's *Essay on Burns*, *David Copperfield*, *Silas Marner*, *The Golden Treasury*—I don't think American literature ever rated seriously in the college entrance stakes, in spite of our reading of *Walden* —in fact, we were given to understand that while American history was a subject we could take pride in, American literature was so comparatively inferior that with a few exceptions like Emerson and Hawthorne it was hardly worth bothering with. But I vividly remember how our teacher, Louis Clough, read to us a strange new poem called "The Congo," by one Vachel Lindsay, and how we listened to its tub-thumping rhythms with an almost trancelike intensity. It was not a recognized academic text, and we hardly knew what we were supposed to make of it, but the power of it seemed very brilliant and almost dangerous. Our tastes were still conventional—we were trained in the orthodox motives and manners of traditional poetry, and the uninhibited sound and fury of "The Congo" gave us the effect of a thrilling plunge into the darkest night of existence. When at college a year or two later I was asked to name a poem I greatly admired I had no hesitation in picking Gray's "Elegy" as my number one favorite, but I had begun to realize that strange new ventures were oc-

curring in the arts. As of today we take "The Congo" as a
sort of native camp-meeting classic, somewhat in the Walt
Whitman vein with great popular appeal, perhaps a little er-
satz or even "racist" in its celebration of black primitivism,
but back in 1917 it seemed to us brave and splendid and somehow challenging.

There were other amenities of school life that I recollect
with more or less pleasure. The ice skating, for example,
seemed quite marvelous, and it was only by chance that I
didn't drown myself. I unwisely went off down the Farming-
ton River on several occasions, and even out across the broad
Connecticut, weaving on smooth ice among the humps and
floes—and was once startled to see a patch of blue open water
ahead of me sparkling in the sun, and I realized that I was out
there alone on the mile-wide expanse and could quite easily
fall in unseen. And again at another time and place I did fall in
—and did not drown—though I was with others, and we
might have all succumbed. It was a day in March, and the
spring floods had overrun all the land for miles round the little hill where the school stood—it was called the "island," and
for a time was cut off from the outside world. The water covered all our playing fields and the farm lands and woods and
pastures, and when it froze to a thickness of three inches or
so we had a few days of the most beautiful skating I have ever
enjoyed. When the flood began to recede a little, the ice settled down to some of the contours of the land, and a skater
could swoop down and over the hills it made, and speed in and
out among the standing trees and over old fences—and the ice
was all black and velvet-smooth, and the skating was like a
wondrous dream. We flew like swallows across the familiar
country, darting along lanes and out over the cornfields in the
flat area to the east—and it was there while I was cutting an
elegant backward outside edge, somewhat apart from my fellows, that I found myself without any warning at all over my
head in icy water. I came up with an emotion of anger at my
predicament, and then proceeded to crawl out unassisted over

the thin edge of the ice—a feat I wouldn't now suppose to be possible, but I did it, and the edge of the ice was strong enough to hold me, and I came away safely before my companions quite realized what had happened. I skated back to shore, and then had to run in my stocking feet all the way to my dormitory where I got out of my ice-cold wet clothes and took a long warm shower and was none the worse, except that the thought of the black icy depths I fell into so abruptly has haunted me ever after. I think by the next day the March weather grew warm, and there was no more cross-country skating—and in fact I doubt if those same conditions have occurred since then.

We had at Loomis a good deal of personal freedom, as can be seen by our behavior. Now and then I went alone or with others by trolley car to Hartford—mainly to go to the movies, but sometimes simply to wander about the city. I once went in to visit a girl who had been a nurse during a spell of German measles at school—and she urged me to come and see her in her apartment afterward, and I did so, bravely at first and then fearfully when I began to realize she had sexual designs on me—and I escaped intact and somewhat bewildered and shocked by the revelation. At sixteen I lived in a bright glow of romantic idealism that hardly took into account the actualities of bodily desire and I could scarcely believe that my charming young nurse had had such intentions—though I suppose she was mostly playing with me. She succeeded in scaring me off, though, and afterward I began to feel that I had behaved properly but had also missed a chance at the experience I secretly desired. But I was much too young for it, as I am sure she realized. I never went back. Some of my more worldly fellows at school used to talk about a certain girl in Windsor, whom I knew, as though she were a whore—and indeed her name still rings with the accent of contempt and wonder we used to give it, but what was really true about her I never knew. The whole sexual drama was for me wrapped up in the darkest mystery, and my ideas about it were drawn

mainly from the romances I constantly read. I of course had
no teaching about it, and was always embarrassed to mention
it in anything but euphemistic terms—even among my more
uninhibited companions—and in truth I am still fixed in the
reticent and fearful habits of my early youth and I can be
readily shocked by the popular candor of our times. At any
rate, most of us made the effort to control our desires and
were conscientiously disturbed when we failed. We at least
had a theory of continence and faithfulness and even true
love, and though we often did otherwise in practice we kept
in mind the traditional hierarchies of virtue and sin. Boarding
schools are often dramatized in terms of their sexual excesses
and abnormalities but in my own experience nothing far-out
ever seemed to occur. A few boasted, or at least intimated that
they knew all about it, and sexy talk was fairly common, but
more of us lived in innocence and hopeful romantic idealism.

It was a time, of course, when religious doctrine prevailed
naturally among us, and we had morning chapel services as
well as Sunday church with organ and choir. Perhaps we
didn't take that sort of thing very seriously—or if we did it
was with sentimental expectations of a good and prosperous
life—but we went through the rituals without rebellion. We
had some eminent preachers—we had our own history teacher,
Arthur Howe, one of the great Yale footballers from its
heroic era, and a manly and muscular and very magnetic
Christian; and we had the celebrated Jewish rabbi Stephen
S. Wise, whose son was our schoolmate and was always addressed as "r-rabbi" with what was considered a heavy Jewish
accent—not invidiously, I might add, but with humorous
good-fellowship and childish candor. The senior Wise used
to preach to us with passionate and dramatic eloquence, and
I can still hear him say the word "evil" with heavy stress on
both syllables—which we repeated to one another for days
afterward: "Do not follow the crowd to do *ee-vill*." I'm
sure it remains the most effective preaching any of us ever
heard. And there was the headmaster of an eminent prep

school who came several times, and whom we all considered the most obnoxious stuffed shirt in existence; he was portly and blandly complacent and presented himself as a model of virtue: "I myself have had no desire to take up smoking," he intoned. "I have had no need to drink." We quoted him with unction and contempt. It seemed impossible that he could be the effective head of a successful school—where he was known, ironically, as the "king"; but in those days schoolmasters were inclined to be self-important and dictatorial, and the world seemed to accept them at their own evaluation. We took it for granted that a certain amount of pretentiousness and even hypocrisy was essential in the proper conduct of life and though we could laugh at and make sport of traditional adult solemnities and could enjoy the entertaining iconoclasm of Bernard Shaw we on the whole remained loyal to the established habit of our tribe.

My best friend at school—and still so some sixty years later—was the elder son of a lady named Mary Ware Dennett who I understood was an advocate of radical causes, notably women's rights and sexual candor—and I naturally assumed that Carl also represented these views. When he took me to see her in their New York apartment I was struck by her eager energy and certainty and her eloquent denunciation of what she considered the predatory imperialism of Theodore Roosevelt, whom in my innocence I had always assumed to be a great and good man. She also spoke warmly on behalf of certain well-known political radicals, and she did it with such persuasive charm that I was incapable of any intelligible response. When I tried to tell my mother about it later she suggested that charm like that must be regarded as dangerous and cautioned me on letting my heart cloud my mind— though of course I knew she didn't know what she was talking about. At school we all had the notion that Carl, as the son of a well-known mother of radical tendencies, was himself inclined to the leftward or sinister fringe, but the only evidence against him was that he always wore red socks and conducted himself with cheerful indifference to many of the solemn rituals of our tribe. He tried to be loyal to his mother's well publicized views, and later stood by her when she was tried and acquitted of "obscenity" on the basis of her pamphlet on sexual practice, but I don't think he ever shared her serious dedication to radical causes. He never actually said very much about his mother or her views, and he was even more reticent about his father, who I gathered was divorced and lived in New Hampshire and in the spring sent him tins of maple sugar which was too sweet and too plentiful for us to eat, but he was at all times outgoing and full of pleasure at the small adventure of daily living. We walked and talked and did things together continually in our school days and during vacations in New York and have been companions and friends through all the vicissitudes of life ever since. He became in time a brilliant teacher of mathematics and an expert and ingenious solver of puzzles and brain-teasers of all sorts, but at school he had some sort of psychological block in the presence of algebra and geometry—and it seems strange to me to remember that I was the one who helped him with his homework problems. He was chiefly baffled by his teachers, I think, and was thoroughly discouraged, when he finally fell into the hands of a man named Windsor who suddenly made everything seem quite clear and understandable to him and from then on he had no more troubles. He is always amused to recall the time when I was the expert and he was the struggling neophyte in the mysteries of elementary mathematics. As I suggested, he developed into a superb teacher of the subject, and operated with wondrous charm and sympathy for all scared or reluctant youngsters. His ingenuity in working out mathematical problems and puzzlers seems to me quite astonishing—and of course it has been a great asset to him as a teacher. He made his students share the ventures and triumphs of discovering the solutions to their apparently unsolvable problems. He had another year at Loomis while I went on to Amherst, but we kept in close touch and shared our vacation times and were companions in many small activities. We walked great distances together, in both city and country, and rode in ferry boats and went to the movies and visited museums and galleries and simply loafed around together with all of life and time at our disposal.

All in all, Loomis like the others of its kind operated with the best of intentions, and I think actually its newness in its field gave it a special quality of youth and discovery that we all shared. It pretty much lived up to its own professed ideals—and no institution professes its ideals more eloquently than a prep school. There was an almost evangelical devotion to honorable and manly behavior, both in and out of the actual schoolrooms. We were taught to be just and fair, and obedient to proper authority and respectful to the venerable traditions of our culture. But though snobbishness of any sort was considered bad form, and we professed a devotion to even-handed democracy, we inevitably took on the unconscious attitudes of an elitist group and tended to adopt the manners and fashions we thought suitable to a high-grade prep school. That rather quaint innocence I had noticed on my first visit did somewhat disappear and we made a point of whistling only the newest show tunes and speaking in the latest fashionable locutions. The distinction between excellence in any absolute or classic sense and the excellences sanctioned by fashion or cult is not obvious, and the values of our prep school world can be attacked or defended with equal effectiveness. The idea of a privileged and self-congratulatory group setting itself up in superiority to ordinary folk is not to be commended, but what if such a group transcends fashion or the level of personal well-being and provides civilized competence? Nothing, of course, can be gained by reducing this question to an either-or conclusion, but at its best the ideal of the high-minded prep school, like that of the private college or university, does try to achieve a classic and culturally essential excellence. And of course the school itself, if it is serious about its professions, is aware of its problems and responsibilities; it seeks out whatever promising human material it can find and offers it opportunity—at least that is part of its policy. Perhaps the system works imperfectly, with resulting inequalities and unfairnesses, but its virtues have been indigenous in our tradition for a long time.

ELEVEN

AMHERST AND CARRIE JOHNSON

I HAD THOUGHT SERIOUSLY about applying at Yale, where the other men of my family had gone since the time of my grandfather, and I had visited my brother there, and the Donaldson boys, and the Hendricksons, but it seemed too large and too shut in by its surrounding city and I craved what I thought would be a simpler and sweeter country existence in a small college in a small town. If I had realized that my great-grandfather had graduated from Williams, I might have applied there as an appropriate gesture—and much later I encouraged my two sons to go there, which they successfully did, but at the time I knew nothing about my great-grandfather and had heard a good deal about Amherst. I had even been invited up there from Loomis for a "sub-freshman" weekend and was given some effective propaganda about it. What I chiefly remember about the visit is that the Alpha Delt house, where I stayed, was having a Saturday night dance to which only local village girls were invited, and the boys were very apologetic and even embarrassed at what they considered the inferior quality of their guests. They were accustomed, they said, to the best of Smith College and this rather impromptu experiment was not working out very well. I was of course impressed by such a lordly attitude, and at the same time felt a twinge of sorrow for those lowly girls who were obviously trying hard to be as nice and attractive as they could be. The Alpha Delts, I was given to understand, were a very superior group indeed.

I don't really remember anything else about that sub-freshman visit—except that Amherst village seemed to be a familiarly pleasant place to live in, and there was plenty of open country round about. So I formally applied, and in due course, after the results of the college board examinations were recorded, was accepted. The only Amherst man I had known up to that time was a white-haired, pink-cheeked gentleman whom my Auntie Leta introduced me to when she took me to the Sunday service at Grace Church in New York during my vacations—she thought he was a delightful character, and he seemed very eager at the idea of my going to Amherst and invited me to come and see him at his office and talk about what a fine place Amherst was. He was so insistent that I agreed, and found him late one afternoon alone in what I remember as a suite of old-fashioned offices—and he welcomed me with embarrassing warmth and then gradually got into the subject of my sexual activity, which he introduced with fatherly candor and sincerity, and finally asked if I would mind very much if he inspected my genitals. At this point his eyes were shining and his lips were red and moist—I remember how elegantly he was dressed, with black suit and starched collar and white piping on his vest and how altogether respectable and genteel he seemed to be, and of course I was in a fog of astonishment and embarrassment at his action. I still lived in a state of elementary sexual inexperience and I found it almost impossible to believe that this kindly white-haired gentleman was avidly yearning for some sort of carnal relationship with me—with his hands actually at work unbuttoning my trousers and his lips glistening with anticipation. He had been so kind and from my point of view so elderly that for a few minutes I actually let him work on me—I was still trying to be respectful to what I assumed was some sort of legitimate adult behavior on his part. He protested his own innocent intentions all along and spoke almost as though he was playing a harmless little game—but something in his avidity frightened me and I turned cold and pulled away, and he looked at me with dog-like yearning and sorrow and then seemed to give up his hope. We parted still on a polite and respectful level. I went off in a state of wonder, not quite able to believe what had occurred. I had heard of such men, of course, and had been told that they were wicked and dangerous, but it struck me that this man with his pious respectability and his fine clothes and his desire to make love with young boys must be somehow pathetic and unfulfilled. What his life was like I never knew. He came to Grace Church alone, I think. I never saw him after that memorable visit. But a year or so later I met a student at Amherst who spoke of him with such a tone of personal warmth that I assumed they were attached to each other by close sexual ties. I never said a word about my own experience —not until the present writing, and actually it is still hard for me to believe that it literally happened as I have described it.

But it was my churchly friend who got me started originally on my idea of going to Amherst, which he assured me was the finest college of all. By the time we came to our denouement I had already been enrolled. If I had realized what sort of a man he was, I might not have taken his recommendation, though I had sense enough to see that he was hardly representative of the place he so warmly favored.

The summer that followed these events was the one in which I worked for a few weeks at the Farm School in Valhalla and then went on to the camp on the Oswegatchie River in the Adirondacks, which I have told about. It was the last summer of the World War, and when I arrived in Amherst the college was in the process of being organized as an army training camp. But before that got started, two days were allotted for the traditional fraternity rushing period, a bewildering and brutal sorting of the incoming freshmen who were chosen or rejected at first sight, as it were—an old Amherst custom of those times, since abandoned. It used to be said in justification of it that this method of arranging the fates of the ins and the outs was so quick and arbitrary that it settled everything with the least possible grief and fuss, and did away with the political maneuverings that could drag along over a period of time. Fraternities included about four fifths of the student population, and the one fifth who were excluded were assumed to be the hopeless undesirables—and the whole issue was decided in those two or three days before the formal opening of the college term. I had, as I said, visited the Alpha Delt fraternity during a sub-freshman weekend the previous spring, but I was wholly unprepared and baffled in the presence of this frantic process of rushing.

From New York in those days one went by train to Springfield and changed for Northampton, and then took a trolley eight miles to Amherst. I think I must have had a trunk, but I can't remember how it was handled—but since everyone had trunks there must have been some system that took care of them. I got off the trolley car with a suitcase at College Corner on the Green and was set upon by a fraternity representative who handed me a schedule of half-hour appointments at the dozen or so Greek lettered houses—and then directed me to the dormitory of South College, where my room was. I lugged my baggage up the hill, found my rooms, with signs of unknown roommates, and looking out of an eastward window saw a bare hilltop a couple of miles away across the valley—and before I quite realized what I was up to I had put on a light sweater and set off to find the hill. It marked the pattern of my college life, for I spent more time and strength climbing hills than doing anything else. It seemed that I had a yearning for hills.

The two days of rushing were strangely mixed in with the effort to turn the college into an officers' training camp, and we were hustled through the rushing ritual in a state of quiet desperation—at least I was. Everyone was in a hurry to get it over with, and we were made to feel that our future depended

on the instant acceptance or rejection—we passed before our
judges like dogs in a show, to be given points on the basis of
our deportment and grooming and the mysterious collegiate
values then in vogue. I had a good share of self-esteem at the
time, but I was not yet seventeen, had blemishes on my skin
and gold braces on my teeth and no reputation as an athlete
and no conversational skill. I didn't quite realize how unprom-
ising I must have seemed, but it was evident that the major
houses were not much interested—not even the Alpha Delts
who had been my hosts the previous spring. They seemed to
take themselves, I must say, very seriously, if not pompously,
and I was made to feel somewhat more at home by a newer,
less pretentious group named Delta Tau Delta, who inhabited a big shabby mansard-roofed dwelling house—and there I
was finally "pledged," as they called it. A mixed rag-tag sort
of group we were, without any special distinctions and a good
deal of rather pathetic ambition to be given collegiate recognition. Our leaders were very fine characters indeed, and gave
us some standing in the community—especially a senior named
John Knox Archibald Brown and a noble-looking junior
named Clermont Cartwright who later became my roommate
and good friend. But I hardly knew what I was getting into,
and because of the army training program everything seemed
disruptive. My new fraternity was hardly functioning, I had
to move out of my dormitory room in South College, I took
part in few collegiate activities—I even arranged to take my
meals at a village boarding house that had no college attachment at all; I dutifully went to classes and did perfunctory
preparation for work that no one seemed to take very seriously, and otherwise I was wholly on my own, and spent one
of the happiest autumns of my life. Almost every afternoon I
ranged off into the country—northward to Mount Toby,
southward to the Holyoke Range, chiefly eastward to the
wilder region of the Pelham hills and Shutesbury, a country of
forest and ancient and primitive farms still struggling with the
ways of an earlier century. The valley farms seemed fertile

and prosperous, but up there in the hills was a quite different world of lost hopes. The little communities of Pelham and Shutesbury had once planted themselves with pioneer courage, with white churches high on the upland ground and a few good and substantial houses, and were now dwindling and decaying—and they seemed to me very dramatic and sad, and I wished I could write their stories. I read *Ethan Frome* that year, and was profoundly moved by it. I kept scouting that hill country in wider and wider sweeps all through my college years and after, over further and further ranges—westward into the Berkshires and northward to Vermont and New Hampshire, driven always by the romantic desire to discover new sights and scenes. But that first autumn in Amherst was the most golden of all.

Shortly after occupying my dormitory room I was told that I had to move out—as an under-eighteen juvenile I had no place among the regular student trainees and had to find lodgings in the town. Actually the college seemed to pay little or no attention to the care and feeding of its students, who were expected to forage for themselves—at least in matters of board. Either dormitory or fraternity rooms were normally available, but at the time I was not a normal case. I think I was actually a minor nuisance. So I had to look for a place, and it turned out that one of my new fraternity brothers needed a partner in renting a couple of rooms—he was a senior who was too nearsighted and frail to qualify for the army, and was one of the outsiders like me. His name was Fairbank, and he was born in China, and was a cheerful eccentric—a very skinny, hollow-chested, somewhat cynical boy, and he took me to room with him in a little old brick house on South Prospect Street owned by Mrs. Arthur Johnson.

In one of my novels, *The Garretson Chronicle*, my young protagonist, Ralph Garretson, stops at a neighboring farm and meets Mrs. Kingsley—and a sudden flame of affection and devotion between them is ignited. It is what happened to me when I saw Mrs. Johnson that day in the little front hall of

her house—and to her too, though of course no such sentiment was ever uttered in the subsequent six or seven years
that we were allotted for our love. She assumed at once that I
was a wayward son in need of maternal management, and I
accepted her on that basis with irresistible delight. She was
about fifty years old, stout and ample of body, gray-haired,
blue-eyed, as full of eagerness and energy as a young girl—
and she remembered everything with dramatic intensity, her
young days as Carrie Gale on a Petersham farm, her old
friends and country adventures, and especially the college
boys who had been her protegés. Her two sons, now grown
and gone away, had been members of my new fraternity, so
she was prejudiced in our favor. She was never sentimental
about her attachments, but shrewd and forthright and humorous and always generous-hearted—though her criticism of my
foolish ways could be quite sharp, and she seldom hesitated to
speak her mind with candid emphasis. Once when I came
back from a day's walk and said I had covered thirty miles, the
boys there scoffed at my story, and she was furious at me for
not "knocking them down" for calling me a liar—she seemed
to think I could do it with one blow right in her front sitting
room. She at least believed my story, though it was the sort of
story I had come to assume that no one would believe. But she
shared with me a delight in exploring the back country, especially eastward toward the region where she lived as a girl,
and she wanted to hear every detail of my discoveries. There
was a small graveyard up in the wildest part of the Pelham
Range with a stone and a famous inscription that she longed to
see—and I discovered it for her and memorized it, and can
still quote it fifty-odd years later:

> Think my friends when this you see
> How my wife has treated me.
> She in some oysters did prepare
> Some poison for my lot and share.
> And of the same I did partake

And on me nature worked its fate.
She before my wife became,
Mary Felton was her name.

I have no recollection of the date or the name of the victim.
She was of course very gratified when I brought back the
words for her.

When I first met her husband, Arthur, I thought he was
another lodger. He seemed very quiet and remote, and she
paid no attention to him—he nodded gravely to me and said
nothing. He was a gaunt and weathered countryman who
operated a small greenhouse and raised a few vegetables in another part of the village, and for a long time we kept on saying nothing at all to each other. She referred to him with a
touch of asperity always as "he." With the certainty of youthful prejudices I assumed that he was not worthy of her and I
somewhat scorned him as crude and insensitive. When he did
speak, it was in cryptic and oblique fragments which at first I
could hardly understand. His voice would break abruptly out
of silence and then stop in the middle of an utterance. "Take
Dan'l Shays," he might say. "Had a cave on Mount Nor-
watuck—said to, leastways. He—" Then he would tip his
head and perhaps sigh or blow a breath through his lips and
his drooping mustache and fall into silence again. It took me a
year or more to get used to him. He was not really shy, in the
ordinary sense, nor was he ever hostile or suspicious, but he
had a lifelong habit of quietness and diffidence, and even in
1920 or so he felt anachronistic and looked backward to the
ways of his fathers. He let his wife do most of the talking and
scheming. He tolerated her whims and impulses, her love of
people of all sorts—especially grown boys, her eager curiosity
about the little world she lived in, her desire for small adventures. He began to tolerate me too, and before long he treated
me as a member of his family, even when I took outrageous
advantage of her affection for me and let her indulge me with
pie and cake and other good things at odd hours.

Her great desire, I found, was to have an automobile which she could drive and "go places" in—and somehow he acquired one. Even by 1919 standards it was an antique: a high-wheeled Rambler touring car, with the driver's seat on the right-hand side and a brass gearshift lever and mechanism on the outside of the car on the right. It started, when it did, with a hand crank. I had had a bit of experience in driving a gearshift car—and like all boys I assumed I had a natural right to drive anything. A year or two earlier I had been visiting the caretaker and his family at a Children's Aid Society convalescent home in Chappaqua, near New York, and had confidently offered to drive children to the Fourth of July parade in the village—and did so for several trips in the Dodge touring car they had, though it was the first time I had ever driven on a public road. So I assured the Johnsons that I could drive their Rambler, which I did, and teach them how, which I failed to do. The cranking and the gearshift were too much for them. But I took them off on a few little trips, and they always loved to "go"—just for the sake of going, but more often than not we broke down and had to be towed home, and I was not much good at fixing the trouble. They had an almost pathetic faith in me, though—and assumed that cars always broke down. I had no idea where he got the Rambler, or why he expected so ungainly and elderly a vehicle to run properly, but when I came back the next year they were waiting for me with a new Model T Ford.

I taught them both to drive it—it was equipped with a self-starter, and it seldom broke down, and for the first time in their lives they could both "go"—and we explored the countryside together. I went with her one day across the ranges northeastward to Petersham, where she had grown up, but none of her family was left there and her old house was burned and gone and our visit was sad, though I relished seeing the places she had lived in. I was by then wholly devoted to her, and felt that she was an embodiment of the region and all its tradition. She had been away for thirty years or more, and was baffled by the changes in the countryside. She used to drive in her father's wagon to the grist mill in Millerton, but when we found it she said she felt like Rip Van Winkle coming home after his twenty-year sleep—except that she was too buoyant a character to let herself be unhappy about it. "His name was Abner Colby," she said. "The miller, I mean. He was short and stout, and they said he was the strongest man anywhere around. He could pick me up by my elbows and hold me right over his head." The place was empty and unused, through the stream still flowed under the foundations and along the leaky sluiceway. We returned that day through the country since inundated by the Quabbin Reservoir, by the villages of Greenwich and Prescott that are now forever drowned or abandoned.

I roomed in her house for the rest of my freshman year, and thereafter moved into the fraternity house, where I shared a study with Cartwright and Walbridge Buffum, but in all my subsequent days at college I let none go by without visiting her. I could have been a burden and a nuisance, but I don't think I was—except that I used to try to cajole her into taking me on as a regular boarder—and now and then she did, but she didn't like to be tied down to it. Often enough I stayed for lunch or supper, and had fresh corn or asparagus from her backyard or young rhubarb—and chocolate pudding, which was one of her specialties. When I didn't have classes I dropped in late in the morning, after picking up my mail in a post office box—with the daily *New York Times* which I could read beside her kitchen stove. For quite a while I boarded in a house right across the street from her—an exclusive six-dollar-a-week place that she arranged for me, with a select few others, where the pineapple pie was locally celebrated (at one time I found an oldtime house that charged four-fifty a week for good and ample food—it stood facing the village common between the Town Hall and the Episcopal Church—but it didn't last long. Seven a week was the going rate for the big boarding houses). On Sundays I always had supper with her, and usually I had spent the day charging through the hill country and came in very parched and hungry.

I speak always of "her," as though "he" had no share in her house or life, but he came in so quietly and shyly that I hardly knew he was there. She was the one who made the plans and led the attack on life—and when she learned to drive the Model T she had a joyous time of it. But in his diffident way he went along with her and relished her energy and eagerness, and like her he was infinitely curious about the life of the region he lived in. They were both keenly alert to the doings of their neighbors and all the affairs of the village and the college. Like all country people they loved gossip: he was amused—and she was indignant—at the report that the president of the college never paid his grocer's bills, and they took pleasure in telling over the story of the Dickinson family, past and present.

For those four college years I behaved as though I had been adopted as part of her family. I dropped in at any time of day, had odd meals, sat by her kitchen stove in the cold weather, played records on her Victrola—she loved Kreisler and Ellman, especially Ellman, and we used to dispute as to their merits, and in general we talked endlessly. I should be quite reluctant now to occupy anyone's time and life as completely as I must have occupied hers, but it seemed to happen so naturally and inevitably that I could somehow not do otherwise. I looked at her with both love and pride—I felt that she was the classic time of our past, and lived with wonderful relish close to the realities of simple and essential things. I have known and loved other New England women since then, and have met them in the books of Sara Orne Jewett and other native writers, but still to me Carrie Gale Johnson is the pure and perfect prototype. Our friendship was one of the major events of my life.

But the aftermath was tragic. I went back to visit for a few years after I graduated—I took my wife to see her the

day after we were married in 1927—and heard nothing more
from her until the news of her death came indirectly. And
when later we stopped at the old house we found a strange
woman in charge, a steely-eyed person who had taken over
the house and property and the hapless widower—as cold
and predatory a creature as I can ever remember. The old
house which had been home-base for me for so long was quite
alien now, and my inarticulate old friend, Arthur Johnson,
was filled with visible misery and shame. Soon afterward he
drowned himself in the mill pond of what we called the Freshman River, thoughtfully tying a rope around one wrist so
that he could be fished out without trouble.

TWELVE

VERMONT

WHAT I CHIEFLY ACQUIRED at Amherst was a firm and romantic attachment to the traditions of old New England. My love for the Johnsons became a major adventure for me, and I carried it off into my widening explorations as though I were destined to make some ultimate secret discovery. Whenever I came on a village hidden away in the hills—like New Salem with its white churches, or Conway or Colrain, I had a sense of mysterious revelation. The sight of a white doorway with fan and sidelights was like a strain of purest Mozartian music, and reassured me that harmony and simple beauty existed there in an order of final perfection. I looked always for the old ways, the remnants of the past in action, the working horses, the axes and hand saws, the gathering and boiling of maple sap, the milking of cows, and though I knew the life and world were harsh and often tragic I had a conviction that old New England had once discovered a classic serenity that could still be perceived. I quested for it like a searcher for the Grail. I rushed across the hills along countless by-ways and little dirt roads. I slept in many a back country farm—sometimes in the barn, more often in the spare bedroom for a small fee, with breakfast of creamed potatoes and cold baked beans. I met the forlorn and defeated hill farmers who were thankful to have my dollar—I slept with bedbugs in dusty bare chambers. But once I found it—

perhaps a glimpse of the Grail itself. It seemed to me like pure felicity.

It was about the first of June of my second year. I had resolved to keep going until I got to Vermont, where I had never been, though I recognized it as the promised land of my romantic visions. I followed the topographical maps, and took what I hoped would be the untraveled roads, crossing the Deerfield River at Bardwell's Ferry (where there was a bridge) and climbing over the hills by Shelburne to Colrain on the North River. Near Shelburne I met a girl with green-gold eyes under a big maple tree, and I fell in love with her—and promised myself I would come back and find her again, which I eventually did on her wedding day (the romance was all on my side). I can't now remember her name, but the picture of her sitting under the great maple in front of her white homestead on that sunny June day is still clear in my mind. She had a collie dog who made friends with me and came along the road as though he would attach himself to me—and I said very casually, "I think it's time you went home, old boy," and he at once turned and trotted off, without a backward glance. I kept going as fast as I could walk, though in the late afternoon I found a secluded place beside the North River and undressed and swam in a pool for a few minutes—and afterward stopped at a roadside farm and negotiated for some supper, a simple fifty-cent transaction in a busy and flexible household. They hardly seemed surprised at an itinerant young stranger.

But I kept going northward along the river road, and almost no cars passed to raise dust and the evening sunlight washed the high pastured hills with shining gold. The air was scented with lilacs and young apple blossoms. In the dusk I came on the state line granite marker, with an M on one side and a V on the other, and observed a ceremonial moment of crossing. There was a big old farm place across the road from the granite marker that seemed to be planted squarely on the state line, and I was told later that it had been put there with the idea of somehow evading taxes, and was now the headquarters of a bootlegging operation—though on that June evening it seemed to merge with its innocent surroundings. This was of course the era of the abortive experiment in prohibition.

But—there was Vermont at last, and I breathed its higher and purer air with relish. In the years to follow I was to see a great deal of it and for a while to feel almost native to it, and I remember my first entrance as though I had had a premonition of events to come. But I hardly expected the absolute beauty of its landscape, the mountains and high hills all arranged by a master designer, with rich green mowings in the valleys and golden pastures on the hills and dark forested mountain ranges folding away into the distances—and little clapboarded villages and white churches under elms and sugar maples and homesteads with great barns, and mowings and plowings and herds of placid cows. Not that I saw all such things in the dusk of that first evening, but everything I did see from then on seemed to have a pristine Vermont quality about it. It all lay there like an immemorial Arcadia, except that it still displayed its old northern wildness, with its mowings and pastures running up into the forests of spruce and fir on the mountain slopes. Even in the blossoming spring I felt the presence of the long winter somewhere in the offing.

When I came to a roadside farm in the early evening I had walked about thirty-five miles, and I decided to ask for a drink of water, and maybe a lodging for the night. It was dark, and I realized I should have stopped earlier—the night grows more sinister as it advances, but nothing had seemed to be right for my purposes, certainly not that state line house with its spooky look six miles or so down the road. This house was a four-square two-story of some dignity, with a big cattle barn attached. It stood fairly close to the road, and the brawling little river ran along the other side of the road—a sound I was to remember many times by day and night thereafter.

When I knocked a woman came, a slender little person with pure white hair and a fair unwrinkled face and bright

TO VERMONT 6ws

brown eyes. It must be evident by now that I had a natural affinity for the old-time New England female, because once again that feeling of kinship seemed to occur to us both. I asked if I could stay the night, and she said no, she didn't take in lodgers. She thought I might find a lodging at Jacksonville, two miles farther up the road, but she looked at me with kindness and compassion for my dusty weariness and gave me glasses of the cold mountain water that ran continuously from a separate pipe in her kitchen sink with a faint tinkling sound that I was also to hear day and night in all the seasons afterward—and then she smiled like a young girl and said she'd be very glad to put me up for the night. It was, of course, the sort of place I had dreamed of—the Vermont homestead with barns and cattle behind, the immaculate housewife of infinite kindliness of spirit, the snug kitchen with wood-burning stove, the rill of icy water always flowing, the quietness and warmth of a long settled way of life.

She brought out milk and cake and sat me down in the dining-living room opening from the kitchen. She moved deftly and quietly, with a little smile of solicitude for my weariness and natural hunger, and I told her who I was and where I had come from, and when I said I had never been in Vermont before she glowed with native pride and certainty that it was the best of all places. She had a manner of tipping her head and speaking out with firm conviction, but she did it very sweetly, with a little smile of conciliation. She would hurt no one's feelings if she could help it. Her house and person and ways seemed immaculate to me, and she made me feel as though I were a long-expected guest and friend.

But when I heard the horse and wagon drive into the yard and on to the barn and she tipped her head and said her husband was home at last from his Masonic meeting I felt uneasy and wondered how he would take a stranger sitting so snugly at his table. He came into the kitchen through the connecting sheds and stood in the doorway, a straight, short man with a gray beard and piercing blue eyes that looked directly at me.

She introduced me and said I was staying for the night. She didn't explain or invite his opinion—she merely announced the fact with the gentle little tip of her head. He at once nodded, said howdy as though it were quite natural to offer a lodging for a strange wayfarer, and took off his jacket and hung it on a peg on the kitchen wall. Then he came in and sat down. He asked no questions, but nodded with interest when I told where I had come from—and he said it was lucky I stopped when I did because the folks up at Jacksonville were all going to bed and there wasn't a real boarding place there anyway. Like her, he took me on faith.

That night, in an upstairs chamber—mostly unused—I lay awake for hours, very comfortable and snug, but unable to sleep. I was tired, of course, but not painfully so, and I lay in a waking doze with the sound of the river loud in my ears— and strangely enough in the many visits I was to make there in the next eighteen years or so, in all seasons of fall and spring and coldest winter, I always lay awake in that bed and that room with the noise of the stream sounding loud even through closed windows—and I used to wonder what it was that kept me awake, since the steady rush of the water was not an unpleasant sound, and was muffled by ice in the winter: perhaps, I thought, it was the adventure of simply being there in that good place that I came to think of with intense pleasure—or perhaps it was something about the bed or the room, or even the twelve hundred foot altitude, though none of these seemed to be a plausible explanation. At any rate, I was none the worse for the hours of wakefulness, and always rejoiced that I could be there at all.

That first morning, after a big breakfast and after she made me a couple of sandwiches for my lunch, I went through a few minutes of intense and self-conscious uncertainty about whether I should offer to pay for my lodging. It now seems to me that I should at least have made the effort, with insistence —and of course at other places under similar circumstances I did, but by the time we had finished breakfast we had become friends for life, we looked at one another with deepest affection, and it seemed impossible for me to mention payment. I did try, I opened my mouth to speak of it, but in the end I couldn't. From the moment she invited me in the previous evening, I had been enveloped in a purely uncalculated hospitality, and my youthful romanticism responded to it as though we were living without regard for anything as lowdown as money. And though I was foolish and sentimental about it, I think in a way they were too—at least they seemed to understand my behavior and agree with it. In all my many visits—ultimately with a wife—I was welcomed by the Hancocks like a returning son, and money was certainly not mentioned or considered. They had a grown son and daughter who lived in Shelburne Falls, and when I met them now and then they welcomed me as though it was natural and right that I should be there, and I played with the young grandchildren and drew pictures for them and on one winter visit I spent some daylight hours with their son cutting trees on the mountainside—both spruce and maple, to be dragged down and sawed and split for stove wood.

So I went off on that June morning with the promise that I would surely come back and visit them again—which I did many times in the next few years. I found various ways of getting there, and learned to follow the less traveled roads. I came in all sorts of weather, including the worst of storms, with rain and snow and sometimes intensest ten-below-zero cold and hard northwest wind. When I went to live in Cambridge I could take a train to Charlemont or Hoosac Tunnel and follow the little country roads up over the hills—and in winter I did it on skis, with very primitive equipment. From Williamstown, where I lived for two years, I could head up the Broad Brook Trail and then go eastward across the Hoosac Range on seldom-used roads—following the Geodetic Survey maps, which I always carried, and eventually after thirty miles or so of ups and downs, come out at the beloved homestead where I was enveloped in the warmth of affection and hot tea and wood-burning stoves. I have arrived there half frozen, sometimes soaked through, in various stages of exhaustion, and always was welcomed and restored. They loved to hear of my trips over the back roads, and were full of anecdotes about the region they lived in. In the evenings we played high-low-jack on the dining table, and sometimes a neighbor named Mr. Murdock came in and joined us—and later on in the maple sugar season I went up to his farm and watched him boiling sap—and eventually I used to buy some of his gallons, and he saved his best first-run for me, which he kept stored under his bed and let go only on special occasions—and once I painted a watercolor of his sugar house which he had reproduced on his label, and he gave me several gallons in payment. My adventures there in Jacksonville seemed to me wonderfully satisfying. When I married I took my wife—by Model T Ford—to visit, and we found an old stone house alone and empty in the hills, and were so delighted with the prospect we agreed to buy it for a few hundred dollars—just as a romantic gesture, and perhaps it was lucky for us that someone else got in just ahead. We had no resources to undertake the restoration of a country house, though in the springtime it was all as beautiful as a dream. And later, when we lived in South Hadley for four years with our three children we used to drive up to the Hancocks' just before Christmas and cut a tree from their mountain—and they had a "sugaring-off" for us, using Mr. Murdock's best syrup for the occasion.

It was some eighteen years after that first visit that I got the news that Mr. Hancock had died, and I drove up from South Hadley through the slush and ice of March to be at his funeral service—a Masonic ritual, it turned out to be, and I sat upstairs with his family while it went on in the downstairs parlor that was ordinarily kept closed and unused. The house was all tidy and decorated with flowers and the stoves were

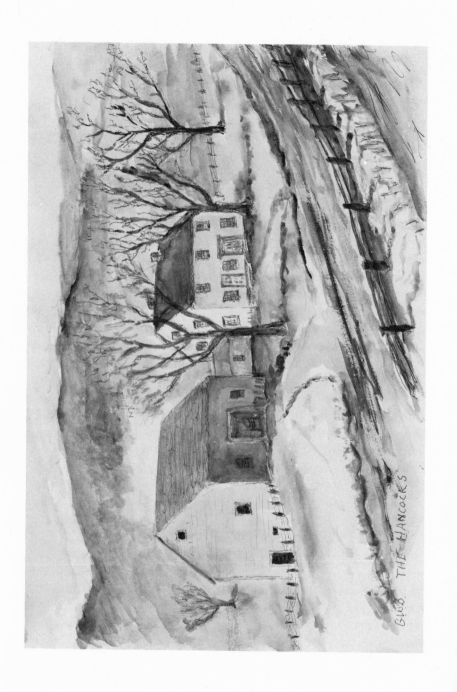

GWD. THE HANCOCK'S

going and the Masons in their funeral clothes stood about the coffin and responded to the ritual with "so mote it be." Afterward all sorts of hot food was served and consumed from casseroles brought in by neighbors and friends—and as much as possible a sense of continuing life and hope was sustained, so that the neighbors and family and the house itself would seem to be keeping up an enduring tradition from past to present to future. But of course we all knew it was an end, not only of life but of a way of life and a time, and we realized that the old house might never again function as completely and well as it did that day. She, of course, had to go off and live with one or the other of her children in Shelburne Falls, twenty miles or so down the river. The house was sold, a bigger and wider road was built by its front door, it grew drab and uncared for, the barns were empty—when I drove past in later years I hardly recognized it. I suppose periods and lives all end in sadness and loss of hope but in our time it seems harder to be reconciled to it than it used to be. The old continuities are destroyed.

I still had at that time a Currier and Ives view of New England and I kept confirming it by my back-country ventures: the folk I saw and met still lived a horse-and-buggy life, with all the work done in the old ways, the milking and wood-cutting, the plowing and hoeing, the sugaring and cider-making in spring and fall, and they carried on their country habits exactly as their fathers and grandfathers had. My beloved Mrs. Johnson in her old village house on South Prospect Street in Amherst represented the classic world of the New England past, and of course my newer friends the Hancocks were still an active part of it. They, the Hancocks, seemed to me perfectly native to their place and tradition, and as serene and confident and competent in what they had to do as it was possible to be—and also as kind and generous and affectionate, though like most old-time Yankees they concealed their stronger feelings with reticence and touches of humor.

"I never knew anyone walked the way you do," he said once. "Except only a feller used to go about collecting spruce gum on the mountains—came up this way from Springfield in the summer—walked it, he said. Had a leather bag on his shoulder. We thought he was touched." But he said it with a dry and kindly twinkle in his blue eyes.

THIRTEEN

ONDAWA FARM

M Y CLOSEST FRIEND and roommate in the fraternity house at Amherst was named Charles Walbridge Buffum—called in times of sober formality Walbridge by his family, and otherwise Bud. He didn't care much for Bud, so perforce I called him Walbridge—though others called him Charlie, which he seemed to care for even less than Bud. He was one of a large and vociferous and strong-minded family who had settled on a back-country farm in the mountains along the Vermont-New York border near a village with the Biblical name Shushan, in New York at the point where the Vermont mountains begin to give way to the rolling open ridges and hills cleared by the patroons and their tenants in pioneer times. The boundary of New England and the state of New York is still a visible division between two old cultural traditions: you can recognize the change from the small farms and woodlots and cozy villages of New England to the wider, more spacious and bare cleared land of New York, with occasional brick Dutch colonial farm dwellings and very few interesting little towns.

When I first met the family they had been living in Buffalo, and their father had been in a hardware concern belonging to his wife's family, I think, but because of financial and other troubles he decided to retire from that and buy a farm—and among them they decided they preferred a picturesque

and mountainous one, which they found in the border country
I have described. There were three girls who all went to
Mount Holyoke, and two boys to Amherst and one to Mid-
dlebury—and their mother was an early graduate of Smith
and their father was in the class of '86 (I think) at Amherst
and played on the baseball team, as he often reminded us—and
now they were all settled on a plain up-country farm with
fields to till and cows to herd and milk. They survived there in
a state of constant family confusion and minor catastrophes
and strongly uttered views on all problems of life. Their aged
car was often broken down, or stuck in mud or snow, and
their goings and comings to church or store or railroad station (sometimes to Eagle Bridge, twelve miles away) were
nearly always events of major crisis. But how I loved to visit
them at all seasons, in mud or snow, sometimes on foot—a
couple of times I walked all the way from Amherst, a hundred miles in two days (stopping for the night at the Hancocks)—and arrived in a state of groggy exhaustion after
battling part way on the Long Trail and even through the
unmarked forest. They always welcomed me like one of their
own. Their view of life was strongly romantic and indi-
vidualistic, and they seemed to take pleasure in my quixotic
habits.

Their natural exuberance was expressed in a fortissimo of
good-natured shouts and family jests and anecdotes—meal-
times were especially loud and hilarious, and they all talked at
once with a sort of Dickensian heartiness and humor. Everything from Mr. Buffum's baseball adventures thirty-odd years
earlier to feeding their lambs from baby bottles was made
part of the day's dramatic dialogue. Mrs. Buffum, a reader of
classics, spoke with indignation of Jonathan Swift's behavior
to Stella—or she commented on the lives of her New England forebears, whom she seemed well acquainted with for
several generations; her interest in the events of the past was a
constant everyday experience for her, and she assumed that
we all were aware of the same sort of continuity. Her six

children had been given full ancestral names—such as Walbridge and Wilder and Samson and Tower and Van Vryling and Noble and Fenwick (the girls all had middle names), and she seemed to have intimate knowledge of the characteristics and qualities of the original owners of the names and could discourse about them with relish. She took an honest pride in the pioneer integrity and competence of the early families—mostly New Englanders—and carried on her life as though she were in their presence.

But what heavy labors she had to perform! She was not cut out to be a drudge—she was equipped with a bright, humorous, eager intelligence, and she loved to read and talk and exchange ideas, but she was faced with the unending task of feeding and taking care of a household of large and always hungry people living on a back-country farm three miles from a village store, with primitive equipment, a coal-burning stove, a black iron sink, and a summer icebox. At times she seemed half-buried in the debris of daily living, with the accumulated stuff of dishes and pots and pans and leftovers piled high on every square inch of available space—and even a crew of helpers to do the washing up hardly seemed to lessen the effect of the chaos. I could never see how she produced meals—always ample and good, day after day unfailingly, with no complaint or touch of self-pity, with in fact apparent good nature and relish for the appetites of her hungry family. She must in fact have been weary and discouraged by the unending trials of her hard life, but she never showed it or admitted any such weakness.

The farm lay in the valley of the Battenkill just where it emerged from the Taconic Mountains of western Vermont, a range including Mount Equinox and Red Mountain near Arlington, and in my many visits for weekends and vacations I scoured the country. I used to dream of catching big trout in the Battenkill, as others were said to do, but the few times I tried it I had no luck—it took more local knowledge than I had to find those famous brown trout. One day in spring I

walked up to the still remote village of Sandgate and climbed
Mount Equinox from the west side, with no trail to follow
and a hard thrash through new-fallen snow—and thence
down eastward and on through Arlington and so back to the
farm—though because I would have been very late for supper I called them up from West Arlington and Walbridge
drove their car to pick me up, which they were all pleased to
consider a surrender to pure weariness on my part. It was certainly a hard day's outing, but at that age I couldn't admit to
any such weakness as being tired from a twenty-odd mile trip
over a snow-covered and partly trackless mountain and insisted that my only intention was to be on time for supper.
Since then the wilderness of Equinox has been tamed by a
road and a lodge of some sort at the top, though I have never
been back to see—nor have I been back to the village of Sandgate, which at that time seemed almost unchanged from what
it was when the rebellious Daniel Shays lived in hiding in the
mountains there long after the rest of the world had forgotten
about him.

During and after my college years I kept returning to Ondawa Farm, as it was named—often on foot, after long treks
across southern Vermont, and I was always made welcome as
though I belonged there, no matter who was at home. From
the Hancocks in Jacksonville to Ondawa there were several
routes to choose from, but I figured the distance in any of
them was about sixty miles, which is a hard day's walk no
matter what the conditions of weather and terrain. I could
average as much as five miles an hour, which included jogging on the down slopes—though on the first trip I was mis-
led by a topographical map and thrashed around the woods
near Somerset Dam until I found some Long Trail markings
and followed it north until it seemed to veer off to the eastward and I decided to risk a more northwesterly course
through the forest—and came out on what was then the little
dirt road running east and west across the mountains from
West Wardsboro to Arlington, past what has since become

the major recreational development at Stratton Mountain. At that time it seemed wild and remote, but the little dirt road was a gladsome sight when I came on it, and I jogged along down the long hills toward East Arlington as dusk closed in. I had used up a couple of hours of my day in the effort to get through to that road. It was nearly eleven that night when I got to Ondawa and found a barn dance going full blast—a project the girls had organized as a way of raising a little money for the Mount Holyoke Endowment Fund, and I had intended to be there early enough to join in, but in fact I was too late and too weary and too hungry and by the time I got cleaned up I was in no mood for dancing. It seems to me that I gave it a try, just to be able to say I had done it, but the bounce had gone from my legs.

In those years when I visited Ondawa Farm I was what Anthony Trollope would have called a hobbledehoy—a very self-conscious creature half way between a boy and a man. I was afflicted with unwarranted vanity. I was full of the best sort of intentions, but I craved recognition as both a particularly sensitive young man and a muscular prodigy. At college, I had achieved the rating of "the second strongest man" in my class, the result of a complicated set of tests, and of course I was very proud as a consequence. My feats of lonesome cross-country endurance gave me great eagerness for the quest— and what I seemed to be questing for was the Arcadian past, the regions and times of my forefathers, the old country life in the hills and mountains and along the seacoast where everything worked together in natural harmony and beauty. I tried to learn the old-time ways of doing things—the handling of horses, the use of an axe and a scythe and all the other hand tools, the farming and longshore operations—I yearned to be indigenous, to be a native and competent part of the region I lived in. But all the time I was in reality a romantic and sentimental observer, an amateur, a college boy, a gentleman's son —at least that is what my friend Anne Buffum seemed to mean when she turned on me with righteous indignation and accused me of complacence. I was blandly dabbling, she implied, in the hard realities of life and using them to play with for my own satisfaction. It cut into my self-esteem, this attack, and I brooded over it, but then I shrugged it off as something I couldn't really do anything about—and I didn't understand what she meant anyway: I told myself that my heart and intentions were pure.

I suppose I did take advantage of my warmhearted friends, the Johnsons, the Hancocks, and the Buffums—and there were others of similar generosity to me—but at least I loved them and took to them as though I had a sort of natural right in their lives. They gave me affection, of course, as well as refuge, and also a sense of the continuing past which I was making an effort to be part of, and though it may have been a romantic vision—or even a sentimental one—it is the kind of vision that can sustain one for a lifetime. They did live, those kindly folk that I came to know so well, with integrity and patience and mutual love and a sustaining belief that a good life is worth struggling for. It is a premise in contemporary writing that virtue is a mask for the evil and corruption which are essential in the human condition, and that it is impossible for even an ordinary person to live well and happily or to be in any way admirable, and though I see that nearly all lives end in tragedy I am ready to argue that my old-fashioned folk lived with honor and decency and devotion to what they believed to be good. They of course had the advantage of the established ways of life, and were not aware of the vast revolutions the world was about to undergo, and they still hopefully clung to the habits of their forefathers—hardly realizing that the cars and electricity they were beginning to use were the forces that would cut off their past and bring in the uncharted future.

I naturally tried to hold on to that past as long as I could—like many others of my age, especially those with country habits, I made a point of being old-fashioned, and resisted every modern device that came along, though in the end I nearly always capitulated. I put my faith in wood-burning stoves and hand-pumped water, in walking and rowing and sailing, in bucksaws and axes, in horses and teams, in lamps and candles, in wooden boats, and all the other traditional materials and arrangements. I tried to follow a Thoreauvian way of life, but not with consistent dedication or a sense of discipleship. I was probably sentimental and whimsical about it, and I lacked the certainty of a true follower, so inevitably I let myself be beguiled and overcome by the instruments of modern progress I professed to despise.

FOURTEEN

FROST, WHICHER, MEIKLEJOHN, AND OTHERS

A S I HAVE SAID, the best part of my Amherst education was not academic. What I really majored in was old-time New England life, as represented chiefly by the Johnsons and the Hancocks, and by the many farmers and villagers I met on my pedestrian travels. But I also took the usual repertory of courses and engaged in some of the minor affairs of the college world, in which I achieved no distinction whatever. My record is without honors—except for a very routine *cum laude* on my degree, which means that I had collected a minimum number of B grades. I tried to be a runner on the track team, without much success—though I did passably well at cross-country; actually the nervous tension brought on by competitive running seemed to drain away my strength and I seldom rose to the occasion. I couldn't in fact even sleep quietly and was jarred all night by the pounding of my heart. The scriptural recommendation that I might rejoice as a strong man to run a race seemed wildly fantastic to me. I dreaded the ordeal of it. I worried myself into a state of debility. It was of course a weakness of character; I was simply not constituted to be an effective competitor, even though I had excellent physical equipment; but I think a capable coach could have understood my problem and helped me to find some solution to it—at least that is what I suppose a good coach tries to do. I have often been defeated by excessive self-consciousness, which has a large measure of simple vanity in it, but with trial and patience I have won some success—in races other than foot races.

At college, however, I remained pretty much a nobody. I tried out for the student newspaper and was not chosen. I sang a little in the glee club, but was not one of their regulars. I went out for the hockey team but got a bad cut in my foot and had to quit. I played a lot of tennis, but not well enough to make the varsity. With all my dreams of glory I had valid expectations of failure—yet I think I kept being hopeful about myself, and preserved more self-esteem than I had a right to. Perhaps it was a deplorable complacence, as Anne had said, but a certain amount of illusion must be allowed us. Without some faith in ourselves, whether warranted or unwarranted, we could hardly endure a lifetime of our own company.

It was really a secret life that I was leading in my travels and explorations into the country of the New England past, with the almost daily visits to the Johnsons and the long voyages through the hills of Pelham and Shutesbury and beyond into Vermont and New Hampshire and the Berkshires—a life that most of my college mates hardly knew about or believed in when I tried to tell them. But though I didn't enhance the reputation of our fraternity, which was considered a primary obligation, they treated me nearly always with tolerance—and once at least two of them, Cartwright and a city boy from New York named Howard Merz, came off with me into the unknown country northeast of Amherst and we supped on bread and cheese and went on through the moonlit spring evening down the long hill east of Shutesbury and across the Swift River and on into the township of Prescott where we asked a man named Grizwold if we could sleep in his barn. It was a Saturday night and Mr. Grizwold was taking a bath in his kitchen, but naked as he was he welcomed us heartily and said sure we could use his barn—it was open, of course, but there was no hay in it, we'd have to make do on the bare planks and he hoped we wouldn't be lighting matches, and he went on with his bath. So we lay on the barn planks, and shivered and ached till daylight—and because the adventure of it was new and strange I think we were quite happy, and I remember how we basked in the early morning sunlight on the wooden bridge over the Swift River on the road from Prescott to Pelham and ate the last of our dry bread and cheese—and how I suddenly realized that plain rat-trap cheese which I had thought I hated was in fact delicious, and I have never since tasted it without remembering that sundrenched spring morning on the little wooden bridge over the Swift River—now long-since lost under the waters of the great Quabbin Reservoir which occupies that whole valley. I think Mr. Grizwold's houses and barns must have been taken away too, along with most of the villages of Prescott and Greenwich.

But though I was happy with the fellowship and mutual well-being of our little adventure, especially that early morning pause for bread and cheese and water in the sunlight of the Swift River bridge, I continued to operate mostly as a loner. I was aware of a sort of passionate folly in my constant questing and escaping—I was almost daft about it in a mild quixotic way, and I couldn't rationally explain it or bring myself to share it with others. I am afraid I could at times be complacent about it, or even arrogant, like other more celebrated loners, as though I were possessed of a virtue too fine for the common world to share. It is the sort of attitude, as I said, that I used to find in Thoreau, and much as I admired and followed him I tried to avoid his know-it-all self-approval. I don't believe I really succeeded.

The book that more than any other excited me was one recommended by my teacher and master, George Whicher—it is Hilaire Belloc's *The Path to Rome*, the most brilliant and delightful record of a solitary pedestrian's adventures that I have ever read. I still see occasional references to it by enthu-

siastic discoverers, and I am sure it will settle in as one of the
literary immortals, but my own attachment to the book was a
matter simply of uncritical and wholehearted love. Its style, its
content, its wit and charm, its whole approach to the adventure of living, seemed to me miraculously and dramatically
right—and now after fifty-odd years I can still remember its
scenes and passages almost to the point of literal quotation.
Hilaire Belloc's adventure as recorded in his book was begun
by his drawing a line on a map from the land of his birthplace
in Alsace down across the Alps and the Appenines to Rome,
followed by a solemn vow that he would walk the whole
way, take advantage of no wheeled vehicle, and hear mass in
St. Peter's. It was a vast and wondrous whim, a game that he
played with a full sense of the absurdity and the reality of the
adventure—and his running commentary on his experience is
in its own way as delightful as that earlier classic of the road,
Laurence Sterne's *A Sentimental Journey*. He also did illustrative sketches for his book which seemed to me almost as
deft and appropriate as his text.

He remained my chief inspiration for many years, and it
was hard for me to break away from his influence. I found, of
course, that he wrote all sorts of things—histories and biog-
raphies and serious essays and light verse, and a book about
cruising in a sailing vessel around Great Britain, and a novel
called *The Missing Masterpiece*, and was generally recognized
as a great writer and always bracketed as a Catholic, especially
vis à vis his contemporary Gilbert Chesterton. But nothing
that he did or wrote ever equaled in my affections *The Path
To Rome*—with perhaps one exception, a very whimsical and
free-spirited book called *The Four Men* which I used to read
and reread with intense secret delight—secret because it appealed so directly to my love of country vagabonding that I
identified with it and was jealous of outsiders and intruders. I
read also George Borrow, the scholar-gypsy of *Lavengro* and
Romany Rye, and the Stevenson of *Travels with a Donkey*
and *An Inland Voyage*, but neither could match Belloc in
evoking the high spirits and humors of youthful adventuring

in an innocent age. Both *The Path to Rome* and *The Four Men* are so incredibly likable, so full of wit and verve and joy of life, that in my mind I made an idol of their author, and elected him as my guide and master, and some years later when he made a speech at Symphony Hall in Boston I went to hear him—but, alas, it was a disillusioning experience. I had thought of him as forever youthful and sparkling with the humors and ironies of his whimsical ventures, but instead he was old and portly and serious-minded and he spoke grimly about the alarming state of international affairs and his audience was made up of Bostonian Catholics who had no romantic notions about him at all. He was introduced by a cleric with a slight brogue as "Hilary Belloc" (accent on the first syllables), a historian and of course a Catholic spokesman. I saw nothing whatever of my imaginative and high-spirited and humorous companion of the open road. And if all this seems naïve to the point of absurdity, it is none the less one of the minor poignant experiences that have remained vivid in my life.

In my sophomore year, I think it was, I met Robert Frost in a small once-a-week class that was probably a section of a larger course in American literature, and he was supposed to teach us about poetry. But it took me two or three years to comprehend him—which may seem strange to a time like the present when he is regarded as almost unfashionably transparent. I had of course been brought up with the rich and romantic melodies of the nineteenth century, and the major poets in my life were Keats and Shelley and Tennyson—though I also remained faithful to Grey's *Elegy*. I thought that was what "poetry" was, a harmony of lovely sounds and images. I hardly recognized the laconic Yankee speech of Frost as poetry, and my youthful idealism rejected what was commonly assumed to be his view of the defeats and tragedies of New England country life, which I still regarded with proprietary concern and affection. In time I realized that he also shared my proprietary concern and affection, but I was at first made skeptical by the general opinion, as expressed by

Amy Lowell, for example, that he was too harsh in his handling of the native material, that he even lacked a sense of humor—in comparison with Alice Brown, for example. Like me
and many others, Amy Lowell was put off by his candor and
plain speaking about the realities of his New Hampshire
world, and she failed to perceive the ironies and the subtleties
of his vision. And as she rightly said, he wrote "in a way to
set the teeth of all the poets of the older schools on edge." It
took us a long time to be reconciled to the flat nasal awkwardness of such a line as "Something there is that doesn't love a
wall," which by now seems as familiar and native to us as any
line in American poetry. And I remember how some of us
mocked the prosiness of "A Hundred Collars," that comedy
of the bookish and nervous professor who was forced to share
a room in a Woodsville Junction hotel with a large hard-
drinking and talkative traveling bill-collector for the Bow
Weekly News—one of the episodes that Miss Lowell may
have missed the humor of, as I think we somewhat did too.
"Call that stuff poetry?" Bilge Tilley said of it, and quoted
passages in facetious accents.

> "Lafe was the name, I think?"
>   "Yes, *Lay*fayette.
> You got it the first time. And yours?"
>   "Magoon.
> Doctor Magoon."
>   "A doctor?"
>   "Well, a teacher."
> "Professor Square-the-circle-till-you're tired?
> Hold on, there's something I don't think of now
> That I had on my mind to ask the first
> Man that knew anything I happened in with.
> I'll ask you later—don't let me forget it."

No, that sort of commonplace talk struck most of us young
romantics as unworthy of the name and nature of poetry.

I don't really remember what went on in those class ses-
sions more than half a century ago, except that he talked in an

uninterrupted and spontaneous monologue, facetious, cryptic, oblique—plain but not always understandable. A book about him by his friend Sidney Cox has as its subtitle the phrase "Original 'Ordinary' Man," and presents him as a man of genius who used the lives and the language of plain country people as the substance of his poetry, as though he himself were one of them—as of course he felt himself to be. He spoke in north-country accents and idioms—and used his speech as the basis of his style, which he always heard in his mind's ear before he allowed himself to write a word on paper. It was the sort of colloquialism we weren't used to, except in the comic distortions of *The Biglow Papers*, say; certainly not as the vehicle for serious poetic expression. The pure Yankee dialogues in the short stories of Alice Brown and Sarah Orne Jewett and Mary Wilkins Freeman were of course familiar to us, and perfect in their intonations and idiom, but they were not "poetry" and belonged in an accepted dramatic category. Frost was speaking his own native language in his own voice, and doing it with calculated poetic intent.

> What kept him from remembering the need
> That brought him to that creaking room was age.
> He stood with barrels round him—at a loss.
> And having scared the cellar under him
> In clomping there, he scared it once again
> In clomping off;—and scared the outer night,
> Which has its sounds, familiar, like the roar
> Of trees and crack of branches, common things. . . .

It is all talk, shaped of course into iambic pentameter lines—it is not a dialect, not a talking-down for quaint or humorous effect, it is a genuine dramatic language with a classic function, deliberately calculated and selected. It is true that Frost "talked like that" most of the time, that he made himself into the sort of "original ordinary man" who was actually and consciously quite extraordinary. He used those idioms and turns of phrase naturally—perhaps he learned them better as he grew older and more certain of his purpose and could make himself into the embodiment of his own poetic theory. Certainly his earliest poems, like "Ghost House" or "Love and a Question" or "A Line-Storm Song," suggest a more conventional romantic lyricism than he would have permitted himself later on when he insisted on what he felt to be his true native style.

Anyway, I got over my reluctance to accept "Mending Wall" or "A Hundred Collars" as admirable, and made myself as far as my sentimental nature allowed a Frost disciple. Not that I ever was close to him, but he treated me from then on with wonderful kindness. I was mostly quite unaware of the harsh self-seeking side of his nature that some of his biographers have described, though of course I never in any way threatened his career as a poet and writer—which I suppose he was maintaining with fierce insistence. He was, I realized, generous and kind to other young writers and admirers besides me. But I recognized him as a man of genius, with an unpredictable temperament and extraordinary individuality who went his own way and built his own poetic life with what could at times be the sort of calculated policy that hardly fitted the image of wise and humorous benevolence that he created for himself. I remember the anguish of his early ardent friend and admirer Sidney Cox, whom he refused to see, and in fact rejected, chiefly I think because Cox's adulation of him seemed so excessive that it was embarrassing and annoying. Sidney, whom I came to know well and counted among my close friends, could be almost overwhelming in his devotion to those he admired, and back when they were both young and unknown, teaching at Plymouth State Normal School in New Hampshire, he had attached himself to Frost and shared in his early successes and his great subsequent fame —but in the end he felt himself pushed off and abandoned by the man he loved and admired more than anyone on earth.

But as I said, Frost always behaved to me as a benevolent friend, and except for borrowing a book or two from his library and inviting him to dinner many years later I never asked anything from him—though I must acknowledge that once in 1934 when I was out of a job in the depth of the Depression I visited him in Amherst, at the suggestion of my professor and his close friend George Whicher, who assured me that Frost would be happy to give me advice and comfort at least—which he did with genuine concern. He told me how he had come back from England feeling broke and abandoned and hopeless about his future, and settled in a farmhouse in Franconia, New Hampshire, and was occasionally asked to speak and read in public, and how scared he was—it was like going into battle, he said. After that I used to see him now and then at some of his lectures at Mount Holyoke (where I got a job that year) and Amherst, and later when I lived in Belmont, near Cambridge, I often called at his dismal little house on Brewster Street, where he seemed to be watched over and taken care of by Mrs. Theodore Morrison. It was from there that he came to dinner with us, and fascinated my children by his speculative nonstop monologue that seemed to increase in depth and strength as the evening went on. He was always most alive at night, and wrote and thought best in the late hours—and I think he would have gone on all night if we hadn't suggested that it was time to go to bed.

One of the last occasions when I saw him was in October 1958 at a lecture at Boston University, where I drove him in my car and introduced him to his very large audience. He was of course throughout most of his career a masterful platform artist, without any apparent qualms or diffidence, as those realized who watched him on that cold and windy day at the inauguration of John F. Kennedy where he read his poem in the glare of sunlight to the thousands—even the millions—of his viewers. At Boston University that evening he told them that he couldn't hear what I had said about him but whatever it was they had better discount it because "we were old friends"—he said it twice to give it emphasis, and I have been pleased to remember it. He could, as I have said, be very kind, at least when nothing else was at stake. And of course he could talk to any size group, small or huge, with a steady flow of homemade wit and wisdom, reinforced by the reading of poems that were made of the same material. The only ones who ever found fault were the serious left-wingers who were put off by his mockery of their hopes for ideal social equality, which he was skeptical about, being himself an old-fashioned Yankee individualist. His thinking was always a speculative game, a playing with probabilities. If we must have a revolution, he said, we'd better "plan to go half way and stop."

> Yes, revolutions are the only salves,
> But they're one thing that should be done by halves.

Another of the semi-facetious couplets that he liked to read in public is the sort that strikes the earnest listeners as much too frivolous:

> It takes all sorts of in and outdoor schooling
> To get adapted to my kind of fooling.

He was not one to take stands on political or social issues—rather, he played with them as illustrative dramas of human experience—as "insights" into the dilemma he always perceived as the everlasting and ironic dichotomy of our lives—where love and need try to coexist, and work is play for mortal stakes. In one of his reflective—and defensive—later poems called "To a Thinker" he wrote,

> It almost scares
> A man the way things come in pairs.

And went on to say,

> I found I never really warmed
> To the reformer or reformed . . .
> So if you find you must repent
> From side to side in argument,

> At least don't use your mind too hard,
> But trust my instinct—I'm a bard.

Yet as he had pointed out in "The White-tailed Hornet," instinct in both men and animals is not to be relied on. He saw us always as poised and balanced between reason and impulse, like his character Meserve in the dramatic poem "Snow" who had to decide whether to stay safely in the Coles' farmhouse in the night of a great blizzard or to risk going on, and he seemed to base his decision on whether the page of an open book on a table turned itself backward or forward—but it stood upright and refused to fall either way, and in the end he went on regardless—because the storm "says I must go on." Impulse wins out in time of storm—or war: "Ask any man" —but that book-page is very characteristic of the balance he liked to maintain in most of his judgments. Lawrance Thompson, in his exhaustive biography, insists on the rooted conservative puritanism of Frost, as though his political and moral decisions were dogmatic and even "reactionary," but in most of his writing and speaking he plays with his ideas ("My kind of fooling," as he says) with such disarming insight that it seems impossible to charge him with conclusive finality of opinion. He was too professionally philosophical, too learned, too cagey, to let himself be caught inside a dogma, though I can see that he leaned toward the conservative Yankee individuality he had been brought up with, an Emersonian self-reliance that took no stock in communal ways of life or even legally enforced equalities. He probably voted Republican, which is the sort of treason his critics make the most of. But his speculative and articulate thinking about all human affairs, past and present, was by far the most compelling I have ever experienced. He said once with his usual touch of irony that "all there is to writing is having ideas," and if any man was ever gifted with "ideas" it was Robert Frost: they flowed from him in a life-long stream, which as he said of West-running Brook "is time, strength, tone, light, life, and love." The smallest details of his daily living were translated into emblems of universal experience—a process common to most good poets and writers but seldom carried out with such discerning insight as Frost again and again achieved—from his earliest "My Butterfly" in 1893 through all the familiar triumphs of his later years, "Mending Wall," "Sitting by a Bush in Broad Sunlight," "On a Bird Singing in Its Sleep," to his death poem "Away!" in his last published volume in 1962:

> Now I out walking
> The world desert,
> And my shoe and my stocking
> Do me no hurt

As I said, my master at Amherst was George Whicher, who along with his brilliant and competent wife Harriet remained good and faithful friends of Frost's—in spite of an early jealous suspicion of them as representing the Amherst academic "establishment" which he seems to have resented, as indicated in a letter to Louis Untermeyer that Thompson has quoted. But it was my impression that he continued on the best of terms with the Whichers, and depended on their support during his Amherst years in the twenties and thirties. They watched over him in his restless goings and comings, and gave him devotion and comfort in his many family problems, and of course they were fully aware of his unique genius as a poet and philosopher. They knew too how prickly and dangerous he could be in protecting his ego against real or fancied rivals, though so far as I could tell they regarded him with affection as well as admiration. They were always amused and fascinated by the unpredictability of his behavior —as for example the occasion when he hailed a taxi in New Haven after a lecture at Yale and had himself driven to Cambridge for an appearance at Harvard—a hundred and fifty miles or so, at great and uncalculated expense, all in a state of desperate impulse. "Poor Robert," they said.

George Whicher was a cool and reserved New Englander, very upright and conscientious, with a rather formal demeanor that I think concealed a natural shyness. His manner of somewhat aloof self-containment rather put off some of his associates and students—he seemed always in full control of himself and the situation, and spoke and acted with professional competence. He was a Columbia Ph.D., and his published thesis was a life and appraisal of an obscure early eighteenth-century English novelist named Eliza Heywood, whom he had selected as an arbitrary academic "subject." His interests were at first quite catholic—he "played the field," as he put it, in doing articles on various minor topics, but he devoted himself more and more to his native region and produced a definitive biography of Emily Dickinson, *This Was a Poet*, which is not only reliable in its details and substance but very rich in its insight into the poetry itself. With his profound understanding of the New England Puritan heritage as well as of what makes poetry poetry, he might have been the ideal biographer of Robert Frost, but he died too soon. He had an enormous interest in and respect for the mysterious quality of creative genius. He seemed, in fact, especially devoted to good poetry, and he used to read it to us, in class and in morning chapel, not in an ordinary conversational voice but in a heightened bardic intonation which seemed at first strange to me but which I can still hear—it was a habit we used to debate pro and con but I came to like it even when he read the colloquial Frost. I remember that the Irish poet William Butler Yeats used to read his poems in much the same way—and he was being very consciously "bardic." It made me remember that Scottish guide on Grand Lake in Maine who raised his voice in the night at the camp fire to intone the ballad of the fair-haired boy who died on the field of battle.

I took various courses with George Whicher, but the best of them was a small seminar in what has come to be called "creative writing"—which of course means any writing that aims at being art. Later in life I conducted many similar classes, and what method I had was mostly his—a wholly informal and spontaneous consideration of selected class writings, and anything else that seemed interesting and relevant. He read to us the wonderful Preface to *The Nigger of the Narcissus* and some of Belloc's *The Path to Rome*, and poems of Chesterton (full of thumping melodrama) and Borrow's tale of his epic fight with the Flaming Tinman in *Lavengro*, and an account by Dorothy Canfield Fisher of the process of writing a story—very discouraging to me, who was trying to write in a similar vein but lacked the experience and the wisdom, though I did produce a story of Maine coast life that he read to the class with mild approval. It was intended to be fearless and a little grim in facing the realities, but in present-day collegiate surroundings it would seem foolishly sentimental. I remember how brilliantly gifted some of the other members of that class seemed to me in comparison to my own uncertainties—especially a youth named "Dickie" Richards who wrote genuinely beautiful poems and was a friend and protegé of Robert Frost's and in 1922, as Lawrance Thompson records it, accompanied Frost on his somewhat abortive expedition on the Long Trail in Vermont. Thompson also points out that it was a Richards poem that gave Frost the idea for writing one of the most philosophical and speculative of all his poems, "West-running Brook."

George Whicher was a good country walker, and he and I took some brisk outings together in the Pelham region to the east of Amherst. We also played tennis a few times, and my recollection is that I had about a seven to five edge on him. And now and then I visited at his house in the evening. There was not much affectionate warmth between us; he was always cool and reserved, but at the same time extraordinarily kind in doing his duty by a naive and persistent student. His intelligence about books and life and our native New England seemed to me infinite in range and depth, and I listened to him with intense respect, hardly realizing how little I had to give him in return for the hours of his time I occupied. It was his example and encouragement that eventually turned me into the way of a student and teacher of English and a writer.

He was the only Amherst teacher I came to know well.

The others all remained at a professorial distance, though most of them operated with competence. There was one instructor who took over George Whicher's course in American poetry and did it so badly that the class rebelled vociferously until Whicher returned and made peace—an unusual sort of demonstration for that more docile era. And there was a Professor Churchill who had been elected to the state senate but who continued to teach a small seminar in Shakespeare and who read to the few of us sitting round the table the most pompous and stupefying lectures I ever listened to—I can still hear him giving us the biographical facts with oratorical solemnity: "Now this woman whom he married was eight years his senior—take note, gentlemen: it was *eight years*—not seven or nine years, but exactly eight years. It is our duty to be accurate about such a fact." None of us around the seminar table ever spoke a word from first to last in the course. It was Professor Churchill, the leading political figure in town, who delivered an eloquent oration on the Common on the occasion of the armistice that ended the World War on November 11, 1918, and I remember how he shouted and gesticulated, but I couldn't hear what he said. It was a solemn event.

In those years the most exciting personality in town was our college president, Alexander Meiklejohn, who had the natural faculty of polarizing the college community into his opponents and proponents. As a student I remained quite innocent concerning the fierce tensions that built up around him, and like most of my fellows I was simply delighted by his eager wit and charm and freshness of mind. He seemed from the start—from the very first assembly of the year—a man of extraordinary magnetism; he came on in all his talks with a very appealing diffidence, as though he couldn't quite think what he wanted to say: he had had a speech all ready and waiting, he implied, but he had lost it or mislaid it—and here he was trying to remember it and not at all sure he could and hoping it would come to him in time. It was an act, I suppose, but he always in the end performed brilliantly, but his tentative beginnings won our sympathy and made us seem to share in the building up of his speech. When he reached his climax and finale he was in full control of his eloquence, and most of us were ready to stand up and cheer him at the end.

But of course he offended the practical and conservative folk, especially those in authority, like the trustees and faculty elders—and Robert Frost, in spite of the indulgence and respect bestowed on him. Frost apparently despised and was jealous of some of the other faculty luminaries, like Stark Young the novelist, whom he considered an immoral mountebank, and he accused Meiklejohn of dangerous radical "intellectualism." It all seemed incomprehensible to me in my innocence that anyone could find fault with a man of such shining candor and good will—and I still feel that the passions that Meiklejohn roused up in his many enemies were brought on by deplorable human perversity and prejudice. I even remember a stupid attack on him by the sports editor of the Boston *Herald* on the ground that his so-called intellectualism would deprive youth of its natural right to play games, as though his emphasis on brainpower were wicked. He was actually an expert tennis player—and one morning in chapel he pleased us by expressing a hope that we would "beat Dartmouth" in baseball that afternoon. But it is true that he roused the ire of the sporting professionals by emphasizing the spirit of amateurism in collegiate athletics. It may be true also that he was not a good practical manager of the daily business of running a college—or his own household. I was aware of local complaints about overdue bills and other confusions; the old-time townsfolk looked at him with a good deal of suspicion. Yet those who loved him did so with passionate loyalty—so much so that at the occasion when at last he was fired, in 1923, a year after I graduated, fourteen of his faculty appointees at once resigned and a large group of seniors refused to accept their degrees and a larger group of juniors transferred to other colleges. I am not one to go in for radical or desperate gestures, but if I had been in the class of 1923, instead of 1922, I should have been strongly tempted to join the rebellion. Like most of my fellows, I was wholly for him. He made all other academic leaders seem dull and stodgy. He imbued us with a spirit of eager adventure in learning and living. He faced us always with quick-minded charm and wit, and set us to laughing at him and ourselves but always with an affectionate and somewhat rueful awareness of his hopes for a better and brighter life for all of us. To the old-line conservatives of his time he seemed impractical and radical—and Frost being himself a conservative turned against him, or so at least Mr. Thompson records in his biography. If I had known of his attitude at the time, it would have shocked me, because I admired and revered both men. I still think of Alexander Meiklejohn as the most gallant and magnetic of intellectual warriors. I think the notion of his sinister "radicalism" was one of the prejudices common to us in the twenties and since; so far as I know, Meiklejohn took no doctrinaire political position at all, but simply encouraged a more Socratic approach to education and more ideological adventures. Three or four years later, he came to speak at Williams College, where I was teaching, and I remember one of the old-timers there declaring that he wouldn't be hired to go and hear him. "I simply dn't want to be *all stirred up*," he said. I thought it was high time someone stirred him up, but being a new instructor I kept quiet.

Meiklejohn pursued his dream of the perfect college to Wisconsin and then to San Francisco, but I fear he was too much the idealist to function effectively in an imperfect world. At the time I used to associate his hopes and efforts and inevitable failures with those of Woodrow Wilson, who was fighting for his vision of the League of Nations in the same era. As I remember it, their styles of speaking were quite similar—except that Meiklejohn had a deprecatory sense of humor and a sparkle that the more serious-minded Wilson lacked.

FIFTEEN

FUSSING

O NE PHASE OF Amherst life in the early twenties was
the ritual of the date. The word is still current, and
remains one of the linguistic absurdities we hardly
take note of any more—like its sequel, "going out with." Our
dates, I must say, involved very little "going out"—except for
a decorous evening walk around the campus grounds of
Mount Holyoke or Smith. We made the preliminary arrangements by mail, since telephoning seemed both chancy and
rather bold—though it could be resorted to in times of need,
and on the chosen day and time—generally right after supper
—we boarded a trolley car and went rocketing and clanking
off either to Northampton eight miles to the west or South
Hadley ten miles to the south—a ten-cent ride, I think. The
South Hadley ride, which I generally took, was a forty-min-
ute uphill and down-dale affair, with a hard grind up one side
of the Holyoke Range and a dizzy coast down the other,
through what seemed like a quite wild and wooded region.
The cars were huge unwieldy affairs, and their dim lighting
and bad air and noisy grinding and rocking seemed almost
purgatorial, especially on the late and dark homeward trip.
But the main event of our evening was the walking and talking—and in bad weather not even walking, but sitting politely
in the large parlor of the dormitory and making conversation.
I think this was the routine for most of us, and boys and girls

together we went through it with patience and a pleasant awareness of the sexual ambience that hovered around us, though we never acknowledged it by word or act. My girls always seemed more sophisticated than I was, and I think were amused at our ritualistic and almost ceremonial meetings. The name given to the operation at that time was "fussing." We went fussing—it was I think a strictly local locution, and has long since died out—though "date" and "dating" are still the common terms for any meeting of the sexes.

We mostly behaved, I can state confidently, with the utmost propriety, though a very few did not—at least they so implied in the sort of boasts that we took to be wild exaggerations of the truth. It is hardly necessary to say that sexual indulgence has always persisted in human affairs, but back in 1920 the restraints were dominant among most of us. We were aware of and afraid of sin, and had no uncertainties about what it was. There was of course a "double standard" that everyone subscribed to, in which it was assumed that the girl must be purer and more continent than the man, and that her indulgence must be consequently more disastrous and unforgivable. Men were after all men, and it was up to the girl to remain inviolable in spite of all urgings and pressures—until the sanction of marriage, which at once altered the whole circumstance. The world had long mocked the motives of Richardson's eighteenth-century novel *Pamela*, wherein matrimony is the one and only key to virtue, but in actuality the code still persisted. The conservative and timid among us still followed it implicitly. Certainly, I was magnetized and excited by girls, but until I met the girl I married I never even kissed one. It was not a question of moral principle, but of the manners and social customs we had been brought up with—though perhaps some sort of theory of moral behavior did make an unseen underpinning to our practice. We took such values for granted. But of course I was a good deal of a prig, which means I was devoted to the idea of virtue without any understanding of the true human forces I was involved in.

We had a fraternity dance two or three times in a year, and I generally invited Anne Buffum, though I think she had a bit too much strength of mind for me. She was a year or so older than I was, and a great deal wiser and more certain in her judgments and she could be very effectively critical of me and others as well. But we always had a fine time together, in a somewhat brother-and-sister fashion—walking in the country and going to the college dances. Sometimes she would match me up with other girls who needed a partner, and once she half facetiously suggested that I would do well to marry her younger sister Mary, whom I was obviously very fond of. I was flattered but not ready for any such commitment.

The fraternity-house dances were very pleasant small-time affairs, with a hired band consisting of one piano, one saxophone, and one set of drums, and the furniture was pushed to the walls in the downstairs rooms, and everything was simple and unconcealed—which means there was no liquor or secret sex activity.

Perhaps those came in a few years later. I do remember a couple of occasions—not at dances—when some of the brothers were drunk enough to make pathetic spectacles of themselves—and of course I was morally outraged, but such events were quite rare. The reputation of the "roaring twenties" was mostly brought on by a small minority, chiefly among the rich and spoiled, like the people introduced by Scott Fitzgerald. But as I said, our parties were carried on with quite innocent pleasure to the melodic music of "Margie" and "Dardanella" and a rousing tune that blended perfectly with the words I can still sing:

> Oh, oh, oh—my sweet Hortense,
> She ain't good lookin' but she's got good sense.
> She's got good teeth in her mouth;
> One points north, the other points south.

There was a lot more about Hortense, but I have forgotten it.

It was a period, too, of the big formal affairs called

"proms," which I gather are no longer part of the college scene. I never went to an Amherst prom—I was too shy and diffident to take on the responsibility of a major blast that went on for two days or more, but I was invited to a couple of Mount Holyoke ones—and a Smith one too—which I think involved spending a night in a hired room and seeing to it that my girl was provided with a suitable corsage of pink rosebuds in time for the main event. There were other events too, of course—plays and games to watch, luncheons and suppers in quaint places—but the big thing was the formal dance that lasted most of the night with a rich ambience of ritual and emotion as though it was the climactic time of our lives. We danced now and then a waltz, but mostly what I think was a foxtrot, a very simple stepping around in time to the music— or sometimes stepping along in what was known as the Castle Walk, named for the professional dancing couple of Irene and Vernon Castle who used to perform in musical shows—and daring ones did it cheek-to-cheek in the early Fred Astaire manner. The Charleston and other absurdities came in a bit later.

But though dancing among the young back in the twenties was a very elementary activity, and took little skill—unlike the older dances such as the waltz and the polka—it was a basic and serious part of life and we engaged in it as an essential ritual. The sanctioned and public embrace of boy and girl, the subdued light and the beguiling melodies of the popular songs with words of love and desire—it all created the illusion of the purest romantic pleasure that was leading us on and up toward some sort of glorious fulfillment. We thought we understood the realities of life—as all do who are one and twenty—but actually we lived in a state of supreme innocence—and when I say "we" I mean most of us. We had hardly absorbed the truth of the World War and its aftermath, and were still reluctant to accept the new intimations of cynicism that were coming in with such a play as *What Price Glory*. We had no dream of the evil future that was almost upon us; we recognized none of the signs of a new time of depression and war and a waste land of moral and social disruption. The illusion of peace was still strong and bright, and we subscribed to the ideal of Woodrow Wilson and his vision of a League of Nations that would make the future safe for democracy. We lived on the whole in the cheerful innocence of a fool's paradise—as I suppose most ordinary people do most of the time, even now after all that has happened for the last half century. But in that decade of the Twenties we were especially devoted to what we all assumed was our national birthright of continuous prosperity and "progress." Like most of my fellows, I took it for granted that we had won the war, and in spite of certain cultural vulgarities as noted in *Main Street* and *Babbitt* we had become the destined leaders of world civilization and we carried on our lives in a state of happy self-congratulation. We assumed that everything was working out for the best, especially of course in the U.S.A. where we were blest with wealth and freedom and what we told ourselves was the know-how. I think for those few years, up to the time of the market crash, at least, we lived in an atmosphere of careless euphoria—and even the depression, along with the rising menace of the communists and fascists and Nazis, seemed irrelevant and foreign to our basic wellbeing. We felt that our nation had become the destined leader of mankind in achieving personal freedom and prosperity and most of all in the natural ability to get things done by dint of technological skill and innovation. "The American way of life" had connotations for us of such happy mastery of the problems of ordinary living as the world had never seen before, and we mostly regarded all other nations and peoples as hopelessly sunk and mired in the ways of the quaint and backward past.

My collegiate social life is hardly worth more detail. Though I lived among chivalric dreams, I engaged in very small ventures indeed. It was a time of acute self-consciousness between the sexes, when freedom seemed to offer itself and yet the old proprieties remained in force and we hardly knew where we were or where we were going. I have no doubt that a similar self-consciousness still exists—at least as it reflects the vanity and rivalry inherent in all sexual equations —but I am sure that it is more openly dealt with and understood, and carried on with less dramatic and bewildering secrecy. I remember the agony of one of my roommates who was deeply in love and refused to admit it even to himself, as though it was a wickedness, and he worried himself into a state of nervous collapse and betraying nightmares which gave rise to cruel jests from all of us who assumed that he was simply making a fool of himself. At that age and time, a nice and conservative and obviously puritanical young man had no right to indulge publicly and frantically in the ordeal of unfulfilled passion. In due time, I am glad to say, he married her, and so far as I know they got along well. But for a while his effort at suppression of his normal desires almost unhinged him. Yet I am old-fashioned enough still to believe that a certain amount of suppression of desire is essential to our wellbeing, both public and private. The question is how much, and when, and how is it to be enforced. The strong taboos and restraints of earlier times seem less disastrous in their consequences than the permissiveness of the present. The pattern of our old ways prescribed behavior that is often so conventional as to be a form of hypocrisy, and we were taught to go through with it with as much acting skill as we could muster, even in the face of disaster and death, like the girl in Amy Lowell's poem who suffered what I am sure was only a temporary lapse when she cried at last, "Christ, what are patterns for?" I think Amy Lowell would herself have found many good reasons for the patterns that her heroine blamed for her tragedy. We still fluctuate between the devil of indulgence and freedom and the deep blue sea of discipline and inhibition, and are lost at either extreme—though of the two choices, the devil is obviously the more popular. Yes, as I said, I had been conditioned for discipline—theoretically, at least—and I re-

sented the notion that people like me were "inhibited," as the
new-fangled Freudian jargon of the time described it, as
though there were something a little shameful about any effort at moral restraint.

But of course I was full of romance and boyish dreams
and delusions. I could not understand how Bernard Shaw, for
example, could balk at the inevitably happy-ever-after con-
summation of the affair between Eliza Doolittle and Henry
Higgins in *Pygmalion*—it struck me as nothing but cynical
perversity on Shaw's part, and I must say it still strikes me that
way, though I can better appreciate the logic of it.

SIXTEEN

LINCOLN

AT AMHERST, in addition to my devotion to the Johnsons and the Hancocks of Vermont and the Buffums of Shushan, New York, and the girls of Mount Holyoke, and Professor Whicher, I made a few friends including the man who became my partner and sidekick and would be still if he hadn't gone to live in San Francisco. His name is Lincoln Fairley, and he along with Carl Dennett has been as faithful and generous as it is possible for one man to be to another in the course of a lifetime. I saw him first on the tennis courts, playing a steady and patient and determined game—and many were the even matches we had in the ten years to come. He was a sophomore, and I a junior, when we met, and since he had not made a fraternity I invited him to visit mine and we agreed to ask him to join us; but he politely and coolly declined. He said he didn't admire Amherst as much as he might have, though his father and an uncle had graduated from it a generation earlier, and he had decided to transfer to Harvard and go as a day student from his home in Jamaica Plain, near Boston. I don't think his nonfraternity status troubled him at all—he has seldom been concerned about his "status" in society—but he already had a professional interest in economics and sociology and he felt he would do better in those areas at Harvard.

On that first visit to our fraternity house I was very

strongly and warmly drawn to him, though for a while he had little to say—he was not a collegiate type, not at least in the conversational fashion of the time. But after some fishing around I gradually discovered that he and his family spent their summers in Penobscot Bay, about six miles from the point on Deer Isle where my family were, at Weir Cove (which he correctly pronounced "Ware") on Cape Rosier. It was one of those little-by-little revelations, where you start off with "The Maine Coast" and then come closer and closer until you pounce on the very spot. Weir Cove! Of course—right next to Horseshoe, right inside Spectacle Island—fancy that! Practically in sight of our house on Dunham's Point. I had already had the feeling that he and I were destined for each other, but this settled it. In the course of time we were almost inseparable.

In writing a memoir such as this I find that however much I may try to be candid I inevitably fail. I cannot bring myself to deal objectively with the human weaknesses of my family and friends—or with those virtues which may strike the skeptical reader as incredible. We live in a time when the weaknesses are prominent and are naturally to be expected even among the best of friends, but the virtues belong with the delusions of our lost innocence. We are reluctant to admit the possibility of the sort of selfless integrity that heroes and saints used to be made of, and that has existed, I am convinced, still in some of the rare mortals I have known—there were, for example, to name a few, my Uncle Jim Croswell, and Dean Briggs of Harvard, and Ellen Coolidge of Boston, and James Fairley and his son Lincoln—and since Lincoln may even some day be reading this I am naturally shy about putting my opinion of him on public view. Like the others, he has lived always with spontaneous and humorous benevolence, has relished the simple and lovely amenities of life, and devoted himself wisely and very competently to what he believes is the common good. Quite early in his life he became aware of the attacks on his high-minded and pacifistic father during and after the First World War, and he began to question the authority of the rich and socially powerful families of the parish in Jamaica Plain. There were more tensions in the affair than I could realize at the time, but eventually James Fairley retired from that old and eminent Unitarian Church and went on to a new community church in White Plains, New York, and Lincoln dedicated himself to the ideals of a socialistic society. It was partly a reaction against the concerted power and privilege that had turned against his too liberal father—the early Twenties was a blindly prejudiced period—and partly a reasoned adoption of a socialistic vision which has grown more sure with him ever since. He became in due course a Harvard Ph.D. in economics, a teacher in various colleges, including the Massachusetts Institute of Technology, and finally the resident authority on all labor problems for the West Coast Longshoremen's Union, whose boss is Harry Bridges. It has been a satisfying career, I think. He has of course been accused of radical subversion, but he remains serene and formidably reasonable in maintaining his position. I used to argue against him with more emotion than logic, and of course time and tide seem to be vindicating his visions. The old world of "free enterprse," which we were taught to consider our private property, is rapidly heading toward self-destruction.

The summer after I met Lincoln we were both in Maine, within easy sailing distance of each other—and naturally we got together as soon as my boat was in commission. She, the boat, was the twenty-eight-foot "knockabout" that my father had bought new from Hand of New Bedford—and for some thirty-seven years she was a valued member of the family. When I was about seventeen I began to take charge of her—at least as far as getting her caulked and scraped and painted and rigged and handled and moored. The actual hauling in and out was mostly done by Ozzie Brown at North Haven—until her latter days when I undertook to do that too at Deer Isle. She was a flat, beamy, spoon-bowed craft, originally with a small fin keel and a centerboard, but the board kept giving trouble and my father had it taken out and added a deeper keel, though even so she drew only three and a half feet, which was not enough for good windward work. She was very fast on all other points of sailing, and handled well even in strong winds, especially after we added a bowsprit and larger jib to ease her weather helm. She was the third boat my father had—all three named after his daughters: *Doreen* for Dorothy, *Eileen* for Eleanor, *Bettina* for Betty. The first two I never saw—I think he had them on the Hudson River at Dobbs Ferry; the third was sailed by her builder along with an eminent sailor named Nutting, from New Bedford around the Cape to Portland, Maine, where my father and mother picked her up and took her on to North Haven. Her lines and an account of her trip around the Cape were published in *Yachting Magazine* in 1902 or 1903—her knockabout rig and flat ends and overhang were considered rather daring in a small boat for offshore use.

Anyway, she was our family pet for many years, and by that summer of 1921 I had taken over her care and maintenance and soon afterward my father formally gave her to me. I used to spend a week or so at North Haven in June getting her caulked and scraped and painted, under the benevolent professional eye of Ozzie Brown, who always seemed to welcome an ignorant young amateur and was patient about giving advice. He was a relaxed and grandfatherly man, and I remember how he tried to teach me to put a burr on a varnish scraper and how hopeless and futile it always seemed when I tried to use it. Scraping old and weathered varnish is one of the more discouraging tasks in boat maintenance, though of course the well preserved bright work, as it is called, has always been the traditional symbol of elegance in a yacht. When I came many years later to plan a new boat for myself, I used no varnish at all. But varnish or no varnish, the maintaining of a wooden vessel, even a small and humble one, is a demanding task, and many a hot and dusty hour have I devoted to it—always aware that I fell in the end far short of the perfection it seemed to expect of me.

Even now, in my seventies, I undertake the annual labor, but with considerably less enthusiasm and strength. I do it out of habit and loyalty to my earlier life when I overflowed with expectations of adventure and the romance of youth and freedom and infinite energy. In that day of long ago I arrived in North Haven on the early morning steamer—usually the *J.T. Morse*, in a blaze of eagerness, and after arranging for room and board in a village house, not in that era unlike the familiar house of Almira Todd in Miss Jewett's book, I got into khaki pants and sneakers and posted down to the boatyard to find Ozzie Brown and get to work on *Bettina*'s old and somewhat weatherbeaten hull. She sat outdoors, of course, in a little field among other boats, with a canvas cover nailed down to her topsides with battens and small shingle nails—and it always seemed an indignity that nails were driven into the white sides, though of course the holes were afterwards carefully filled with putty and sanded smooth and painted. The whole boat, top and bottom, stem to stern, had to be scraped and sanded, the seams payed with linseed oil, and caulked where needed and puttied and sanded again and finally painted—with oil paint or varnish or antifouling paint as was required. And each year there were critical repairs to make—a new canvas deck, or new chain plates for the shrouds, or sprung planks to be fastened, or bobstay fittings, with many consultations with Ozzie and his two faithful expert helpers, Forrest and Izri, who could do anything that had to be done. I am not by nature a painstaking workman, but I learned from them what good boat-work involved.

It was of course a still unmechanized period. The gasoline motors were becoming common, even as auxiliaries in sailing craft, and the steamships had been operating for many decades, but most of the routine work was still done by hand: there were no convenient power saws and drills and sanders, nor any electricity to drive them. Major force was applied by tackles and winches, sometimes with a horse or an ox. The hauling and launching there was done with a four-part tackle and a drum windlass with stout hickory handles to turn for an inch by inch advantage—and of course birch rollers on planks under the cradle—all carried on with shouts and gestures and a good many obstacles and crises to be surmounted. *Bettina*, weighing less than two tons, was no problem for these veteran professionals, but getting her launched and afloat seemed to me always a great victory, and I was full of a sense of glorious achievement as though she had phoenix-like renewed her life and youth and strength.

That summer of my first cruise with Lincoln when we sailed eastward to Passamaquoddy Bay, *Bettina* took a hard beating, especially in the head winds on the return. We had pulled out the splice of one of the starboard shrouds in a northwester off Machias Bay, and had carried away the bowsprit in a heavy southwester off Petit Manan (both of which troubles we luckily survived and temporarily repaired), and the last day we came from Bass Harbor to Naskeag in an easterly gale, close reefed, no jib, our tender swamped behind us and the boat leaking like an old basket. Back at Weir Cove at last, still shaky with fatigue and strain, we grounded her out in a little inlet where she could rest against a convenient granite face, and at low water I applied a few screw fastenings to the sprung planks and hammered in some twists of caulking cotton and new putty—and hoped for miraculous improvements. Youth, as Conrad and others have said, has no sense about the dangers and troubles of life, especially in the presence of boats and the sea, and after *Bettina* floated again and seemed to leak only moderately I felt wholly confident that all was well. It was a sequence I was to go through many times in the remaining seventeen years or so of her life.

My partnership with Lincoln continued strongly through the next academic year, even though he had left Amherst to go to Harvard and live at home in Jamaica Plain—and once or twice I went to visit him—and was made as welcome in his house as though I belonged there. It was my extraordinary fortune to fall among the kindest and most hospitable people in the world and to share their lives and ways with wonderful mutual affection. I especially admired and loved Lincoln's father, who was a man of humor and warmth and granite-like integrity, together with a quick and subtle intelligence that played over philosophical and historical motives in a spirit of adventurous inquiry. He maintained what is now regarded as an attitude of stern moral stringency, but he did so with compassion and a recognition of the folly that underlies most of our pretensions. He had the carriage and countenance of a major prophet but I have never known anyone more kind and approachable and altogether humane. That he should have been attacked by some of the well-to-do gentry who were in charge of the proprieties of his day, on the ground that he was too pacifistic and Christian in his preachments, was the sort of grim irony I found it hard to accept. Back in the Twenties the fear of any radicalism, even of Woodrow Wilson's enlightened proposal of a League of Nations, was especially strong among the old propertied families, for whose attitude the word "reactionary" was coined—which implied a looking backward to the safety and stability of an earlier time and an objection to any change. For all his moral stringency, James Fairley was a liberal in the old-fashioned sense—that is, he believed that if men were given freedom and justice and opportunity they could flourish together in decency and peace, and he protested at the monopoly of money and power that brought on the social inequalities and the miseries of poverty. It was, as I said, the critical view of a hopeful liberal, and it appealed to me as clearly just and sound, but in time it seems to be a position that is attacked by both the left and the right as based on nothing more than wishful thinking. But apparently even such honest Christian hopefulness was not quite acceptable in the opinion of his more conservative and influential parishoners.

SEVENTEEN

ABROAD

I N THE SPRING OF 1922, before my graduation from Amherst, I arbitrarily decided that I would study architecture. I had already applied for and been awarded a fellowship for the study of history at Columbia, and had the notion of living at home with my family on Park Avenue, but for reasons that don't now seem very cogent I declined the Columbia opportunity in favor of the Harvard Architectural School, which admitted me without very seriously questioning my qualifications. In a history course at Amherst on the Renaissance I had written and presented a term paper on Italian architecture of the Palladian period, and had been flattered by the praise of my professor, Crock Thompson, who was pleased enough to applaud when I finished. He was a very stout, hearty, enthusiastic man who gave us little talks on the virtues of physical exercise and "getting up a sweat" every day; I used to see him playing tennis doubles with Meiklejohn and others—but I'm sorry to say that he died soon afterward. I think the final examination for his course was the same every year: "Explain what the Renaissance was and why it occurred when it did."

Another course that encouraged my architectural interest was "Greek Civilization," conducted by Harry DeForest Smith—called always Mike Smith—who I discovered later

was not only an eminent classicist but a close boyhood friend
of the poet Edwin Arlington Robinson in Gardner, Maine.
He was also a friend and admirer of Uncle Lincoln Hendrickson of Yale. It always surprised me that a learned classical
scholar such as he was should have retained the Maine accent
of his youth, and I used to wonder if Robinson had done so
too, though I never had a chance to hear him speak. But Mike
Smith overflowed with the glories of Greece and gave us a
thorough grounding in the orders and forms of ancient architecture. We all took note of the innumerable classic imitations
and perpetuations in the buildings of the college and the surrounding town. When at the celebration of the college's Centennial a formal Doric entablature was erected as a ceremonial
gateway to the campus he was outraged and embarrassed by
its basic errors of design, wherein the architrave was made to
overhang the outermost column rather than terminate directly
above it. It seemed to him a glaring disgrace, especially in a
college with a proud classical heritage; he couldn't understand how it had happened, though he realized that it was a
common mistake among careless amateurs.

This devotion to the classical and neoclassical traditions,
including what we called the "colonial," was the fixed attitude of the early twentieth century. The so-called Bauhaus
style had not yet come in to upset the conventions, and while
the true Gothic was looked upon with a devotion akin to worship—especially in view of the discovery of Henry Adams'
Mont St. Michel and Chartres—the Victorian effort to repro-
duce the Gothic seemed like a travesty. Nothing, we thought,
could be more absurd and false than the gables and turrets
and vaults and stained glass and gingerbread decorations that
the previous century had left for us. Such a house as Ches-
knoll, which my grandfather had had built, already seemed
hard to believe in as a real part of my own active experience,
though as a specimen of the domestic Hudson River gothic it
was relatively modest: but still it belonged to an age and time

now lost and gone. We learned to use the term "mid-Victorian" to relegate all that into the junkyard of the immediate past. We skipped back over a full century to the simple white-painted classical orders and balanced rectangles of the colonial and federal eras and the brief period of the Greek revival. At least, I did so; I felt an extraordinary appeal in the purity of those forms of the late eighteenth and early nineteenth centuries, and my heart leaped up whenever I beheld one of the genuine old ones with fan-lighted doorway and small-paned windows and the familiar ancient details of cornice or pediment or pilaster. Even the house of my dear friends the Johnsons had the date of 1820 carved into a joist in the attic, and therefore qualified as one of the true hundred-year-old aristocrats, though it was a perfectly plain little rectangular brick box. I never could enter it without an awareness of my kinship with that faroff time when life must have been carried on with simple and sensible dignity.

When I graduated in 1922 I skipped the commencement ceremony entirely. I had booked passage to France in the ship *Rotterdam*—paid for of course by my generous father, who loved to travel in Europe and had taken the rest of his family on various occasions. It hardly occurred to me that it was an evasion of duty to depart before my degree was properly bestowed, but I did make a habit of avoiding as many academic and other formalities as possible—and actually I never attended any college commencement exercises until I was on the Mount Holyoke faculty a dozen years later. All my earned degrees, one from Amherst and two from Harvard, were mailed to me, though I remember being somewhat taken aback by the strongly worded letter from President Olds of Amherst who regretted my decision. I hadn't somehow realized that if all of my classmates behaved the way I did there would be no graduation ceremony at all. It is stipulated, I observe, in the giving of honorary degrees that the recipient must be on hand in person: otherwise, no degree. But in those days the commencement exercise came in mid-June and even later, and I couldn't bring myself to squander the golden days of summer waiting around for what I thought were superfluous rituals.

So after my last exam I shipped off my trunk, underwent a somewhat muffled and sad farewell with the Johnsons, shook hands with some of my housemates, and boarded the trolley car for Northampton and the railway station. I was filled with tireless energy and enthusiasm and good intentions and self-esteem. I took it for granted that I was destined to live happily ever after and I accepted my opportunities and privileges without question or analysis, as if I had a natural right to them —though I don't think I was arrogant. Complacent, yes— more than I realized or would admit, but eager to be useful and helpful and respectful to my elders and betters. I had a naïve devotion to what I conceived to be the old-fashioned and handmade ways of life as followed by the country people I had come to idealize and love, and in a romantic way I aspired to live the way they did—though it was mostly a dream, I suppose. I had an overwhelming yearning for the world of mountains and sea, and for the wondrous adventures I thought they held for me, and I had a sense of enormous physical energy that could cope with any challenges or emergencies. I was happy too to be embarking alone. I was of course unfamiliar with the ways of foreign travel, but I had all the innocent confidence of youth and faith in my own specially appointed destiny.

At Amherst each year the seniors used to sing—and possibly still sing—a happy-sad song of parting that is full of old-time sentiment and haunting words and melody that continue to "linger in each heart," as the lyric puts it:

> We have climbed
> Together up the pathway
> On to the goal

Where life doth lie
Where in bright
And beckoning fields of promise
Lieth fame or fate. . . .

In a day given over to black humor, like so much of the present, this may be written off as somewhat boozy nostalgia, but those of us who gathered to sing the song on spring evenings long ago can hardly forget the hopes and visions it created in us. I for one, and I am sure others, had a sense of mysterious personal destiny and we saw our lives as a progress onward and upward toward that shining promised land—and for me it was always quite literally a vision of forest or seacoast or delectable mountains.

About this time I discovered Euripides in Gilbert Murray's translation, especially *Iphigenia in Tauris*, and the rich romantic yearning in it overflowed in my heart. I memorized some of the choral chants and could sing them to improvised tunes:

A flash of the foam, a flash of the foam,
A wave on the oarblade welling,
And out they passed to the heart of the blue:
A chariot shell that the wild winds drew.

I thought I had never read anything so filled with the mystery of the longings of youth—and one of its repeated lines—"O youth and the days that were"—has echoed in my memory ever since, with varying implications.

The guiding oar abaft
It rippled and it dinned,
And now the west wind laughed
And now the southwest wind. . . .

And ghostly Achilles raceth there
Far in the Friendless Waters.

Ever since I had read Hawthorne's *Tanglewood Tales*—and reread them again and again—I had seen the Greek myths as pure romantic mysteries, with great heroes doing great deeds, and this play of Euripides seemed the most beautiful of all the old stories in its evocation of a world of sea and ships and the splendid rescue and deliverance of Iphigenia by her brother Orestes. I am told by Greek scholars that Gilbert Murray translated the original Greek into a sort of Tennysonian romanticism, and it may be so, but whatever the source—Hawthorne or Tennyson or Murray, or even Homer and Euripides themselves—my imagination responded with belief, and I lived in a dream of beautiful lands and seas and heroic adventures. And I suppose many young men at times dream such dreams, and see themselves climbing great mountains or reaching the secret places of primeval forest or sailing off through the Friendless Waters or finding the perfect seas for surfing or the endless downhill run in powder snow and they think of their lives as heroic and touched with godlike splendor—at least they thought so in the innocent age of my early youth, perhaps more than they do now that the old illusions are no longer permissible, though in many ways competitive prowess and heroism are more intense and demanding among the young than ever. What is lost is the illusion of transcendent mystery that used to keep beckoning us onward toward these bright fields of promise, the belief that divinity itself was somehow waiting for us there.

On that voyage in the *Rotterdam* I spent a good many of my waking hours talking about these and other matters with a very cultivated and charming young man named Graves, and it seems to me now that I have never spoken with anyone more intimately and eloquently. I am not naturally a ready talker—as life goes on I seem to have less and less to say about it—but with Graves on that trip I simply overflowed, as he did too. We walked the decks together and sat together, and we talked about everything in the world—he with much greater wisdom and experience and with what seemed to me wonderful charm and tolerance for my youth and ignorance. He was a graduate of the University of Pennsylvania, I think, and a veteran traveler and man of the world—though I never knew exactly what else he did. During the eight days or so of our passage the rapport between us was wholly natural and pleasant, without any overtone, so far as I could tell, of sexual inclination such as I had experienced with the gentleman from Grace Church, or as I had been rather faintly made aware of on one or two other occasions. But I was flattered and charmed by being treated as an adult and an equal by a man of such cultivation, who knew all about everything and came on like someone in a Henry James novel.

It turned out that he was a social friend of my Auntie Emma in Philadelphia, and therefore was a person of the utmost distinction. But such are the habits of men that after the eight days of the closest rapport we said farewell, he went on to Rotterdam, I disembarked at Boulogne, and I never saw him again. Friendships at sea do turn out that way, of course; the intense intimacy seems a little embarrassing after the voyage is over and we return to the more ordinary habits, but for fifty years I have been grateful to Graves for his company and all the kindly wisdom and thoughtfulness he offered to me. He spoke without condescension and listened appreciatively and seemed never to tire of my company, and together we considered all things great and small. Afterward I kept thinking I would see him again, and at Harvard in the fall I ran into his younger brother in the commons at Memorial Hall where we had meals, and for some reason we didn't take to each other at all and I was shy about expressing my feeling about my shipboard companion and so we let time and our lives go by without renewing our connection. I have no idea what sort of life he led afterwards or what he may have achieved in it. I do regret that I lost touch with him.

I also met on the voyage a Harvard architectural student named George Howe who seemed to me very competent and confident, especially in contrast to my own innocence in the field. He was one of a large and celebrated family from Bristol, Rhode Island, and has since been very successful in his profession. After we landed at Boulogne, he piloted me on to Amiens and Rouen to see the cathedrals, which he knew all about in full detail—as he also knew about all the other architectural exhibits dating from later periods. I was aware of my ignorance, of course, but the experience of Amiens was for me one of the major dramatic moments of my life. The mystery of its great size and the infinite ingenuity of its structural details and decorations seemed to me a good deal more astonishing than I had actually expected, though I was all ready to be impressed. I have since then many times had that experience of pure gothic awe, but never quite as intensely as at that sight of my first major cathedral. For a young romantic still imbued with the miraculous possibilities in human achievement it was an experience of genuine religious revelation. I thought it transcended all rational explanations; if God could inspire men to do such work there could seem to be no doubt as to His place in the scheme of the cosmos. At the time I actually had few convictions about the mysteries of creation, but I was inclined to be respectful in the presence of time-honored faith, especially when it manifested itself in so sublime a wonder as the cathedral of Amiens—as well as the many others I came to know afterward.

I don't remember the minor details of those stopovers on the way to Paris—what I did about luggage or where I ate or how long I stayed with George Howe (it was not long, I am quite sure). I saw the Cathedral at Rouen, which seemed dark and strange, and the great church there of Saint Ouen, which was brighter and more beautiful, and when I got to Paris I must have taken a taxicab to the hotel on the rue des Saint Pères, where my sister Eleanor was staying—and she knew all about Paris and spoke French, which I could do only in stumbling schoolboy fashion. We saw a few sights together (some of the Louvre, of course, and Chartres and Versailles), and I found that both wine and beer set my head to reeling, to my chagrin, and I bought a straight razor *"pour une barbe dur,"* but I think it was not a good one—at least I could never achieve a perfect edge on it, though I kept trying for a number of years. It was my step-cousin Norman Donaldson who assured me that a straight razor was the only kind a really manly man ought to use, and for four decades thereafter I struggled with one—in fact I acquired several, and applied them with unpredictable results in all conditions, on land and sea—until I surrendered to an electric shaver. It is one of the many little surrenders to technological convenience I have been guilty of —and I feel a small twinge of shame when I think of those tempered steel blades lying unused and touched with rust, and the slick leather strops and the brush with its Chinese bristles and the crockery mug that held the round cake of barber's soap. The ritual was actually a nuisance and a bore, but I took some small pride in performing it, especially at the times when the razor was perfectly honed.

So far as I could actually see, the traces of the great war that had ended four years earlier were pretty well obliterated, though we didn't visit the battlefields or the cemeteries. In general life seemed to go on as though it had always been that way, prices were low, there were no crowds, Americans were welcomed, no hostilities or bitterness was displayed. My sister and I always got along happily, I being eleven years or so younger, and we both relished the felicities of that timeless world that seemed to play for our benefit like a divinely arranged pageant. In spite of the upheaval of the war, the rituals of social stability remained in force, and tourists like us were treated with old-fashioned deference, and the daily adventures of places and people were a delight. It was still from our point of view the world of Henry James in which the chief goal of existence was the awareness and practice of the sort of good manners and good taste best manifested in the European scene. Not that we engaged in very much actual social intercourse but we took part in the show as spectators and shared some of the stage at least. Most of us at that time,

Americans and Europeans as well, believed that peace and stability had come to pass on earth and the good old ways were restored forever. We thought that the war had been so appallingly evil and futile that nothing like it could happen again: it was the war to end all wars—so we were told and so we mostly believed. The world had been made safe for civilization—if not for democracy. The forces of a new disruption were not visible to us as yet—only a rumor of fascists in Italy, which we took to be a comic opera, and more dimly of revolution in Russia which was far too remote and irrelevant to count.

After a week or so we took a train from Paris to Geneva, and I think we frugally sat up all night in a second-class compartment, the other occupants of which permitted no breath of fresh air to enter during the whole trip. It is my impression that the European (not the English) traveler would rather die in a state of comfortable suffocation than risk the touch of cool and breathable air. The English, of course, provided they can wind a long woolen muffler around their throats, consider themselves impervious to cold and air, but I recollect no English aboard the Geneva train that night. At daylight I was standing in the corridor outside the compartment hoping to see Alps and noting that the country looked instead very much like my native New England hill country—which of course gave me pleasure. No high Alps were visible. I had never seen big mountains and I was full of tremendous expectations. But I had to wait.

We followed the course of the Rhone River and came into Geneva, and there must have transferred ourselves to a suburban train to take us out a few miles along the northern shore of Lake Geneva to the village called Creux de Genthod, where our sister Betty was living with her husband Huntington Gilchrist and their year-old son Johnnie. Their house had the impressive name of the Chalet de l'Aîle and was a suburban adaptation of a traditional Swiss chalet. Huntington at the time was a member of the secretariat of the newly organized League of Nations, and with his other cohorts there was dedicated heart and soul to the cause of bringing permanent peace to the nations of the world. He and Betty were caught up in a busy round of international friendship and social affairs, and were full of enthusiasm and faith in what they were striving for. It was an exciting and hopeful time for both of them.

After a week or so Eleanor and I made ready for our tour of the Alps: we equipped ourselves with rucksacks and mountain boots and alpenstocks and a set of detailed maps and we figured out a general itinerary and we sent our heavy suitcases ahead by mail—at very low rates. We took a steamer to the head of Lake Geneva (passing the Castle of Chillon) and a train that ran from Montreux straight up eastward into the mountains—and got off somewhere and started walking. From there on for three our four weeks we lived and moved as close to heaven as I have ever come. Everything seemed to be blessed—the cool sunny weather, the clean welcoming inns, the paths through the Alpen meadows and over the high passes, the cream-colored cows, the hay-makers with their scythes and rakes, above all the shining ice-white peaks of the Bernese Oberland and eventually the Tyrol. It seemed as though all my dreams of mountain felicity had come true. It was a pristine world, all pure and uncorrupted, and it was arranged somehow just for us, like a celestial pageant in which we were the chosen guests and spectators: day after day we made our way eastward, staying at the half empty village hotels, having lunch perhaps at a lonely *gasthaus* at the crossing of a mountain range—always appearing where it was most needed. From Gstaad to Lenk to Adelboden to Kandersteg to Mürren to Lauterbrunnen we followed the old winding foot-trails, meeting now and then the native herdsmen and mountain dwellers and very few outlanders like ourselves. It was a time when the old Alpine ways still went on in seclusion and peace in the midst of the most beautiful scenery I had ever imagined.

It was after leaving Gstaad that we came suddenly, without a moment's warning, face to face with the major snow peaks of the Bernese Oberland. In that pre-ski era, Gstaad was a secluded mountain village—though doubtless like most of the others it had even then a "Grand Hotel," but with very few customers. We had no trouble finding lodgings—and I remember the good honey and native Gruyere cheese we had at breakfast—and the rich hot chocolate. And so we set out on the eastward trail, marked I think with little pointing signs —one perhaps saying "Lenk, 5 St.," which meant five hours of walking: Swiss distances in the mountains were always measured in *Stunden*, and in my youth and vigor I found the rate of speed they proposed absurdly slow. But there was a path, winding up and up toward a far mountain wall with a little notch cut in it like a scoop; it was an old well-beaten way, and it zigged and zagged up over the green Alpine meadows and pastures, and all about us was a lovely region of modest mountains rising to gray summits above the green— and ahead of us the rampart wall and the little notch in it where the trail went through, perhaps six or seven thousand feet above sea level. And all unsuspecting, in perfect innocence, I stepped up into the notch—and there in front was a deep gulf of space and above it the absolute whiteness of the biggest mountain I had ever seen.

Nothing seemed to exist between me and the mountain. Even the rocks I stood on seemed to vanish under me, and I was somehow carried off into that great gulf of space and I had to reach back and cling to the ledge and command my legs to hold up firmly. For a few minutes I felt faint and powerless. We both did, I think. We couldn't speak. I remembered at once how Hilaire Belloc had written that the most stunning view of a high mountain is to be had from an elevation about half its height, so that you are looking both up and down— and of course I saw that he was right. The whole height and depth of it filled the space with immensity, from the far hidden bottom of the valley where a little stream flashed in the sunlight up past the alpine meadows and forests and lesser ridges and summits to the dazzle of white snow high and pure in the blue—all hanging there in absolute silence.

It was called the Wildhorn, and was part of the great range that marched away eastward toward where the Jungfrau and the Finsteraarhorn shone dimly white in the far distance. The map gives its height as 3,248 metres, which is a mere ten thousand or so feet, but it was not only the first snow peak I had ever been close to, it hung right there before me with nothing but air between us, with no foreground to hold on to. The sense of its silent and motionless vastness seemed almost overwhelming. We sat there in that narrow mountain notch for a long time before we were able to gather enough fortitude to take the rocky path downward toward the deeply hidden valley.

I must add that that snow peak, or one like it, has been in and out of my dreams ever since. It looms there as a sort of ultimate goal, and again and again I have approached it—though I rarely get to its actual summit. The dream of it is a genuine sleep-time dream, and I am exalted by the possibility of achieving such a climb as I have longed for, and I am at the same time saddened by the knowledge that I am alone and probably incompetent to cope with the technical difficulties of a major climb. I wake up in a state of triumph and frustration. I see the way ahead of me up the icy steeps, I am almost there, I feel brave and competent, I have a sense that the wondrous adventure is at last being brought off—and then almost invariably the vision recedes and seems to crumble away and I am left with the poignant awareness that the adventure has once more eluded me and I am back in my own limited life again. But I can never forget the mountain as it looms up silently and whitely in my dream.

The mountains, the forest, the sea, have been the illusions that I lived with—mostly in my younger days when I read the romantic poets like Byron and responded emotionally to the music of Wagner and saw man and nature sharing together a tremendous cosmic drama that gave metaphysical meaning and purpose to life. I saw myself as ready to play a part in some sort of transcendental revelation in which the beauty and splendor of the natural world would make itself known to me and I could in truth drink the milk of paradise. I knew exactly what Wordsworth meant when he said the sounding cataract haunted him like a passion. I could echo Childe Harold's sentiments when he put them down as rhetorical questions:

> Are not the mountains, waves, and skies a part
> Of me and of my soul, as I of them?
> Is not the love of these deep in my heart
> With a pure passion? Should I not condemn
> All objects, if compared with these?

I shared that early Byronic conviction that these immortal grandeurs, with the implication of a conscious and deliberate Almighty above them, operated in some mysterious way for the benefit of those who could most admire them—among whom of course I had special status. I felt that my soul was in tune with and even favored by the power who created and controlled the firmamental pageant. I even felt that all this transcendent splendor was designed somehow for me, and it made me both humble and exalted. I think most young romantics used to feel this way about the great natural world; it was a century-old legacy inspired by the poetic fervor of Byron and Wordsworth and their followers. Wordsworth had announced that "Nature never did betray the heart that loved her," and I responded with approval and agreement. This "Nature" was surely to be both loved and worshipped, and I knew that I had been somehow specially designated as one of its acolytes. I scorned the eighteenth century gentlefolk like Addison and Horace Walpole who called the high mountains "horrid"—and I equally resisted the later pessimism of Thomas Hardy and the "Naturalistic school" of Zola and many others who saw man as the victim of cosmic oppression or cruelty. I was convinced that what I regarded as the sublime beauty of the world was a manifestation of the heavenly grace that surrounded me.

So day after day we walked eastward the length of Switzerland. We crossed the Grimsel Pass and the Furka Pass, and the Oberalp Pass and eventually struck southeastward over the Julier Pass and came to Silvaplana, the village just below St. Moritz. The days were all beautiful and cool and the inns and hotels were quiet and hospitable. There were no automobiles on the roads, no dust, no noise. Now and then we telephoned back to Betty and Huntington—and once when we did they were having dinner with friends and the telephone operator found out where they were and called them for us at their friends' house—and they said that's how things were done in Switzerland. The whole beautiful country seemed to be arranged for the convenience and delight of its people, both natives and strangers—and certainly at that time, in the early Twenties, the destructive forces of the modern world were hardly apparent.

St. Moritz was the place where my sisters, Eleanor and Dorothy, along with the Croswells and John Donaldson, had been caught in the first weeks of the first World War—and stayed on at the elegant Suvretta House, which extended them unlimited credit until they were able to make their way to Genoa and sail for home aboard the *Adriatic*. It was there also that John and Dorothy climbed a mountain called Piz Nair, and he proposed to her and was accepted—and ever after he pronounced the name of Piz Nair with fervent remembrance; he was never much of a climber, but he counted that as one of the pinnacles of his success in life. And it was at St. Moritz that my grandfather, the first Charles Loring Brace, died and was buried in the little Protestant churchyard in 1893—and we found his headstone more or less neglected there, and I fear by now it is altogether neglected and probably lost. In 1955 my son, his namesake, looked for it on a winter day, but there was deep snow and he could find no trace of it.

But, as I said, we stayed this time at Silvaplana in a modest and pleasant chalet. The Suvretta House was too elegant and too expensive for us, though we visited it long enough to have tea one day. At this time we were joined by Douglas Gilchrist, a younger brother of Huntington, and he and I ventured on what seemed to me a splendid if quite unplanned climb. A snowy peak called the Piz Corvatsch loomed up in the east, and we set out toward it one day with more enthusiasm than knowledge. We were both full of youth and strength, and we charged up the steep trails, gulping the thin mountain air, and presently we came to the snow fields. Ahead of us a line of climbers plodded downward all roped together and carrying alpenstocks, moving very slowly and deliberately, and we dashed past them with the ritualistic hail of *"Grüss Gott"* and on up the steep beaten trail to the top of a high narrow edge with a bit of a cornice on our right and a drop-off into sheer space below it. It seemed to me as I stepped along that ridge that at any moment I might go through the snow cornice and pitch downward into empty air, but we made it to the rocky top—and I suppose it was a very minor sort of achievement for a real Alpinist, but to us innocents it seemed like a triumph. We had not really expected to get all the way to the summit. From below those Alpine snows seemed unreachable by ordinary walkers like us; they existed in a lofty unassailable heaven of their own, up among the clouds and the infinite blue where only trained climbers with special equipment could hope to penetrate.

The Corvatsch is an 11,000-foot mountain, and from the summit we could see a vast range of peaks in all directions, many higher and whiter in the clear sunlight, like the Bernina to the south and the Stelvio to the east, and far in the west the dim summits of the Bernese Oberland where we had come from; but actually the mountains seemed innumerable in all directions, and I had a sense of being for the moment on equal terms with them, as though I were admitted into their fellowship. It is, of course, a heady and exalted illusion that occurs even in the lives of small adventurers in the wild regions of the world.

On the down trail we crept softly along the knife-edge with its cornice on our left and then down to the steep snow slopes where we could *glissade* for long stretches on the corn snow surface. It seemed like a triumphant descent.

A few days later we took one of the wonderful mountain trains eastward, up over the high Stelvio Pass and on into what had recently become part of Italy. Somewhere near Bolzano, which up to the end of the war had been Bozen, in Austria, we got off the train and set off up a steep mountain cart track. We were navigating entirely by map—and the topographical maps of the region were very detailed and reliable. I don't remember the name of the station where we got off, but I remember how our little stony cart track climbed up the mountain range eastward, and how about half way up we came to a genuine medieval castle, with crumbling turrets and crenellations and a courtyard with old farm wagons and rakes and some chickens pecking on the barren ground and a general air of desolation and poverty that hardly fitted in with my notion of a castle. But it held a commanding position above the valley below, which was the main north-south route between Italy and Austria, and I assumed a romantic history of a predatory baron who exacted tribute from the travelers on the valley road. It still comes as a shock to Americans to discover such relics of antiquity half-hidden in the innocent and timeless countryside.

So we kept on up the cart track and over the first mountain ridge eastward and came into a perfect dreamland of high pastures and steep mowings and enormous mountains rising above them in spires and pinnacles and gray walls of stone with patches of snow caught in the crevices far up against the sky. The whole place might have been designed and built eons ago by a race of titans, and left to mellow in the weather of time. The Dolomites, cloud gray and touched with pink in the afternoon light, like splendid ruined buildings rose to heights of nine or ten thousand feet, their still vertical walls looking unassailable as though they were marble curtains hung there above the green alpine meadows. And high up on those grassy slopes the haymakers were at work, the men with ancient scythes, swinging and stepping along in a rank, one behind and a bit to the left of another, and in other places girls in dirndl skirts were raking what had been mowed earlier, and now and then a man would pick up a great mass of hay in his pitchfork and totter off with it and disappear far below in the valleys where the haycocks were built and stored —and they all worked with smiling good nature as though they were posing for a child's story, and greeted us cheerily as we passed, and in the late afternoon with sunlight slanting from the west they gathered in a little group on the high uplands and following a man with a brass baritone horn they marched off in formal procession, with rakes and scythes on their shoulders, singing as they wound their way downward toward their summer chalets in the valley—I remember how the notes of the horn floated eerily up through the evening air long after the marchers had disappeared below us.

I don't know whether such a world and life really exist anymore, but the place itself must go on through the years, with its lovely steep alpine meadows and those grey towers and spires of the Dolomites standing above them against the pale blue sky. It may still be an idyll of peaceful and festive haymakers moving in the sunlight of those heaven-touching meadows and singing their way homeward at day's end to the music of a baritone horn, but it all seems to me like one of the legends of a long-gone world.

And some of that mountain paradise had already been strangely marked by the war. We saw where roads had been cut in zig-zags to drag guns up the steepest crags—up into the very snows of the high mountains, and barbed wire fenc-

DOLOMITES

ing had been set up on the high and improbable pitches and
and bunkers and emplacements established on the narrow-
est ledges. In the midst of that serene and idyllic beauty the
desperation of the effort to carry on the war seemed unreal
and incredible, as though the whole thing had been pushed to
a preposterous extreme. We saw where clean-up crews had
rigged aerial cables a couple of thousand feet long so that
bundles of junked wire and other metal relics could be sent
straight down to the valley floor with a rush and a crash at
the bottom. It was almost impossible to realize that the destructive madness of war had been a reality in that lovely region only four years or so earlier. But in that summer of 1922
life there seemed to have returned to its age-old ways of peace
and serenity, and what I best remember is the singing of the
haymakers as they came downward from the mountain meadows in the late afternoon, and the cushiony thumpings of the
horn that accompanied them.

That part of the Dolomites had been annexed by Italy
after the war, but the people who lived there were fair-
skinned and blue-eyed—at least some of them were. They
looked and acted like the mountain folk of Switzerland. They
seemed reticent and cool, though not at all unfriendly. In the
towns, like Bozen and Cortina, we saw Italian policemen,
generally smaller and darker than the natives, dressed in fancy
blue uniforms with cocked hats and holsters for pistols, and
always walking about in pairs, and no one so far as I know
gave them any sort of trouble. But already rumors were in the
air of new political forces at work underground, and we began to hear of the *Fascisti* and a young demagogue named
Mussolini. The possibilities seemed trifling and even comic,
especially in this mountain region.

We stayed a week or so in a Cortina hotel, right in the village. There were more tourists here than there had been in
Switzerland—I think because prices were lower. I had to sleep
in a sort of upstairs storeroom. I don't remember that Douglas Gilchrist was still with us then; I think he went off on his

own somewhere and rejoined us later in Venice. We spent our days walking and climbing in the idyllic mountain country round about and we admired the 11,000-foot Marmolada and other high peaks that stood like ancient towers and spires above the steep meadows and pastures. Now and then we met other walkers, particularly the groups of stout and earnest Germans who seemed to occupy the center of the path and plodded dutifully upward exclaiming *schön, schön* at intervals and elbowing others aside. At this particular time in recent history the German tourists were not making themselves popular in other countries, though there seemed to be a good many of them. But even so, compared with later times there were relatively few of any sort, and the mountain country seemed wholly serene and unspoiled.

Except that already there were a few motorcars in the little village of Cortina, brought in by the Italians, who drove fiercely up and down the narrow streets with machine-gun roars from open mufflers as an announcement of their power and importance. The Italians didn't seem to walk in the mountains very much; rather they sat about on the piazzas and lounges and drank aperitifs and admired and loved their beautiful dark-eyed children—when, that is, they weren't driving up and down the street with their cut-outs wide open. They seldom seemed to go to bed at night, not even the children.

I met there a lovely Danish girl with blue eyes and white-gold hair, who I think was being a governess for some children, and I persuaded her to climb a small mountain with me. As a newly graduated BA I was impressed by what I supposed was my learning and wisdom but I found out that my Danish girl was wiser and a lot more learned—and could speak very good English besides. We never really got to be friends —in the boy-and-girl way—but I have always kept a bright image in my mind of her beauty and charm and have wondered how she has fared over the fifty years that have passed since then. I never saw her after we left Cortina.

We went on to Venice and spent a week or so there in a

hotel that had been one of the great palaces on the Grand
Canal, near the Piazza. I don't remember that we had any res-
ervations; I think we simply got into a gondola at the railroad
station and were wafted along to the hotel, where Eleanor
had stayed once before, and we were received respectfully
and given rooms on a third or fourth floor—the whole event
unfolded like scenes from a pageant, which of course is what
Venice was. The ceiling of the dining room in our hotel was a
vast Tiepolo painting with angels and cherubs floating about
in it. The gondolas passed and repassed in the Canal in front,
and some boats loaded with fruit and other provender, and
now and then a tenor voice was lifted in operatic song, and
the waves rippled and splashed on the front steps, and the
buildings along the Canal seemed filled with mystery and antique beauty.

We went about like bemused but dutiful tourists, and saw
the churches and palaces and galleries and the paintings by
Titian and Tintoretto and Veronese and Bellini and others,
and the wondrous pageant seemed to go on peacefully and
permanently—except that once or twice in the evening we
heard the sound of marching feet in the Piazza and voices
raised in a song we were told was the fascist hymn, but it was
shrugged off by the hotel staff as merely a passing folly. Nothing else interfered with our serenity. I walked about the little
streets and alleys, crossed innumerable bridges—and I remember once when I was heading as I thought back to the hotel
and dodging along with speed and certainty I passed a little
shop and it came over me strangely that I had seen that same
shop only a few minutes before and I realized with a shock of
recognition that I had unknowingly gone around in a circle
and was about to do it again—which seemed an ignominy to
one who took pride in his sense of direction. It was a small
event indeed, but it shook my confidence. I have never forgotten the moment when I strode past that shop door, and became suddenly aware of what I had been unconsciously doing.
Venice was put together like a maze.

I watched the gondoliers with avid curiosity. I thought I was good with an oar and a paddle, but I had never seen such mastery as they exhibited in driving those great cumbersome gondolas through the windings of the crowded canals. He, the gondolier, stood on the high stern overhang and manipulated a single heavy ten-foot oar that rested not in an oarlock, but on a bit of a ledge near the top of a stand on the starboard side built up a couple of feet above the level of the deck. On the forward stroke, the oar bore against the stand and pushed the craft forward—and of course turned it in a circle, so that in the act of rowing he had to counteract the turning motion by a quick scoop of the blade, with the result that the flat bottomed gondola tended to sidle along in a somewhat slanting course, turning a little at each stroke and being partly straightened by the scoop at the end. The oar itself was very heavy and awkward, and had a bend in the middle of its length to give added leverage to the essential scooping motion.

I couldn't of course rest until I tried it, and it took a powerful diplomatic offensive along with some essential money to persuade the gondolier to let me do it. He fumed and fussed and called on his saints to witness my folly, but I persisted— and discovered the technique was even more difficult than I had expected. At the first pause or hesitation in the application of the oar it slipped off its little ledge on the pedestal and fell downward against the gunwale and trailed in the water behind —and then of course had to be lifted and restored to its niche again: it was an operation that the gondolier performed with an effortless and fluid familiarity but for a while I felt quite flummoxed—and of course the gondolier offered nothing but unintelligible imprecations. He was convinced that my effort was ludicrous and hopeless, and expressed himself in pantomime as well as language. But I did persist and began to get the hang of it and I managed to scoop and sidle the ship down the Grand Canal at a fairly respectable rate, with no collisions or sensations or interceptions by the police patrol. The tendency of the oar to slip out of its niche and trail astern was a repeated difficulty for me, and it took me a while to master the trick of restoring it to its proper place by boldly throwing my weight against it and maintaining forward pressure on it. But I kept safely to the broad highway of the Grand Canal. Only a lifetime professional could thread his way among the networks of the minor canals where he had to twist and turn through spaces with hardly an inch or two to spare. In the end our gondolier managed some nods and smiles of approval and pocketed his tip with good cheer. I expect by now it is strictly against the law for a passenger and an amateur to operate a gondola on the canals of Venice: perhaps it was then, but I was too innocent to realize it.

We traveled from Venice to the Lakes of Como and Maggiore, and for two or three days were there. It was the church in the town of Como that I had used as a basic illustration for my history paper on Renaissance architecture in Crock Thompson's class at Amherst, so I studied it with a proprietary eye—though it seemed less impressive than I had somehow expected. But the scene of the lakes and the mountains round about was of course more beautiful than anything I had imagined—and again as it had been in the Alps and the Tyrol and Venice it all was more like a dream vision than like the actual world I ordinarily lived in. Everything there, near and far, seemed to be bathed in a tranquil brightness, like a Claude Lorraine painting, with the quiet waters of the lakes stretching away into intensities of deeper blue, and the mountains in the north standing against the luminous pale blue of the sky, and the shores and little islands mysterious with old pines and cypresses and glimpses of hidden tile-roofed villas. Like the other regions we had been visiting, this one seemed to have been designed and arranged as an immemorial pageant to give mankind a foretaste of paradise—and it was all perfectly preserved, as though it were being kept under some sort of celestial glass. I remembered the little rectangular mirror that my Aunt Leta had at Deer Isle—called the Claude

THE WILDHORN
1922

Lorraine mirror because in some mysterious ways it intensi-
fied the colors of the land and sea and sky and gave them a
magic sort of glow—and the afternoon light on Lake Como
was like that too. It was then a quiet place, with no roaring
engines, but rowboats and cargo barges with square sails and
small passenger steamers that slid silently along.

This was all more than half a century ago.

So we took a train back under the Alps through the Sim-
plon Tunnel and on to Geneva, and stayed a few days with
Betty and Huntington Gilchrist at Genthod, and then returned to Paris in a long night-time trip in a second-class compartment full of suffocating bad air—and soon after we took
the boat train to LeHavre and embarked on the old *Maure-
tania*, which was still the speed champion of the Atlantic. We
arrived in New York on my twenty-first birthday.